WATER

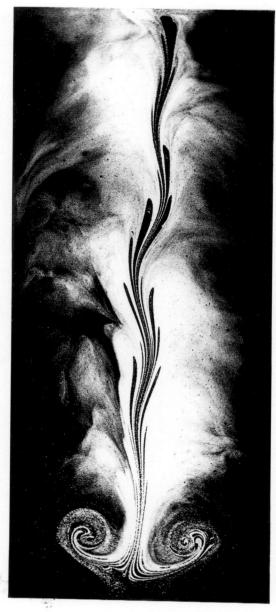

THEODOR SCHWENK • *Shapes Formed by Water Responding
to Rod Being Drawn Slowly Through Viscuous Liquid,
Das sensibles Chaos*, Verlag Freies Geistesleben,
Stuttgart, 1962 (*Sensitive Chaos*, Rudolf Steiner Press,
London, 1996) • Modern Silver Gelatin Print

STEVEN BENSON • *Rain, Daning River, China*, 1999 • SILVER GELATIN PRINT

ROBERT DAWSON • *POLLUTED NEW RIVER, MEXICAN/AMERICAN BORDER, CALEXICO, CA, 1989* • SILVER GELATIN PRINT

ELLEN LAND-WEBER • *CATACEAN SIGHTING AT ARCATA MARSH*, 1999 • IRIS INKJET PRINT

SPONSORS

MAJOR INSTITUTIONAL SPONSORS

Houston Endowment, Inc.

Nan Tucker McEvoy Foundation

National Endowment for the Arts

Manzanita Creative-GoBase2

Axiom Design, Houston

Vine Street Studios—
Margaret Regan and Fletcher
Thorne-Thomsen, Jr,

City of Houston and Texas
Commission for the Arts through
the Cultural Arts Council of
Houston/Harris County

Continental Airlines—
The Official Airline of FotoFest
and FotoFest 2004

The Brown Foundation Inc.,
Houston

William Stamps Farish Fund

Trust for Mutual Understanding

The Houston Chronicle

The Warwick Hotel ·

The Station—James and Ann
Harithas

Texas Commission on the Arts

Verizon Wireless

The Bruni Smothers Foundation

The Wortham Foundation

H-E-B Grocery

KUHF88.7FM

Buffalo Bayou ArtPark

Buffalo Bayou Partnership

Rice University

Rice University Department of
Visual Arts and Abrams, Scott
& Bickley LLP

Houston Downtown Management
District

Department of Foreign Affairs and
International Trade of Canada /
Minstère des Affaires étrangères et
du Commerce international du
Canada

ADDITIONAL INSTITUTIONAL SUPPORT

Cultural Services of the French
Embassy in the U.S.

Cultural Services of the French
Consulate in Houston

The George and Mary Josephine
Hamman Foundation

The Clayton Fund

New World Museum – Armando
Palacios and Cinda Ward

ArtsHouston

British Art Council

PaperCity Magazine

George Mitchell Interests

The Oshman Foundation

Joan and Stanford Alexander
Foundation

The Samuels Foundation of The
Endowment Fund of the Jewish
Community of Houston

Project Row Houses

Lawndale Art Center

SPECIAL IN-KIND SUPPORT

Hines—Williams Tower Gallery

Weingarten Realty

McCord Development—
One City Centre

Century Development—
Reliant Energy Plaza at 1000 Main

Crescent Real Estate Equities—
One Houston Center

Trizec Office Properties—
One and Two Allen Center and
Continental Center One

J.P. Morgan Chase—Heritage
Gallery

Sotheby's, New York—Denise
Bethel

Sicardi Gallery

The Wealth Group—
Erie City Ironworks

New World Museum—
Armando Palacios and Cinda Ward

Houston Community College,
Central Art Department

Gremillion & Co. Fine Art Inc.

Aurora Picture Show

Microcinema International

Rudolf Steiner Foundation

SPONSORS

Rice University Media Center,
Film Program

KUHT-PBS Channel 8

Southwest Alternate Media Project

Voices Breaking Boundaries

The Artery

DiverseWorks Artspace

Angelika Film Center

Museum of Fine Arts, Houston—
Film Program

SPECIAL SPONSORSHIPS
THE GLOAL FORUM

Rice University

George and Cynthia Mitchell
Foundation

Stewart Title

R. Gamble and Judith Baldwin

Apache Oil

Turner, Collie & Braden Inc.

HARC
(Houston Advanced Research
Center)

2004 CATALOGUE

Eleanor and Frank Freed
Foundation

FILM AND VIDEO

aue design

FINE PRINT AUCTION

The Warwick Hotel

Sotheby's, New York—
Denise Bethel

MindOH!—
Beth Carls and Amy Looper

PaperCity Magazine

Tanqueray

Continental Airlines

Louisa Stude Sarofim

Charles E. Butt

Kelly Gale Amen

Susie and Sanford Criner,
Auction Chairpersons

Joan and Sanford Alexander

Eddie and Chinhui Allen

David and Allison Ayers

Blair and Janice Bouchier

The Casey Family

Julie and Markley Crosswell

DeSantos Gallery

Bill England and Sonny Garza

Eve France and Howard Maisel

Cabanne and Mary Gilbreath &
David and Dianne Modesett

Slavka B.and Miles Glaser

Diana and Russell Hawkins

Carola and John Herrin

Rosalie and William M. Hitchcock

Wendy and Mavis Kelsey

James C. and Sherry Kempner

Mavis and Wendy Kelsey

James and Debra Maloney

Jane B.Owen

John Roberson and John Blackmon

Sicardi Gallery

Harry Zuber and William Bomar

Greentree Foundation

Sara Dodd-Spickelmier and
Keith Spickelmier

Gregory M. Spier,
JP Morgan Chase

Terry and Alice Thomas

ORGANIZERS

Frederick Baldwin and Wendy Watriss, *Artistic Direction and General Management*

FOTOFEST STAFF

Mary Doyle Glover, *Director, Literacy Through Photography*

Patrick McGinnis, *Volunteer Coordinator and Executive Assistant*

CONSULTANTS

Martha Skow, *Coordinator, Global Water Forum and Fine Print Auction*

Marta Sánchez Philippe, *Co-Coordinator, International Meeting Place, International Press and Special Projects*

Jenny Antill, *Coordinator, International Meeting Place*

Vinod Hopson, *Press and Public Relations Coordinator*

Jennifer Ward, *Exhibitions Coordinator*

Eileen Maxson, *Coordinator, Film & Video Programs*

Christine Rosales, *Special Projects and Publications Assistant*

Susannah Huggins, *Exhibitions Assistant*

Mary Stark Love, *Global Water Forum*

David Lerch, Axiom Design Group, *Graphic Design—Catalogue and Promotional Materials*

GoBase2-Manzanita Alliance, *FotoFest Web Site Design*

Dancie Perugini Ware Public Relations, *Media Coordination and Opening Night Events*
Dancie Ware, Marta Fredricks, Christy Guth, Jami Mabile

Janice Van Dyke Walden, Van Dyke Walden Assocs., *Public Relations, The Global Forum*

Masterpiece Litho-Printing, *Auction Catalogue, Film & Video Brochure*

Lisa Lerch, *Production Director, 2004 Catalogue, Map, and Calendar*

Mountain Dog Design, Haesun Kim Lerch, *Design, Special Publications*

aue design, *Design, Film and Video Calendar*

Jim Kanan, Kanan Construction, *Biennial Production*

Keith Hollingsworth, Hollingsworth Art Services, *Exhibition Matting/Framing*

Mark Larsen, *Facets, Exhibition Installation*

Lucille Graham, *Special Events Coordinator*

Rolf Eberlein, *Exhibition Lighting*

Mark Larson, Facets, *Exhibition Installation*

ttweak, *Multi-media Installation*, David Thompson, Randy Twaddle

Lucinda Cobley, *Matting/Framing Assistant*

Ruth Antonius, The Travel Solution, *Travel Coordination*

John Abrash, Destination Houston, *Houston Transportation*

Jeff Johnson, Brilliant Computers, *Computer Management*

Alex Kapadia, Brilliant Computers, *Computer Consultant*

Karen Whitaker, *Biennial Office Manager*

Lambros Papanikolatos, *Biennial Assistant*

Water is not only essential to all life and the survival of the planet, it is a vital part of spiritual and creative expression. Water, however, is an endangered resource. Fresh water resources are being misused, contaminated, and destroyed. Oceans are being polluted and depleted of life. Fresh water consumption is growing at twice the rate of population. Since 1950, fresh water demands have tripled and already over half of the world's accessible fresh water resources are being used. 1.1 billion people, 20 % of the world's population, still do not have access to safe drinking water. In the ocean, over 90% of the large fish species population has been killed off. Estuaries and reefs are disappearing. The state of Water in Texas and Houston is a microcosm of the world situation.

2004 WATER

Liquid water has been on our planet for at least 3 billion years ... Water moves in closed cycles that operate over vastly different scales of time and space.. But only in the past century and particularly within the past fifty years, has the scale of human impacts on the earth's water cycle reached global proportions.

Sandra Postel, *Natural History Magazine*

We view the land and the sea as separate worlds, when in fact they are closely linked. If we continue to combine a 19th century attitude with 21st century technology, little worth protecting will be left in the oceans.

Leon Panetta, *The Washington Post*

Looking back into the distant past as far as our awareness reaches, we find that water was the object of human veneration, a veneration amounting to religious worship. Every great culture felt water to be connected with the loftiest gods. It was considered holy, an element not to be tampered with in its purity.

Theodor Schwenk, *Sensitive Chaos; The Creation of Flowing Forms in Water and Air*

If there is magic on this planet, it is contained in water.

Dr. Loren Eiseley, *The Immense Journey*

There is no way that human society can or will refrain from imposing its will on the waterways of the world, fresh water and the oceans. It is our belief, however, that humankind must come to a new accommodation with the natural environment—an accommodation that respects the needs and equilibrium of the natural environment, on its own terms. An accommodation that is defined by stewardship, not unfettered conquest.

For scientists, technicians, artists, urban designers, economists, and ecologists studying Water around the world, there is no question that there is a crisis. Fresh Water sources are being consumed faster than the earth can recharge them. The consumption of Water scarcity is growing across the world. Commercial privatization and cross-national transport of water are increasing. Fresh Water reserves are not infinite. Clean, accessible fresh Water is becoming the "oil" of the new century.

In most industrially developed societies, however, Water is taken for granted. There is little general awareness about the looming crisis. Public understanding of the politics and ecology of Water is still at the beginning of the knowledge curve.

With FotoFest 2004, FotoFest is bringing science, art, and policy together to explore one of defining issues of this century—Water.

The programs include: Four-day Global Forum with scientists, policymakers, and humanists working on global and local issues of Water. Twenty-nine exhibitions and installations of classical photography and mixed media art about Water—curated and commissioned by FotoFest. Thirty-five independently curated exhibitions about Water. Film and video series about Water. School-based, student projects on Water. Special edition of the prestigious international art magazine European Photography dedicated to Water and FotoFest 2004

These programs address:

~ *The Global Perspective:* Water as a determinant of human history. The state of the world's water.

~ *The Environment:* Water as the underlying resource of all life on earth

~ *The Community Perspective:* Water and the quality of life. Water's potential for enrichment and destruction.

~ *The Personal View:* Water as a catalyst for creative and spiritual expression.

FotoFest 2004 reflects a deep and longtime interest of FotoFest's founders about the impacts of human society on the natural environment and use of Water in particular. Six years ago, we began a worldwide search for photo-based art projects relating to water. To reflect the breadth and complexity of the subject, we expanded the exhibitions into the realm of film and video. The Global Forum brings the information and analysis of science, economics, technology, urban design, humanistic philosophy, and social policy into the framework of art.

What is the state of Water in the world today?

How much of the ecosystem is being affected by the way we are managing water?

Can technology solve the growing crises?

What does the privatization of Water mean?

What are the economics of Water?

Locally, are the Water Wars of Texas a mirror of the world situation?

Can all people have access to clean Water?

What is Water? What does it need to survive?

It is time for a new 'vision' of Water.

FotoFest 2004 is designed to address these questions and look to the future.

Wendy Watriss and **Frederick Baldwin**
FotoFest

Many, many people have been important to making this FotoFest a reality. We thank these individuals later in this catalogue. Here we would particularly like to thank the staff, consultants and Board of FotoFest as well as the co-organizers of the Global Forum from Rice University — Paul Harcombe, Walter Isle, Neal Lane, Mark Wiesner, Jim Blackburn, and Christian Holmes. We would also like to thank longtime friends and colleagues who, in very different ways, made it possible to do FotoFest 2004—Senator Tim Wirth, Wren Wirth, Nan Tucker McEvoy, Ambassador William Luers, and Wendy Luers. We thank the artists whose work are the basis for these exhibitions about Water.

FACTS ABOUT WATER

The world is now using 52% of the available fresh water.

Water consumption is growing at twice the rate of population.

About 60% of the human body is made up of water.

70% of the human brain is made up of water.

Over 20% of the world's population (more than one billion people) lack access to safe drinking water. —Center for New American Dream, *Enough!*, quarterly report.

By 2025, nearly 50% of the world's population (at least 3.5 billion people) will face water scarcity. —*World Resources Institute*

Annually, Americans consume more water per capita (1677 cubic meters), than any other country in the world, including India and China combined.—The Center for Economic and Social Rights, *Right to Water Fact Sheet #1.*

Half the world's rivers and lakes are seriously polluted. —*Khalid Mohtadullah, Executive Secretary of the Global Water Partnership, World Water Day*

90% of large fish population in the oceans are gone, due to commercial fishing.

"At least 20% of the Earth's 10,000 fresh water fish species are now endangered, threatened with extinction or already extinct."
—*Sandra Postel, Hydro Dynamics*, Natural History

On average, people have built four dams a day, for the past half century.

In many cultures, water represents, birth, renewal, cleansing and purifying.

Texas law allows landowners to capture and sell any and all water found directly under their properties, even if that water comes from a shared resources and even if doing so poses a threat to the share supply.

Oceans, unlike land, cannot be placed in a private trust for conservation. The oceans are a public trust.

Enough water evaporates from Lake Powell each year to supply Los Angeles with water for the same period of time.

U.S. and Canada have jointly cleaned up Lake Erie. I 1970, it was literally dying. Now, fish life is flourishing.

A gallon of bottled water costs more than a gallon of oil.

Wetlands in the U.S. are becoming wastelands due to dumping, upstream water draw-off, water diversion, and urban development.

Each year, Louisiana loses 35 square miles of bayous to the Gulf of Mexico due to erosion, urban development, oil and gas drilling and silt diversion from levees and canals on the Mississippi River.

More than 100 dams have been removed in the U.S., reviving rivers and aquatic habitat.

Fishermen in California have led efforts to restore salmon habitats and improve management of squid fisheries.

Headwater advantage: upstream agriculture has siphoned off enough water so that two major rivers in the American West—the Colorado and the Rio Grande —no longer reach the sea.

Up to 3.5 million Americans get sick from fetid water each year.

In 20 years, Denver, Salt Lake City, Albuquerque, Las Vegas, Houston and other western cities will be in the grip of severe water shortages. —*U.S. Dept. of Interior*

Texas has almost as much surface water as the land of 10,000 lakes, Minnesota, which has some 4,790 square miles of surface water.

Texas has 9 major aquifers and 11,247 named streams. —*Texas Almanac and U.S. Geological Survey.*

Texas' surface water belongs to the state; its ground-water belongs to the landowner.

About 60% of the water used yearly in Texas derives from underground formations. —*Texas Almanac*

In 1990, Texas and California had the highest water withdrawals rates in the United States.

"Water is a finite resource that requires careful and proactive management: the era of plentiful and inexpensive water in Texas is ending." —*From the introduction to An Assessment of Water Conservation in Texas, done for the 78th Texas Legislature (2003) by the Texas State Soil and Water Conservation Board and Texas Water Development Board.*

COMPILED BY JANICE VAN DYKE WALDEN. 2004

CONTENTS

PETER GOIN • *CP61–VIEW DOWN THE CANYON AT LAST LIGHT, WILLOW CREEK CANYON, ESCALANTE RIVER, LAKE POWELL, JUNE 2003* • CHROMOGENIC DEVELOPMENT PRINT

FOTOFEST EXHIBITS—WATER

FOTOFEST EXHIBITIONS 1

INSTITUTE OF FLOW SCIENCES

The Language of Water

INSTITUTE OF FLOW SCIENCES

Water is mobile
Water is sensitive
Water is open

Water is always found in circulation

Life on earth is irrevocably linked to water,
to fluid water

If one does not understand fluid water
One cannot understand life[1]

This important collaboration with the German Institute of Flow Sciences [Institut für Strömungswissenschaften] illustrates the way science and art are able to intersect to find a new way to "see" water through water's capacity for movement. The Institute of Flow Sciences in Herrischried, Germany, has pioneered methods of visually recording the internal movements and shape-forming processes of fresh water. A major goal of the Institute's work is to bring forth a new understanding of the sensitivity and complexity of water and to establish new benchmarks for judging the purity of water on the basis of its positive characteristics.

"We are concerned that the natural sources of water be cared for and appreciated by the public both for their public utility and their essential beauty," says Wolfram Schwenk, a principal researcher and one of the directors of the Institute. *"Wherever water appears, as moisture in the soil from which it runs as brooks, streams, and rivers to fill up ponds, lakes, and even oceans, water becomes the life-giver, and simultaneously provides a viable environment for an endless number of microorganisms, plants and animals.*

"The central subject of our concern is understanding what good water is and how it changes during the various cycles. Once water is brought into motion, it reveals a wide variety of activities. It becomes the medium for all different sorts of shape-forming processes and the place wherein there is an inexhaustible activity of renewal and recreation of forms.

"The characteristics distinguishing water as a means for sustaining life become activated when water is in motion, and water's mobility is one of its most important characteristics. When water is mobile, it has the potential to reorganize itself. If we incorporate mobility as a factor to be included in qualitative analyses of given samples of water, then we can expand efforts beyond traditional chemical analyses to determine water's quality and its organizational potential.

"Through methods pioneered by my father, Theodor Schwenk, we have developed a systematic way of looking at the internal behavior of water and documenting its movements. Through his Drop-Picture Method, we have been able to develop a scientifically reliable procedure for revealing this aspect of water. And we have been able to establish a benchmark that can be used in conjunction with other analyses to determine the positive characteristics of purity in different kinds of water."[2]

Amongst the green, tree-covered hills of the southern Black Forest, German engineer Theodor Schwenk found clear spring water that demonstrated water's wondrous capacity for movement—the ability of the tiniest drop of water to form infinitely varied and beautiful shapes.

The images produced by the Institute in recent years enable people to see movements of water normally invisible to the human eye. Uncontaminated by pollutants,

Theodor Schwenk • *Train of Vortices*, c. 1960, from *Das sensible Chaos*, Verlag
Freies Geistesleben, Stuttgart *(Sensitive Chaos)*, 1962 • Modern Silver
Gelatin Print

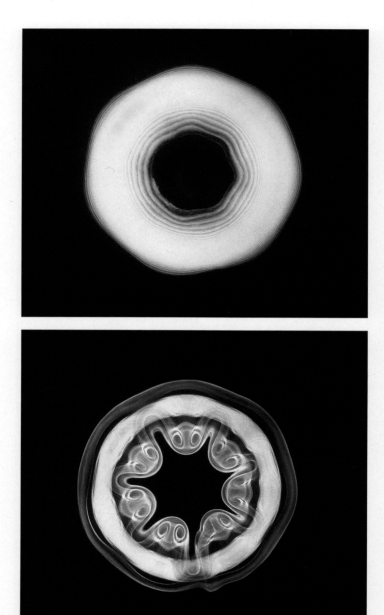

INSTITUTE OF FLOW SCIENCES • *RISING RING VORTEX*, 2004 • COLOR
TRANSPARENCY • VORTICES SEEN FROM ABOVE.

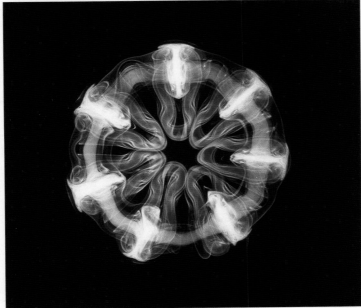

INSTITUTE OF FLOW SCIENCES • *RISING RING VORTEX*, 2004 • COLOR
TRANSPARENCY • VORTICES SEEN FROM ABOVE.

fresh spring water shows an almost infinite capacity for continuous and multi-formed movement, creating an enormous variety of complex shapes. As one radiating circular form follows another in the Drop-Pictures, it is clear that the internal movements of water are never linear. The images create an enhanced understanding of water and its simultaneous ability to both mold its surroundings and adapt itself to the external forms that surround it.

The refinement of the Drop-Picture methodology is attracting an increasing number of waterworks professionals to the Institute to find new ways to enhance more traditional measurements of municipal water quality. The city of Amsterdam is one beneficiary of the Institute's investigations.

The Institute is also studying how water's capacity for movement can affect water's capacity for self-purification after its contamination with pollutants. In the mid 1990s, the Institute participated in a study (published in the 1990s) of the Mettma, a small Black Forest stream contaminated upstream by brewery and domestic wastewater. The contents of the water and its organic life were analyzed over an eight-kilometer (five-mile) stretch downstream from the point of wastewater discharge. Taking water samples at various distances from the source of pollution and putting these samples through the Drop-Picture process resulted in a remarkable documentation of the relationship between water quality and the differentiation of organic life in polluted and less polluted water. The images show a clear correlation between the point where the stream water was able to regain its pre-pollution condition and the development of more sophisticated life forms.

"Our concern is to help people 'see' water in a new way," says Wolfram Schwenk. *"The work at the Institute of Flow Sciences, should be understood as 'research for a new consciousness of water,' to appreciate its complexity and capacity to generate and serve life.*

"The research is not simply an end in itself to enjoy the beauty of water phenomena, but rather to learn to understand what, in nature, acts as both beautiful and healing, in order to incorporate health and beauty into our fashioning of the world. To find the middle between extremes, while granting each its right, and to mediate between opposites. We can learn all of this from water."* [3]

The philosophy and work of the Institute has also inspired the work of German artist and urban designer Herbert Dreiseitl, whose use of water in urban environments is attracting the attention of cities throughout the world, and top architects such as Sir Norman Foster and Renzo Piano.

Wendy Watriss
FotoFest

This text is excerpted from the book *Understanding Water* by Wolfram Schwenk, Andreas Wilkens, and Michael Jacobi in the series *Sensibles Wasser* published by the Institut für Strömungswissenschaften in Herrischried, Germany, 1995. The ongoing work of the Institute is based on the research and writings of German fluid-mechanical engineer Theodor Schwenk (1910–1986) whose book *Sensitive Chaos* was first published in 1962 by Verlag Freies Geistesleben, Stuttgart, Germany. Theodor Schwenk was a founder of the Institute in 1960 and its director for many years.

The exhibition was co-curated by FotoFest with Wolfram Schwenk and Andreas Wilkens of the Institute of Flow Sciences. FotoFest's work with the Institute was coordinated and assisted by The Water Research Institute of Blue Hill, Maine, and its director, Jennifer Greene. Greene has worked with the Institute of Flow Sciences for many years to promote an understanding of water, including presentations at World Water Forums in The Hague, Netherlands (2000) and Kyoto, Japan (2003).

This exhibition received special support from the Rudolf Steiner Foundation in San Francisco, CA and from Margaret Regan and Fletcher Thorne-Thomsen, Jr., of Vine Street Studios.

[1]Wolfram Schwenk, Andreas Wilkens, and Michael Jacobi, *Understanding Water,* from the series *Sensibles Wasser* (Herrischried, Germany: Institut für Strömungswissenschaften, 1995), Prologue.

[2]*From Conversations with Wolfram Schwenk*, August 2003, in Herrischried, Germany and *Water as a Life-Giving Element in Understanding Water*, pgs. 67-75.

[3]*Understanding Water*, pp. 22-23, 27-28, 67-75

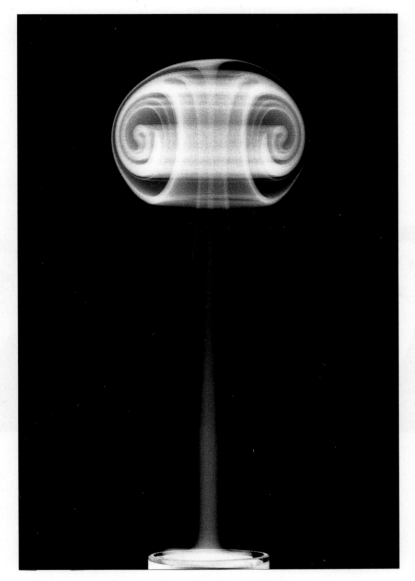

INSTITUTE OF FLOW SCIENCES • *RISING RING VORTEX*, 2004 •COLOR
TRANSPARENCY • VORTICES SEEN FROM THE SIDE.

INSTITUTE OF FLOW SCIENCES • *TRAIN OF VORTICES*, 2004 • COLOR PRINT

Looking at a naturally flowing stream we notice the winding course it takes through the valley. It never flows straight ahead. Are these meanderings in the very nature of water?

The rhythm of its meanders is a part of the individual nature of a river. In a wide valley, a river will swing in far-flung curves, whereas a narrow valley will cause it to wind to and fro in a faster rhythm. A brook running through a meadow makes many small, often only tentative bends....

Research on canalized rivers, for instance the Rhine in its lower reaches, revealed decades ago that the natural course of water is rhythmical meandering. Even between straightened banks the river tries, with what remaining strength it has, to realize this form of movement by flowing in a meandering rhythm between the straight banks. Not even the strongest walled banks can hold out indefinitely against this "will" of the river and wherever they offer a chance they will be torn down. The river tries to turn the unnatural, straight course into its own natural one.

Theodor Schwenk, *Sensitive Chaos: The Creation of Flowing Forms in Water and Air* (reprint: Rudolf Steiner Press, London England 1996), pp. 16–18.

INSTITUTE OF FLOW SCIENCES • *TRAIN OF VORTICES*, 2004 • COLOR PRINT

RIVERGLASS

A River Ballet in Four Seasons

ARTIST: ANDREJ ZDRAVIC

R*iverglass* is a poem to one of the most beautiful rivers in the world—the Soca. Clear, cold, and buoyant, the Soca dances in the Julian Alps of Slovenia.

Riverglass is not a documentary about the Soca but rather an experiential film—a poetic river ballet to the music of natural sounds. Unlike conventional films that rely on facts and stories about nature as told by humans, *Riverglass* conveys a story without words or human presence: the story is the river itself.

The message of the Soca lies in its primal, aerial clarity, a true treasure that surprises and inspires anew. I devised a special tool to capture the river from a unique perspective: through the liquid lens of crystalline water, we perceive, perhaps for the first time, the magical underwater world of turquoise volumes, flying bubbles, pulsating sun membranes, and dancing stones. The vivid colors and rhythms of the river become a source of philosophical and spiritual insight. Four years in the making, *Riverglass* is a reflection of my endless fascination with the forces of nature, forces that contain universal principles of life and the seeds for a new kind of narrative cinema.

I have been studying and filming water (rivers and oceans) ever since I made my first film three decades ago. Water is effortless power and grace, the elixir of life. Chinese philosophers of millennia ago regarded water as a supreme mediator of truth. They recognized in the fluid element the principles governing all life and also the precept for human conduct. Theodor Schwenk's seminal book *Sensitive Chaos: The Creation of Flowing Forms in Water and Air* (reprint; New York: Schocken Books, 1987) also greatly inspired me. My involvement in medical filmmaking (namely plastic surgery and microsurgery) opened a whole new world to me. It also gave me a new perspective on the devastating effects of physical and mental violence in films. Our intuition is being short-circuited by an overload of contradictory information produced by the media and advertising, polluting the environment and our minds. Indeed filmmakers have a special responsibility nowadays. At present, education about the Earth is more urgently needed than ever. It is only by promoting a sensitized comprehension of nature that we can hope to create better prospects for nature's (and our own) survival.

I believe my function is to funnel the energy of things at their elemental level, for I feel it is simplicity that holds true revelation. This is a great challenge and the pursuit of my life.

Andrej Zdravic

This exhibition received support from the Trust for Mutual Understanding.

Andrej Zdravic • *Riverglass*, 1997 • Video Still

WATER IN THE WEST

ARTISTS: LAURIE BROWN, ROBERT DAWSON, TERRY EVANS, GEOFFREY FRICKER, PETER GOIN, WANDA HAMMERBECK, SANT KHALSA, MARK KLETT, ELLEN LAND-WEBER, SHARON STEWART, MARTIN STUPICH

One could select the individual work of any one of these 11 artists. Each one of them has multiple bodies of work related to land, water, and the relationship of human society to these natural resources. Their work has focused on the arid U.S. West, where land and water have been shaped and reshaped, worked and re-worked, managed and mismanaged, created, destroyed and re-created.

Diverse, different, and deeply informed about their own individual work, these artists found themselves drawn together for over nearly a decade. They set a framework that would define projects, sponsor exhibits and forums, make presentations, publish books, discuss the meaning of what each of them was doing, and, finally, establish a permanent point of reference, an archive. They came together to share their work: to create a better understanding about the nature of the physical world in which they lived, the meaning and memory of 19th century exploration and conquest, and the impact of human society on the shape of the land and its resources.

In their work, there is a sense of time passing, of bearing witness. There is an appreciation of the importance of history and the ambiguities of its meanings. Each artist has his/her own physical, spiritual, and political connections to land, and, through land, to Water. Like Water, the collective energy of *Water In The West* has ebbed and flowed, occasionally coming to rest and then moving on and away. As individuals and artists, they resist easy definition.

They are diverse and multiple voices, revealing the complexity of Water itself and the paradoxes of human relationship to Water. There is an underlying passion in their work—a shared concern about what is happening to the natural environment and the imprint of human society. This exhibit is a revisiting of their work, their individual and collective commitments to the shape of Land and Water in the West.

Wendy Watriss
FotoFest

The installation of *Water in the West* at FotoFest 2004 was made possible by Hines, Williams Tower Gallery. Special thanks go to Sally Sprout, Gallery Director. Exhibition research was done at the Center for Creative Photography, Tucson, AZ.

FOTOFEST EXHIBITIONS

WANDA HAMMERBECK • UNTITLED, 1997 • COLOR PHOTOGRAPH

FOTOFEST EXHIBITIONS

WATER IN THE WEST

Following the Water

ARTIST: MARK KLETT

Mark Twain once said whisky is for drinking, and water is for fighting. That is the position water plays in the developed West. But water can also be seen as a metaphor for contemplating time and space, a natural force turned into a kind of nature/culture/time coordinate system for tracking an era of change. Landscape photographs then become maps in four dimensions.

Arizona is a dry state among dry states, and the presence or absence of water is not without consequence. Following the water is one way to gauge the flow of power in this part of the world, determining how people connect with their environment and shape their histories. It is a moving focus point where aspirations, land, and artifacts collide.

But water is not my real subject. Although my work has often centered on a place, or on an issue such as water, I am more interested in creating a larger suite of works that concentrates on an idea, a methodology, or an investigation. I am drawn to the construction of time and place, and the way that the natural world influences both. This is an inquiry for which photography is particularly well suited.

My work has led me to search for ways that photographs can fold and unfold time. Water provides a basis for asking questions, and the most important ones for me concern the relationship between time and change. Water is perhaps the most visible symbol of the changing landscapes in the arid West. Yet, the passage of time is not a reliable measure of this change. What if the past changes depending on how we see it? Can time then be experienced as a having backwards flow? Can this perception alter our views of the past as well as our course for the future? Is the movement of time really constant or does change itself become the true measure of time? I believe following the water will give the answers.

Mark Klett

MARK KLETT • *VIEWING THOMAS MORAN AT THE SOURCE, ARTIST'S POINT, YELLOWSTONE*, 2000 • PIGMENTED INK JET

WATER IN THE WEST

ARTIST: WANDA HAMMERBECK

More than oil or gold, our rearrangement of water has altered the landscape of the American West. Beyond the 100th meridian, the West begins—that vast territory defined by the need for irrigation in order to grow substantial crops. We have created man-made rivers with our aqueducts. We have created lakes where there were none with our reservoirs. We have even made our water flow uphill pushed by powerful pumps. Without seeing the full ramification of our actions, we have taken water from seven Western states and Mexico and made it flow to Los Angeles.

By the beginning of the 20th century, Los Angeles had embarked on the largest water-seeking venture in the history of the world. Angelenos realized they would need more water to become the city they wanted to be. This venture, which after 100 years is still under way, radically altered the visual landscape, natural resources, economy, politics, and culture of the American West. The prosperity of California has been built upon this massive rearrangement of the natural environment through water diversion. California's economy, now ranked between fourth and sixth among all nations, leads the United States in agricultural and industrial output.

When I moved to Los Angeles in 1986, I was shocked to see the concrete flood channel of the Los Angeles River. Thus began my interest in Los Angeles water. For the past 18 years, I have researched, explored, and photographed the appropriated water landscape of the Owens River Basin, the Colorado River Basin, the California State Water Project, and the Los Angeles River Basin. These four areas, encompassing seven western states, provide water for the city and county of Los Angeles, and their natural resources have been transformed significantly as Los Angeles has searched for water, clashed with local communities, and vied with governments for power.

Wanda Hammerbeck

WANDA HAMMERBECK • UNTITLED, 1981-1996 • COLOR PHOTOGRAPH

WATER IN THE WEST

ARTIST: ROBERT DAWSON

The images presented here are from the *Water in the West* Project—a collaborative photographic response to the use and abuse of water in the western United States. These photographs were taken over a 24-year period, from 1979 to 2003.

While the water crisis is global, the other photographers in this project and I have chosen to focus on the U.S. American West. It is here that the impact of the rapid development of arid lands is most visible in the landscape.

In the *Water in the West* Project, a core group of 10 photographers, a curator/historian, and I have worked to evaluate and address issues surrounding the western landscape and the escalating water crisis. The project has established a photo archive, which will serve as a resource for people interested in water issues. The archive is permanently housed at the Center for Creative Photography at the University of Arizona in Tucson. Publications from the project include *A River Too Far: The Past and Future of the Arid West* (Reno: Univ. of Nevada Press, 1991) and *Arid Waters: Photographs From the Water in the West Project* (Reno: Univ. of Nevada Press, 1992)

My photographs in the *Water in the West* Project have evolved from my travels throughout the West looking at our culture's relationship to water. The work is concerned about our attitudes toward growth and related environmental controversies. Some of the work addresses the issues with irony. Some of it looks at our culture's desire to possess, control, and shape the land and water to our needs. Certain photographs document abuse, while others examine the complex, evolving relationship to water that I hope to influence with this work.

Robert Dawson

ROBERT DAWSON • *Pipe Carrying Most of San Francisco's Water, Near Mather, CA*, 1992 • Silver Gelatin Print

FOTOFEST EXHIBITIONS

MARTIN STUPICH • *ELEPHANT BUTTE DAM, NEW MEXICO,* 1991 • SILVER GELATIN PRINT

WATER IN THE WEST

ARTIST: MARTIN STUPICH

Raised in the upper Rust Belt just as the good times there ended, I spent Saturdays and summers during my childhood roaming the rail yards and Lake Michigan docks that connected Milwaukee to the world. "Landscapes" meant industrial landscapes. Later in art school, I learned that there was a romantic version of landscape that included cows and trees and pastorale. But for me that romantic view of the world was (and remains) as saccharine as a Strauss waltz.

Intuitively, I was sure that the cultural landscape, the engineered environment, was not only sufficient, but was really the only true place—the only subject matter there is. After the invention of cartography, nothing (not even portraits) escaped the grid, avoided being property or object. Given this frame of mind, Yosemite as the subject of serious pictures seemed a joke to this young photographer. Edouard Baldus, Eugene Atget, Walker Evans, Charles Sheeler, Robert Frank, Linda Connor, and Lee Friedlander were closer to the point. They showed me that evidence of human activity and ambition, the built world, is eloquent. It is our autobiography, and it cannot lie.

Early I decided that if I wanted my pictures to have value, or even simply be interesting, photographing only what I knew would render a slim portfolio indeed. But photographing what is huge and complicated seemed a good bet and could teach me something.

When in 1980 I found a job documenting historic 19th-century Nevada mining sites, I saw finally that all the elements of landscapes can be reduced to earth below the horizon, sky above it, and water, and that good human drama usually unfolds around the water. Cities rise below dams. Mines and agribusinesses claim, then deplete, aquifers. The mirage of abundance becomes a little quivery and transparent—and the tale, more compelling.

The arid West is my home and my primary subject. Water in the West as metaphor remains useful and leads me now to the Red Desert in southern Wyoming's Great Divide Basin. There, in the next decade, hundreds of gas wells will pock the desert, displacing elk, horse, antelope, and the ink-black night. Drilling will draw down tiny lakes, leaving alkali pans. Streams that do flow will course with exotic toxins. The balance, already delicate everywhere, will shift. And one more broad swath of the world will have, literally, the life sucked out of it. This fact, in its austere simplicity, deserves attention. So I photograph.

Martin Stupich

WATER IN THE WEST

Lake Powell

ARTIST: PETER GOIN

Throughout history, people have altered the Earth's air, water, and soil in order to survive and to thrive as a species. The consequences are pervasive. In the United States, meandering rivers and their oxbows are too often dredged into channels along straight lines, while remote mountain ranges are seen from 30,000 feet above to be crisscrossed with spider webs that must be roads. Yellow-brown haze blurs many horizons, burns our lungs, and kills the trees downwind with acidic precision. Rivers and aquifers become oversubscribed, and large cities such as Las Vegas, Los Angeles, and Phoenix negotiate allocations for water flow that may never materialize or be equitably distributed.

Human tampering with the natural world has made the Earth itself an artifact, for the process of civilization has been one of domesticating environments. In the American West, perhaps the most apparent human effort to control nature is the management of water, particularly the Colorado River, which descends from the Rocky Mountains and concludes its 1,500-mile journey at the Gulf of California. This great river with its unparalleled rapids is oversubscribed. It suffers from dangerously high levels of salinity and is restrained by the Glen Canyon Dam and the Hoover Dam, creating the huge reservoirs Lake Powell and Lake Mead, respectively. Its remote canyons and wilderness have sparked the American imagination, yet its modern notoriety derives from the fact

that the Colorado River is likely the most legislated, most debated, and most litigated river in the world. Decisions about the flow and volume of this once wild river are made according to the peaks and valleys of urban hydroelectric power demands, while entitlements are challenged through the justice system. The Grand Canyon was once one of the most inaccessible wilderness areas in the United States; now whitewater enthusiasts and hikers seeking wilderness must incorporate the water-release schedules in their departure times and camping locations.

Lake Powell has 1,960 miles of shoreline, and its side canyons, coves, and straits are extremely popular with pleasure boaters, anglers, scuba divers, and water skiers. Glen Canyon, a geological calendar of red rock, muddy shale, pink or white sandstone, and limestone, is clearly a spectacular oasis, incongruous within the vast aridity defining the American Southwest.

The Colorado River has thus become a symbol of the hope, conflict, and dilemma of managing nature's aridity.

Peter Goin

This essay has been paraphrased from Peter Goin's book *Humanature* (Austin: University of Texas Press, 1996).

PETER GOIN • *CHAIR, FIRELIGHT, AND CANYON VIEW AT LAST LIGHT, DAVIS GULCH, ESCALANTED RIVER, LAKE POWELL, JUNE 2003* • CHROMOGENIC PRINT

WATER IN THE WEST

River, Words, and Culture: Language, Text, Voices

ARTIST: GEOFFREY FRICKER

The photographs in this show reflect my interest in our relationship to land and water. The landscape includes human histories of how we value and use water. Each photograph accordingly has text below it that identifies with various voices—political, economic, recreational. Without the text, the viewer can freely give his or her own meaning to the landscape. With the text, however, the viewer begins to apprehend another perspective or voice to contemplate.

As a time-based medium, photography freezes a scene at one point in time. I like to include in my photographs man-made things or structures (e.g., bridges, canoes) because as cultural artifacts they suggest our values at a given point in time. The quotes that accompany the images are selected from public documents that mirror the values of a wide range of organizations within our community. They also point to cultural attitudes dominant at a particular time in our human history. Taken as a whole, the photographs and text help to outline the diversity of perspectives that define the complexity of water in our community.

Text or language often simplifies issues, isolates facts, and creates a linear narrative. But with regard to water and land issues, words seem to develop a rich and contradictory complexity, creating a convoluted and circuitous language that is much like the natural meander of the river itself. This freely meandering river demonstrates what Stephen J. Gould describes as the "rich raw material of any evolving system: variation itself."

The human productions of art, science, and language are also a part of that raw material of evolving systems. They too are a part of the mercurial surprise of this naturally meandering river.

Geoffrey Fricker

GEOFFREY FRICKER • *WESTER CANAL, WATER DISTRICT DAM,* 1994 • SILVER GELATIN PRINT

Geoffrey Fricker • *Disabled Space*, 1995 • Silver Gelatin Print

WATER IN THE WEST

The Arcata Marsh

ARTIST: ELLEN LAND-WEBER

The Arcata Marsh is a much studied work of constructed artifice designed to treat secondary wastewater for the city of Arcata, population 17,000, on California's far north coast. Built on an abandoned industrial and dump site, the Marsh is a series of carefully monitored man-made ponds that utilize the natural filtration properties of brackish and freshwater organisms to do a job normally accomplished by large machinery and unsightly, sprawling, maintenance-intensive installations.

Since its initial construction in the late 1970s, the Marsh's enhanced wetland habitat has quietly evolved into a successful wildlife sanctuary. Located under the Pacific Flyway, the Marsh has become favored ground for over 200 species of waterfowl, shore birds, and migratory birds, enough to satisfy a resident flock of appreciative, binocular-toting humans.

To a person strolling the Marsh trails, cues to its artificial origin and purpose are not readily detected. It appears that birds and other small animals are equally clueless. Representing a positive and clearly beneficial intersection of nature and human endeavor, the idea of the Marsh begs the question, what is natural about nature?

My *Water in the West* series—a project of photographic ollages with its own evolutionary time frame—takes note of this question. It purports to show what animal species might be found at the Marsh following prolonged global warming, global cooling, genetic engineering of animal and plant species, or all three.

I became a member of the Water in the West Photographers Collaborative because I have lived the best half of my life in the West, in a place known for cool weather and much rain. On a clear day from my bedroom window, I have about a six-inch view of Humboldt Bay and the Pacific Ocean beyond. Water and its multiple meanings along the spectrum from basic necessity to spiritual succor are never far from consciousness. Making photographs that embody water as subject and content has always seemed a natural thing to do.

Ellen Land-Weber

ELLEN LAND-WEBER • *ELEPHANT FAMILY WITH FLAMINGO AT THE ARCATA MARSH*, 1999 • IRIS INKJET PRINT

ELLEN LAND-WEBER • *A FRENCH SEA LION AT THE ARCATA MARSH*, 2003 • IRIS INKJET PRINT

WATER IN THE WEST

El Cerrito Y La Acequia Madre [The Little Hill and the Mother Ditch]

ARTIST: SHARON STEWART

In a region of ghostly presences, the Spanish Land Grant village of El Cerrito has endured through centuries. This black and white photographic survey that began in 1992 presents a village life portrait illustrated by the people's interdependence on water from the community irrigation ditch, or *acequia*. No one in El Cerrito can remember hearing about the origins of the *acequia*, lending to speculation that the ditch was created by Native Americans who first settled this Pecos River Valley. Others believe its existence can be ascribed, like other of the 1,000 *acequias* in New Mexico, to the efforts of Franciscan priests who, when colonizing the area for Spain, were directed to establish two vital elements of village life—faith and water. Very likely a confluence of efforts created this hand-dug, one and a half-mile gravity-flow irrigation system that now sustains the village.

Acequia also refers to the association of users that honors water as a community resource rather than a commodity. The *parciantes*, water rights holders, for generations have shared in the responsibility of maintaining a waterway that feeds their families, orchards, gardens, fields, and livestock. While recharging watersheds, *acequias* also provide a rich riparian zone for wildlife, shade trees, and native plants, many used in traditional medicines. Each spring the *limpia*, or cleaning, of the *acequia* is the responsibility of the *parciantes*. In a self-governing system

dating to the Moors, who established acequias in Spain during their seven-century occupation, the caretaker, or *mayordomo*, is chosen by the *parciantes* to oversee the maintenance of the acequia throughout the year, particularly during the spring *limpia*. The *limpia* is the one social gathering outside the rare wedding and more common funeral for which all manner of people come to El Cerrito.

Seeing the universal in the specific, this exploration of the survival of El Cerrito gives insights into sustainability through cooperation, two concepts continually offered as harmonious solutions to the dissonance created by our time's reigning consumption-driven, individualistic life style.

The availability of water looks to be the defining issue of our nascent century. Monetary pressures are strong on rural Hispanic villagers to sell their water rights. This would effectively severe ties to water and the land that are the most cherished cultural component of the region's agrarian communities such as El Cerrito. In resisting, villagers ensure the vitality of the Southwest's oldest extant water system while reinforcing this universal truism:

Agua es vida. Water is life.

Sharon Stewart

SHARON STEWART • *EL CERRITO Y LA ACEQUIA MADRE: ACEQUIA FLOW,* 1994 • SELENIUM SILVER TONED PRINT

FOTOFEST EXHIBITIONS

WATER IN THE WEST

ARTIST: LAURIE BROWN

My photographs have always focused on our culture's relationship to the land in the Southwest. Desert regions make up a large percentage of the American Southwest, and in this dry terrain the scarcity of water is always a defining factor. In the Las Vegas series, I am looking at visual evidence of the suburban growth taking place on the city's outlying edges, where there has been relentless development of, and expansion into, the rural or wild tracts of the surrounding desert. (For the past several years, Las Vegas has been one of the top two fastest growing cities in the nation.)

When photographing for this series, which I call *Las Vegas Peripheries*, I am drawn to juxtapose the natural terrain, with its extreme aridity and sparse vegetation, against the new built environment, with its human marks, signs, and structures. Amazingly, this ongoing expansion often includes man-made lakes and canals, with lush golf courses and waterfront living.

My continuing interest in the history of our culture's connections to the western landscape stems partly from the fact that in 1864 my great-grandfather brought his family to California in a covered wagon. They came to homestead and started a new life in the "promised land" of the West.

Over the years I have continued to record the imprint of this part of the human story as it relates to settling the land of the Southwest. While recording the spaces and stark details of our own specific time and place on this land, I also find it fascinating to explore and consider the history of our past and the implications for the future.

Laurie Brown

Laurie Brown • *Waterfront Living, Northwest Las Vegas*, 1991 • Cibachrome Print

Laurie Brown • *Green at Man-made Lake, Las Vegas*, 1996 • Cibachrome Print

WATER IN THE WEST

ARTIST: SANT KHALSA

My photographs and installations create a contemplative space where one may consider the subtle and profound connections between humanity, nature, and our constructed environments. The subject of water provides endless material for ideas and artworks that bring greater awareness of the interdependence of human beings and the natural world. My artwork develops from the myriad meanings, mythologies, and metaphors associated with water, the universal solve(nt), integrated with ideas about nature, the body, and art experienced as a "sacred site." The installation *Watershed* and the photographic project

SANT KHALSA • *WATERSHED PRODUCTS*, 2000 • INSTALLATION

Western Waters address the commodification of nature, water as a consumer product, and human desire—a never-ending thirst.

Watershed is constructed solely with everyday materials and involves the most basic and necessary of life experiences, the drinking of water. The installation includes a shedlike structure of corrugated boxes holding bottled water, point-of-purchase displays, and product information, including a mission statement and market research. The words used as water product names (creativity, inspiration, change, balance, integrity, harmony, and grace) represent attributes found in the natural world as well as desirable human qualities. The *Watershed* "product" gives viewers/consumers what they physically require—health—and psychologically desire—happiness (by playing off the notion that we consume to feel better about ourselves). The artwork is a "critical commodity"— a consumer good that critiques its own existence. The installation invites participation in the physical consumption of water, as well as in art and ideas, with the hope of activating a "watershed" experience.

Western Waters photographically documents the growing business of retail water stores throughout the southwestern United States. The stores are located in regions where more water is necessary for survival, but less naturally available. In southern California, many of these businesses are in low-income neighborhoods and/or locations with large immigrant populations, while in Arizona, New Mexico, and southern Nevada, stores appear most often in retirement communities and in regions where tap water has a very high sodium and mineral content. The success of these stores is based on consumers' fear that their tap water is not safe to drink and on providing a less expensive alternative to bottled water.

What most interests me is both the necessity and the absurdity of these stores, and the way these venues have come to represent the source of a natural experience. Of course, these stores are merely elements of entrepreneurial enterprise—constructed sites to provide the consumer with the most essential requirement for life and survival. Today plastic bottles have replaced earthen vessels, and to fetch our water, we travel in polluting automobiles to and from this fabricated representation of a river, well, or spring. The photographs will serve in the future as a historical document, either registering a fleeting fad or laying the foundation of what will have become commonplace in our society.

Sant Khalsa

SANT KHALSA • *WATERSHED*, 2000 • INSTALLATION

WATER IN THE WEST

ARTIST: TERRY EVANS

Water is not my subject, or rather water is not my only subject. These photographs are selected from a larger body of work in progress about Chicago and the surrounding region stretching into Indiana and Michigan and up to Wisconsin. Entitled *Revealing Chicago*, this series will be an exhibition of 80 to100 40 by 40-inch prints shown outdoors in downtown Chicago's Millennium Park in the summer of 2005. A book and documentary film will accompany the exhibition. My intention, and the intention of my collaborators from Openlands and Metropolis 2020, is to show the beauty and complexity of the city and region while raising questionabout land use, urban sprawl, transportation, development, water, and more. My hope is that viewers will come to see the interconnectedness of the region and thus see themselves as citizens of the region, responsible for its future.

Water issues are deeply woven into the complicated tapestry of Chicago, which developed into a major city in large part because of the construction in 1848 of the Illinois and Michigan Canal, which connected the Great Lakes and the Mississippi River, thus enabling Chicago to become a major shipping port. So, though Chicago grew up on, and was nurtured by, rich prairie lands, water also played a strong role in bringing the city to power. Water will be a major character in this project as we explore its role in the lives of the people of the region, all of whom live relatively close to the shores of Lake Michigan. One irony is that Chicago currently has flooding problems due to development patterns that have not retained enough natural drainage. And though we live at the edge of a huge body of water, we must consider it a limited natural resource as we plan for future water quality and use.

Revealing Chicago is organized by Openlands Project and Metropolis 2020 and the Chicago Cultural Commission.

Terry Evans

Terry Evans • *Frankfort, Illinois, September 2003* • Archival Inkjet Print

FOTOFEST EXHIBITIONS

WAVES
Kevin Griffin

KEVIN GRIFFIN • *WAVE 12*, 2000 • LAMDA PRINT

KEVIN GRIFFIN • *WAVE 16*, 2000 • LAMDA PRINT

ARTIST: KEVIN GRIFFIN

I must down to the seas again, for the call of the running tide
Is a wild call and a clear call that may not be denied;
And all I ask is a windy day with the white clouds flying,
And the flung spray and the blown spume, and the sea-gulls crying.
from "Sea Fever" by John Masefield (1878–1967)

Surprisingly, a single human being shares much in common with the vast expanse of the world's oceans. Viewed from space, our world appears as "The Blue Planet" with seas covering over 71 percent of the land. Correspondingly, our own bodies are made up of a similar proportion of water; blood and muscles are 90 percent water. Before birth we are cocooned in liquid in the womb. Without water, human existence is simply not possible. When we breathe and move the body gently, we balance and harmonize the internal water throughout the water-filled tissues and passageways of the body, just as the seas and oceans glide across the Earth's surface.

The lure of the world's oceans has presented an irresistible challenge since the first seafarers set out to discover the unknown and found to their amazement that the ocean's waterways allowed circumnavigation of the globe! This extraordinary breakthrough led to trade, both good and bad, and a global awareness of different cultures—food, religion, clothes, and customs. To this day, the challenge of pitting their limited abilities against the mighty forces of the seas continues to excite people to take up more and more daring endeavors.

In the same way that our human lives are in a constant state of flux and change, both physically and emotionally, so are the oceans in a continual state of motion. Water is the bridge between the physical and energetic domains of the human system, the interface between the living matrix and nature. As we step into the sea and move across this bridge, we come closer to understanding our own true nature. Wind-driven currents move in swirling circular movements that affect the world's climate. Waves pound the shores in a never-ending cycle. And with their constant pounding of the land, they erode soil and rocks, which are turned to sand—then carried to a distant shore. Tides, governed by the pull of the sun and moon, ebb and flow in a rhythmic and reassuring pattern. The capturing of the photographic image is empowering: it is after all such a tremendous force, and for that split second the tremendous force is yours.

Leads me, lures me, calls me
To salt green tossing sea;
A road without earth's road-dust
Is the right road for me.

A wet road heaving, shining,
And wild with seagull's cries,
A mad salt sea-wind blowing
The salt spray in my eyes.

from "Roadways" by John Masefield

Kevin Griffin

The presentation of this exhibition by FotoFest 2004 was made possible by the support of Crescent Real Estate Equities. Special thanks go to Frank Staats, Vice President, Property Management, and Kimberly Gauss, Assistant Property Manager.

KEVIN GRIFFIN • *WAVE 16*, 2000 • LAMDA PRINT

FREE ELEMENT

The Seascapes of DoDo Jin Ming

ARTIST: DODO JIN MING

Free Element is the term that DoDo Jin Ming chose for titling the series of seascapes she made between 2001 and 2003. Though most of the pictures in this series were made along the coasts of Maine, Nova Scotia, or Hong Kong, the title speaks of the elusive and emotional side of nature, rather than specifics about a particular ocean or place. Conveying the awesome power and drama found only in the sea, DoDo Jin Ming's images transport the viewer to a precipice about to be submerged under a cascade of water, and to achieve this effect, she often imperiled her own safety to gain access to the ocean from jetties and rocks.

DoDo Jin Ming uses a Graflex camera and black and white Polaroid film to give her both an instant negative and an instant positive. In some pictures, she has exposed the frames twice; other images were made with two negatives montaged into a single image. Although this technique of multiple printing harks back to the mid 19th century, specifically the majestic seascapes of Gustave LeGray, the resultant imagery is more reminiscent of the turbulent landscapes of the painter J. M. W. Turner or the dramatic seas painted by Winslow Homer than anything photographic. They also bring to mind certain literary connotations, such as Dante's account of his descent into hell or adventure novels such as Daniel Defoe's *Robinson Crusoe.*

After training as a classical violinist in her native Beijing, DoDo Jin Ming moved to Hong Kong, where she began making photographs in 1988. Early in her career, she chose subjects that encouraged her to explore more deeply the interconnections between people and nature. In her *Sunflowers* series made in Blois, France, in 1994, she accentuated the nobility and mystery of the tall plants in the final stages of their flowering, demonstrating a passion for making eternal mysteries tangible. The *Free Element* series is a natural, yet more complicated extension of this pursuit. It reveals not only an artist in command of her medium, but one who has forged a path for both herself and her viewers to contemplate the sea's restlessness, power, and eternal mystery.

Vicki Harris
Director
Laurence Miller Gallery, New York

The presentation of this exhibition by FotoFest 2004 was made possible by the support of Crescent Real Estate Equities. Special thanks go to Frank Staats, Vice President, Property Management, and Kimberly Gauss, Assistant Property Manager.

DoDo Jin Ming • *Free Element Plate VI(A)*, 2000 • Silver Gelatin Print
Courtesy of Laurence Miller Gallery

DoDo Jin Ming • *Free Element Plate XI*, 2000 • Silver Gelatin Print
Courtesy of Laurence Miller Gallery

DoDo Jin Ming • *Free Element Plate VII, 2000* • Silver Gelatin Print
Courtesy of Laurence Miller Gallery

SHIPBREAKING

Radiant Monoliths: Edward Burtynsky's Shipbreaking

EDWARD BURTYNSKY • *SHIPBREAKING #9A, CHITTAGONG, BANGLADESH,* 2000 • COLOR PHOTOGRAPH

EDWARD BURTYNSKY • *SHIPBREAKING #4, CHITTAGONG, BANGLADESH*, 2000 • COLOR PHOTOGRAPH

ARTIST: EDWARD BURTYNSKY

More than 71 percent of the Earth's surface is covered by water. Whether for trade, exploration, or conquest, the oceans, rivers, and other waterways of the world have historically been our principal means of transportation. It is no accident, then, that many of the world's thriving urban centers have emerged in close proximity to major bodies of water. A city's growth and development often hinge on its strategic access to the world's waterways. But such communities, sheltered in harbors or river mouths, can also be vulnerable to invasion and exploitation.

Chittagong is one such city. Located at the mouth of the Karnaphuli River near the Bay of Bengal in southeastern Bangladesh, Chittagong is the commercial center for the surrounding agricultural region. Following a long history of European colonization and annexation by neighboring countries, Chittagong has been part of the nation of Bangladesh since its formation in 1971. The region's tumultuous history, combined with its natural propensity for drought and famine, has rendered it one of the world's poorest nations. Chittagong's unique location, in combination with these political and economic factors, have made it, along with certain regions of India, Pakistan, and Turkey, one of the world's optimum sites for the development of the ship-breaking industry.

Ship-breaking is the dismantling of decommissioned oceangoing vessels in order to salvage the materials for reuse and recycling. Canadian photographer Edward Burtynsky's remarkable series *Shipbreaking* artfully documents the entire working process, from the arrival of the obsolete ships on Chittagong's beaches and the removal of all gear and equipment to the physical breaking down of the ship's structure and the reconstitution of the steel into rebar. A challenging activity under the best of circumstances, ship-breaking is conducted on the beaches of Bangladesh without the use of a pier, dry dock, or slip. During the monthly high tide, and in contradiction to all seafaring principles, the ships are taken 50 kilometers (31 miles) offshore where they are driven directly toward land at full speed. After the ships are thus lodged on the effluvial flats of the Ganges River, the receding tide gives workers ready access to them.

Ship-breaking is one of the world's most hazardous industries. Chittagong's workers, equipped only with hand tools, begin by cutting off the ship's propeller. They then remove any diesel fuel and oil—a mere spark can result in an explosion—before extracting the engine. The ship's structure is then broken down, and using successive high tides, the workers drag the steel pieces further inland. As the work progresses, the non-reusable materials, such as machinery parts, oil rags, and leaking barrels, are abandoned along the beaches.

The ship-breaking industry was spawned in part by the Exxon Valdez oil spill disaster in 1989. The risk to the environment of using single-hulled oil tankers has resulted in U.S. legislation requiring oil tankers to be double-hulled. The workers on the ship-breaking beaches of Bangladesh dismantle approximately 60 to 80 of the now decommissioned single-hulled oil tankers each year, while hundreds more are broken down in neighboring countries. The sense of satisfaction at the implementation of these environmental improvements and the fact that Chittagong's laborers no longer live in extreme poverty is necessarily diminished by much needed environmental and worker safety legislation yet to be enacted. Ship-breaking continues to be an exceptionally dangerous activity, with a high risk of injury or death to workers and damage to Asian marine ecosystems from asbestos, PCBs, lead, and other hazardous chemicals and materials.

Edward Burtynsky's *Shipbreaking* captures this industry in all its complexity: butchered fragments of ships' hulls loom on the beach in the early morning light with the emotional power of an ancient ruin or a Richard Serra sculpture; particles of rust suspended in the air paint the sky a pale pink; the surface of the tidal flats shimmers with oil. The appeal of Burtynsky's photographs lies in the tension between the extraordinary beauty of his photographic representation and the suggestion in the diminutive human figures contrasted against such monumental industrial objects of the sheer catastrophic potential. As Rosemary Donegan has written, Burtynsky "depicts an industrial and economic system that has lost its rationality, and a hypocritical politics of waste that is now a global problem. What [his] photographs brilliantly elucidate is the underside of our global economy: dumping waste, whether it is molten copper tailings or old oil tankers, is an ongoing reality of global, industrial detritus. He visually brings the contradictions and consequences of our actions back to us in awesome and ambiguous images."

Scott McLeod
Prefix Photo Publishing

EDWARD BURTYNSKY • *SHIPBREAKING #9B, CHITTAGONG, BANGLADESH*, 2000 • COLOR PHOTOGRAPH

The author wishes to thank Edward Burtynsky for the insights into the ship-breaking industry and his artistic practice that he offered in several interviews conducted between 2001 and 2003.

The presentation of this exhibition at FotoFest 2004 was made possible with the support of the Department of Foreign Affairs and International Trade of Canada / avec l'appui du Ministère des Affaires étrangères et du Commerce international du Canada. The presentation in Reliant Energy Plaza was made possible through the assistance of Century Property Management. Special thanks go to Joyce Harberson, Vice President, Century Property Management.

O CAMINHO DAS ÁQUAS

Waterfall Series — Valdir Cruz

VALDIR CRUZ • *QUEDAS DE IGUAÇU, # XI FROM THE WATERFALL SERIES, FÓZ DE IGUAÇU, PARANÁ – BRAZIL,* 2002 • PIGMENT ON SOMERSET VELVET PAPER
COURTESY OF THROCKMORTON FINE ART GALLERY, NEW YORK

VALDIR CRUZ • *SALTO CURUCACA, #1 FOR THE GUARAPUAVA-WATERFALL SERIES, GUARAPUAVA, PARANÁ – BRAZIL*, 2002
• PIGMENT ON SOMERSET VELVET PAPER • COURTESY OF THROCKMORTON FINE ART GALLERY, NEW YORK

ARTIST: VALDIR CRUZ

O CAMINHO DAS ÁGUAS

Photographer Valdir Cruz is internationally recognized for his sensitive images of the daily life of the indigenous people of the Latin American rainforest, an ongoing study that has commanded much of his attention and resources for years. Since 1981, he has also devoted his efforts to the creation of an interpretive photographic record of the region around the agrarian city of Guarapuava in the southern state of Paraná, Brazil, where he was born. Photographs from the project's early years show specific interest in images of cattle raising and the life of the Brazilian cowboy. More recently, he has turned his attention to the creation of *O Caminho das Águas*, a portfolio that further explores the region through the waterfalls that dramatically figure in its landscape. Part of the patrimony of the country, many of these waterfalls are known principally to the people who live in their vicinity.

In the late 1960s, Valdir Cruz first came to these sites on hunting and fishing expeditions along the Jordão River, which flows through and on past Guarapuava to create the remote, remarkably beautiful falls of Salto Vaca Branca and Salto Curucaca. The photographs included in O Caminho das Águas concern these and others of the many waterfalls that extend from the capital of Paraná at Curitiba to Fóz de Iguaçu in the western tip of the state, at the junction of Paraguay and Argentina, a distance of about 400 miles. Valdir Cruz photographed these waterfalls in 1994, when he visited the cascades of Salto Vaca Branca as part of his broader Guarapuava project. Pleased with the work, he decided to visit and record all the waterfalls from there to the city of Prudentópolis in what is appropriately called the Land of Giant Waterfalls and on to the famous falls of Iguaçu, sometimes regarded as the eighth natural wonder of the world.

The cataracts of Fóz de Iguaçu first became known outside of the country through the Spanish explorer Alvar Núñez Cabeza de Vaca, who headed an expedition towards the Rio de la Plata and Paraguay after spending eight years in the Gulf region of what is today Texas. While three-quarters of the falls lie within Argentina, those considered most beautiful are viewed from Brazil. There in high season, Iguaçu numbers around 270 falls spanning up to 1.6 miles, spilling down over cliffs as high as 24-story buildings.

An important factor in the utilization of the waters of the region, the power plant of Itaipú, developed by both Brazil and Paraguay, is on the Paraná River in the Fóz de Iguaçu area. In recent years, Itaipú has produced one-quarter of the energy supply in Brazil and three-quarters of the energy in Paraguay, and it is annually visited by up to nine million people from 162 countries. Over the years, Valdir Cruz has witnessed the slow disappearance of waterfalls and entire river landscapes due to the construction of dams for power plants. On the other hand, he appreciates what those plants have done economically for the region. Knowing that some of the falls in the region may fall prey to future economic development, Valdir Cruz regards this opportunity to document a landscape of such beauty as a trust, an obligation. His photographs serve as witness to the beauty of what is there now.

Given that Valdir Cruz is widely known for the almost tactile quality and tonalities of his silver gelatin, platinum, and palladium prints, there is something new and immediate about these waterfall images. As he continues to work with nondigital cameras in the field, he produces large format, 4 by 5-inch negatives to facilitate the best possible scanning, making possible the production of digital prints of astonishing detail, size, and quality. His newest book, *O Caminho das Águas*, is forthcoming.

Edward Leffingwell

VALDIR CRUZ• *SALTO SÃO FRANCISCO, # 1, FROM THE GUARAPUAVA-WATERFALL SERIES, GUARAPUAVA, PARANÁ – BRAZIL*, 2001 • PIGMENT ON SOMERSET VELVET PAPER
COURTESY OF THROCKMORTON FINE ART GALLERY, NEW YORK

SUSAN DERGES

River and Shorelines

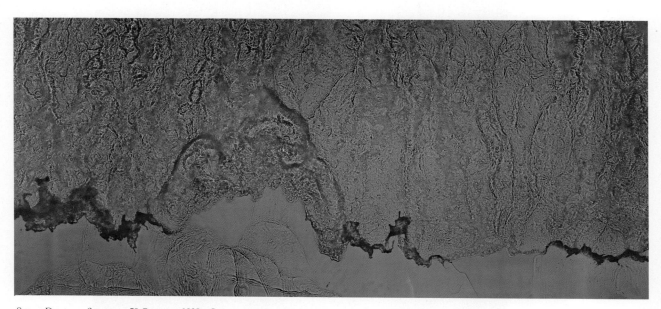

SUSAN DERGES • *SHORELINE*, 30 OCTOBER 1998 • CIBACHROME PHOTOGRAM

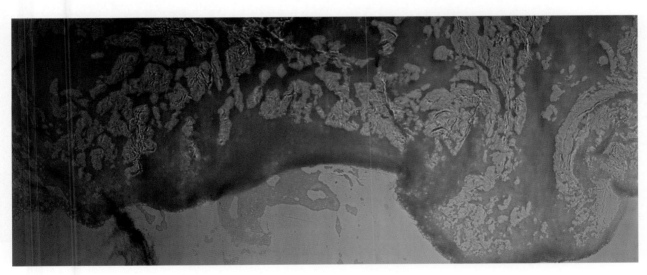

Susan Derges • *Shoreline*, 2 October 1998 • Cibachrome Photogram

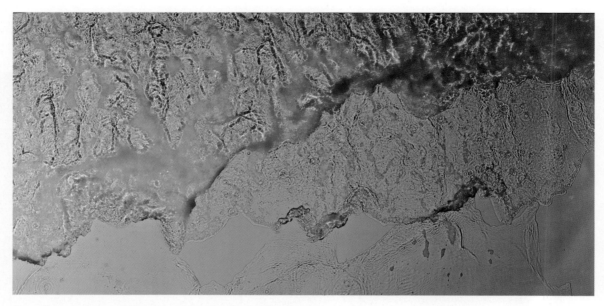

Susan Derges • *Shoreline,* 5 November 1998 • Cibachrome Photogram

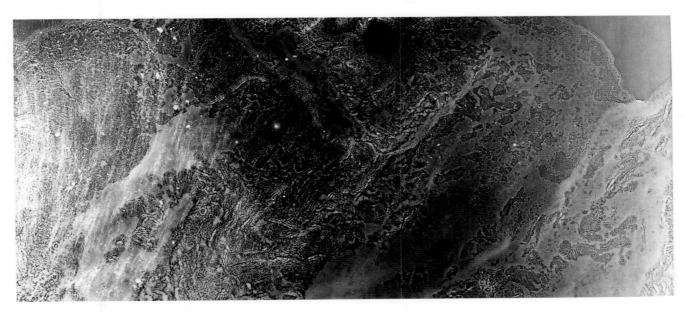

Susan Derges • *Shoreline*, 20 June 1998 • Silver Gelatin Photogram

ARTIST: SUSAN DERGES

...both the artist and the scientist are prompted by the same creative urge to find a perceptible image of the hidden forces in nature of which they both are aware.   Naum Gabo

Light-sensitive photographic paper is taken at night to a point on the river or the seashore near the river's mouth. There it is submerged in the water and exposed. A flash directed from above the water's surface is enough to register on the paper, what is caught for that fraction of a second between light source and paper: the river's eddy, flow and turbulence, the edge of the incoming wave as it flows in and the drag of sand behind it. Before that moment of incandescence, the paper has been exposed over a longer period to whatever dim light may be refracted and magnified by the water; there is always some glimmer even in the darkest night, starlight or moonlight or the ambient light from a nearby town reflected downwards from clouds. In each complex and beautiful image is thus inscribed a dual time scale: moments of dark nighttime and the brilliant instant of the flashlight.

What we have in front of us, then, is a direct index, the trace of the thing itself whose image we contemplate. "Indexes establish their meaning along the axis of a physical relationship to their referents. They are the marks or traces of a particular cause, and that cause is the thing to which they refer, the object they signify." We are looking at an actuality revealed, a moment of the process of reality apprehended, what Wallace Stevens has called the "incessant creation" of nature brought into visibility; a marvelous fact is presented, not represented, to the viewer. Presented, it must be said, in a particular way: as a work of art. We are used to the idea of the work of art as the work of conventional signs, marks, and gestures, images created with expressive intention. Photograms

(photographic images achieved without a camera, which is to say more precisely, outside the "little room" of the dark box) are by definition not communicative signs but traces of the real, of the raw material upon which the imagination works. How does Susan Derges's work differ from that of the scientific investigator using photographic means to examine reality?

Scientists use indices in figuring causes for which they may seek effects as a clue to the consequences of causation; they are seeking to explain the world, to find patterns in processes. Scientists, like artists, are concerned with tracing resemblances. The advanced technologies of photography—microscopic, telescopic, slow-motion, high-speed, time-lapse, flashlight, infrared, and ultraviolet—are extensions of the eye which have revealed to us that cosmic, atmospheric, and oceanic dynamics correspond to those that may be traced in the microcosmos of the body. These "factors of invariance, of similarity in the midst of difference," we perceive as analogies that enable us to comprehend the harmonics of the universe. The countercurrent turbulence in the Devon River configures like the whorl of the spiral nebula; in the apparent chaos of diverse events and constant motion, we sense order. Where the scientist seeks to bring into practical understanding what technologies of observation have discovered, the artist has a different purpose: to create and nurture a sense of wonder at the phenomenal world, and to intensify our imaginative experience of it. These photograms of river and shoreline waters, and the sky seen through them, are at once revelations of a particular and unrepeatable moment in nature, and images that invite our recognition of resemblance and analogy. Framing them and setting them upright, giving them no captions but the date of their making, Susan Derges removes them from the systems of science and places them within the poetics of vision.

The resemblance between things, wrote Wallace Stevens, constitutes one of the "significant components of the structure of reality." This structure is at once something outside us, in the material and dynamic configurations of the world, and inside us, as an imaginative response to the world, an active construction of personal realities, a collaborative work in constant progress. "There is nothing in nature that is not in us," wrote Naum Gabo, who thought as deeply as anyone in this century about the relation of art to science. "Whatever exists in nature, exists in us in the form of our awareness of its existence." These beautiful images of Susan Derges's, taken from the heart of a landscape and revealing to the eye what no eye has seen, are yet strangely familiar. We see, with the surprise and delight of recognition, things we have seen before: the variable currents of the river's "watery transparency," and the flow and drag of the shoreline wave, have the look of fire, their elemental opposite; the river's surface, seen against light, tessellates, lacelike, the way ice forms upon a pane; and the edge of a wave, seen from below, seems to imitate the sweep and curve of the coastline upon which it breaks, as it might be seen from the sky above.

In art we have seen this tracing of elemental correspondences most notably in the light, air, fire, and watery turmoil in the late, cosmic paintings of J. M. W. Turner, of which these images also remind us. Of one of these (*Snow Storm Steamboat off a Harbour's Mouth*), Turner wrote: "I did not paint it to be understood, but I wished to show what such a scene was like…. I felt bound to record it." Lashed to the mast, Turner was the human eye of the storm; his record of it, a brilliant fiction. Beneath the living water of river or shore, the light-sensitive paper acts as the eye of nature itself, composing in an instant a brilliant fact. Fiction and fact alike are necessary to the adventure of the poetic imagination as it seeks to comprehend a marvelous world.

Mel Gooding

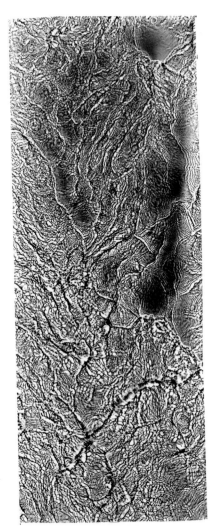

SUSAN DERGES • *RIVER TAW, 17 APRIL 1997* • SILVER GELATIN PHOTOGRAM

The presentation of this exhibition by FotoFest 2004 was made possible through the assistance of the British Art Council and the support of Armando Palacios and Cinda Ward of the New World Museum.

NEVSKY BAPTISTRY

The Eternal Baptistry—Andrey Chezhin

ANDREY CHEZHIN • UNTITLED FROM THE *NEVSKY BAPTISTRY SERIES*, 1994 • SILVER GELATIN PHOTOGRAPH
COURTESY OF NAILYA ALEXANDER, WASHINGTON, D.C. AND NEW YORK

Andrey Chezhin • Untitled from the *Nevsky Baptistry Series*, 1994 • Silver Gelatin Photograph
Courtesy of Nailya Alexander, Washington, D.C. and New York

ARTIST: ANDREY CHEZHIN

St. Petersburg was built early in the 18th century. A city having a European look thus appeared in Russia, a country steeped in ancient tradition. According to a legend dating to the time of its construction, the city is destined to go down with the waters of the river on whose banks it has been built, taking away as it does so all of the city's pains and sins. St. Petersburg, indeed, was flooded again and again until the dam to protect it began construction in the 20th century. Before that, floods used to wash away houses and, with them, any remnants of reason, leaving city dwellers with a mindless fear.

Andrey Chezhin belongs to his native city. He is part of it, as well as its photographer and singer. As a photographer, he pursues the subject of the young city's adjustment to the preceding centuries of cultural tradition, a subject that was particularly exciting for the Romantic poets of the 19th century. This subject takes Andrey Chezhin from the high water in his native city to the motif of St. Petersburg as a "Northern Venice" and from the echoes of the Old Russian lays to the depths of the ancient Christian tradition of redemptive baptism. In *The Neva Baptistry* series, cleansing by water turns into a sacrament with no people present, and the picture, which is beautiful in its phantasmagoric weirdness, is made terrifying by the absence of humans.

The artist became interested in the subject of St. Petersburg's floods as early as the 1990s. He looked through hundreds of photos that showed majestic floods dating from the mid 19th century in archives and museums, and he himself then photographed the stones showing the water levels reached. But nothing he found matched his own vision of a flood reaching to the points of the city's spires. In his vision, the palaces are hardly seen

among the waves, while the monuments project from the flow like ghosts, punctuating the dramatic turns taken by the city in the course of history.

Two events of the past, one real and one artistic, prompted the postmodernist photographer's discovery of the sought-for image. The artistic event in question came from the realm of literature: Aleksandr Pushkin's poem *The Brass Horseman* published in 1833. In the poem, the famous Peter the Great Monument chases the poem's humble and miserable protagonist through the flooding waves. The monument chases him through the waves of his dreams and madness, confusing both the literary character and the reader, and depriving them of a way of telling reality from fiction.

The second event that served as an inspiration for *The Neva Baptistry* was a crucial "reconstruction" of the ancient Russian legend of the city of Kitzeh, which, as the legend has it, sank into the waters of the lake together with its dwellers, houses, churches, and belfries before the very eyes of its foes. This legend was literally reconstructed in Soviet times by water reservoir designers. As a result of this engineering effort, scores of ancient towns went under. As it happened, their belfries continued to tower over the water for decades, which struck the eyewitnesses of storms on the artificial water basins more powerfully than an encounter with Charon's boat would probably have done. What had no historical or cultural allusions for those who built those reservoirs acquired new meaning for the generations of their children and grandchildren.

In the earlier half of the 1990s, the time when *The Neva Baptistry* was created, the subject of repentance was dominant in Russian society's consciousness. This "summing up" led many an artist to create works that symbolized and endeavored to interpret the striving for repentance, a striving deeply rooted in the Russian spiritual tradition. Gradually, this desire to influence society through art

ANDREY CHEZHIN • UNTITLED FROM THE *NEVSKY BAPTISTRY SERIES*, 1994 • SILVER GELATIN PHOTOGRAPH
COURTESY OF NAILYA ALEXANDER, WASHINGTON, D.C. AND NEW YORK

routed itself towards the theosophical dimension, leaving us with works of art whose associative potential was determined by the belief of their creators in the power of faith. Now, a decade later, the trends once prevalent in Russia's consciousness seem to have been washed away by subsequent political events, but the works of this artist who was so deeply involved with the changes in post-Soviet thinking remain a monument to that unaccomplished repentance.

Irina Tchmyreva
Head Researcher, Moscow Museum of Modern Art

This exhibition was done with the assistance of Evgeny Berezner, Deputy Director, Museum of Modern Art, Moscow. Support was provided by the Trust for Mutual Understanding, Anya Tish Gallery, Houston, and Nailya Alexander Gallery, Washington D.C. and New York.

TIME STANDING STILL

The City of Moist Silver

ARTIST: ALEXEY TITARENKO

The most important thing about photographer Alexey Titarenko is probably that in his work he has attained and explored the "third" dimension. In the literal sense, this third dimension is the dimension of airiness, of the depth of the image, of dampness and tangibility, of the "density" of the atmosphere imprinted in the silver layer of his works. Figuratively, Alexey Titarenko's third dimension is the dimension of history relayed through the connotations of 19th-century photography.

The heartbreaking association with the ephemeral nature of times past in faithful reproductions of reality can provoke in the viewer an intense absorption that would seem rather more fitting for the reader engrossed in a volume by Marcel Proust. Yet, the visual and cultural experience of the artist from St. Petersburg enables him to produce the illusion of an immersion in the realm of time on a par with the power of a literary illusion.

The artist's visual experience lies in his incessant observation of elements of St. Petersburg's decaying classical architecture, dilapidated Baroque facades, and simply attired pedestrians who seem to step onto today's pavements from gateways behind which both the 19th century and the mid 20th century are still alive. This fusion of times is evoked in the blurred moving figures captured on negatives by his large old camera.

The photographer's cultural experience taps into a museum space that is saturated with images of the transparent Venetian landscape and Rembrandt's chiaroscuro. St. Petersburg, like no other city in the world, emanates a misty spirit of the past that fills its canals and Neva embankments. As an artifact, it has outstripped Las Vegas by two centuries in boasting the most daring "postmodern" architectural fantasies in its precise simulation of the European look. But in contrast to the playfulness of today's games with art, St. Petersburg has never lost the sobriety of a museum copy. People find the city hard to live in. They appear to inhabit a city of cards, and not the one distorted by Friedrich Murnau's will, where the people are the most harmonious entities in a fragmented world, but rather one where the inhabitants of an immense, harmoniously built theatre are dwarfed by the stage set.

Alexey Titarenko's photos appear to visualize the literary experience of St. Petersburg that a reader of Fyodor Dostoyevsky possesses: "It seemed, then, that this entire world, with all of its inhabitants, weak and strong, and all of its habitations, be it beggars' shelters or gilded places, looked in the dusk like a fantastic, magic dream, a dream that would soon disappear too, going in wisps to the dark-blue sky."[1]

All of Alexey Titarenko's photos seem to be permeated with the perspiration of this mad, phantasmagoric city. Water sprays fuse together, turning movements of indi-

ALEXEY TITARENKO • UNTITLED FROM THE *BLACK AND WHITE MAGIC OF ST. PETERSBURG* SERIES, 1995 • SILVER GELATIN PRINT • COURTESY OF NAILYA ALEXANDER, WASHINGTON, D.C. AND NEW YORK

vidual people and of whole human masses into flows of water and time as the frozen beauty of St. Petersburg's architecture is reflected in the water. Silvery water drops suspended in the air are like dust shaken from a curtain hanging over a theatre stage. Water finally becomes part of his photographic process—if it were not for "wet" printing, his images wouldn't carry on the Impressionist or even the Pictorialist tradition of "gray tonality," no black or white, nothing but close tones of silver-blue and silver-yellow that resemble noble old printing.

The temporal categories in Alexey Titarenko's photography are fluid, filling images with various allusions. The blend of the literal, visual, and figurative embedded in literary tradition, which is inherent in his work, is a rare quality. This seems illogical and artificial although it is a given, like the very existence of St. Petersburg itself.

Irina Tchmyreva
Head Researcher, Moscow Museum of Modern Arr

This exhibition has been done with the help of Evgeny Berezner, Deputy Director, Moscow Museum of Modern Art, and Nailya Alexander, Washington D.C. and New York, and the Trust for Mutual Understanding.

[1]Feodor Dostoevsky, *The Petersburg Dreams in Verses and Prose*,1860, from Feodor Mikhailovich Dostoevsky, *Complete Works*, Vol. 19, p. 69, Moscow, 1979.

ALEXEY TITARENKO • UNTITLED FROM THE *BLACK AND WHITE MAGIC OF ST. PETERSBURG* SERIES, 1995 • SILVER GELATIN PRINT • COURTESY OF NAILYA ALEXANDER, WASHINGTON, D.C. AND NEW YORK

ALEXEY TITARENKO • UNTITLED FROM THE *CITY OF SHADOWS* SERIES, 1993 • SILVER GELATIN PRINT
COURTESY OF NAILYA ALEXANDER, WASHINGTON, D.C. AND NEW YORK

ALEXEY TITARENKO • UNTITLED FROM THE *CITY OF SHADOWS* SERIES, 1993 • SILVER GELATIN PRINT
COURTESY OF NAILYA ALEXANDER, WASHINGTON, D.C. AND NEW YORK

WATER WASTELAND

Manuel Piña

MANUEL PIÑA • *WATER WASTELANDS*, 1992-2001 • BLACK AND WHITE C-PRINT
COURTESY OF MARVELLI GALLERY, NEW YORK

Manuel Piña • *Water Wastelands*, 1992-2001 • Black and White C-Print
Courtesy of Marvelli Gallery, New York

ARTIST: MANUEL PIÑA

My grandfather made my first kite. It was a memorable day when we first sent it aloft from a small hill not far from my school. I made the second kite. I myself. I spent a week working on the wooden slats, and on Sunday I went to the little hill. The problem was not with the strips of wood. It was the paper. It was very heavy. The kite didn't fly. Luckily there were no other boys around so I saved myself from being the object of their jokes. It was that day, when I was all alone, that I discovered the sky. I am talking about being able to feel the sky. Of course had I asked about it a thousand times and about how far away it was, But to enjoy it alone was something else, to throw myself on the ground, to forget the notion of time, to forget my failure. That was the first day I really felt the sky.

....

I couldn't believe that my grandmother let me go. Alone with two friends. It wasn't just the beach, it was the coast: the reefs, the unknown bottom, dangerous and deep— the sea. Getting there, the road seemed to go by in an instant, and once there, with my shoes and very cautiously, I ventured into the sea. But my secret was soon reavealed: the sea coast is not merciful, when you know nothing about it. To my chagrin, I had to yell for help. Although afraid, when I got to shore, I felt their ridicule. Everyone was laughing, the entire universe was making a joke of me. But then slowly it began to wear away. The interminable coming and going of the water and the sensation of its immensity absorbed everything around me. This same sea that tried to swallow me, now trapped me in another way, soft, gentler, uplifting … and for all time.

....

There was a photograph from the 1920s of the 'paseo' along the Malecón, the sea wall. As a photograph, it was nothing special: the avenue viewed from above, the wall with the sea on the left, and the fortress (El Morro) in the background. What was impressive was the traffic. Cars and vehicles pulled by horses. They filled the entre street. One after the other, from one end to the other. The entire city was on parade, everyone waiting for a turn to be next to the sea. It was such a contradiction that, at that same moment, they were building the Wall. A concrete embankment that would separate the earth from the water. Marking a border between land and water. The relationship of Havana to the sea is just that. Havana was not a coastal town that became a city. Nothing depended on the sea. The city was born with the port, and from the port, it grew rich. The port was part of the city, not the sea. The sea was something else. For that reason, when the city shut its doors, it also closed its port. The sea, however, stayed, and the city closed itself off even more from the sea, and what the sea brought with it—storms and assaults. The sea was more a source of danger than life. This is what marked the relationship. Intimacy and distance, attraction and fear. The Malecón, the sea wall, was the manifestation of this relationship, making it obvious. It was a wall that you could not ignore, omnipresent and separating us from the sea. Concrete and steel. Each time the sea tried to destroy it, the city rebuilt it. There have been few borders more tangible than this one. But the attraction remained, and the wall became a balcony. From the asphyxiation of the city, its narrow streets, its noise and interminable lines, we went to the sea as a refuge. To feel the immediacy of its infiniteness. You and it, face to face. The peace, the silence, life, death, pleasure, emptiness, eternity ….

....

In the mid 1990s, Havana faced an abyss. Everything that we had believed in turned upside down. There was no future, and step by step the past was being erased. Then, once again, we went to the sea. Sitting on the wall, the sea became another option for us. It was like being stopped at the edge, held between what we had been and an uncertain future. Many of us jumped. We did it so obsessively that it was difficult to say whether it was death or the

certainty of another land that moved us. But perhaps that is not what was important. What was important was to escape.

....

At that time, my life seemed to converge with the life of my city. In one moment, everything changed, and I suddenly found myself facing emptiness. Almost without being aware of it, as if something was taking me there, I arrived at the Malecón. I rediscovered the sky and the sea. One more time, they helped me escape, and one more time they saved me.

This series comes from that time.

Manuel Piña

Translated from the Spanish by FotoFest

The presentation at FotoFest 2004 has been made possible by Trizec Office Properties. Special thanks go to Joanna Chain, Director of Tenant Relations and Marvelli Gallery, New York.

THE SEA I DREAMT / MY SEA

ARTIST: HAN SUNGPIL

The Sea I Dreamt...

Burying all my pain, hatred, and sorrow,
Sinking my yearning and regret,
Sailing my hopes and dreams —
I glance at the sea.

The sea for me carries memories of my personal experience and
history:

At the age of 15, I for the first time saw the sea.

On one August afternoon,
under the scorching sun,
everything suddenly appeared as I came out of a pine forest
As if I were able to embrace its entirety.

The sea that I saw possessed me with a feeling of awe.

A vague place where the sky and the sea touch one another,
It was filled with insolvable mysteries —
Like a Möbius strip, having eternal continuity.

The sea that I saw at the age of 15
Is still the dream in the film of memory deep in my heart.

Han Sungpil

HAN, SUNGPIL • *MY SEA 001*, 2001 • C-TYPE

HAN, SUNGPIL • *MY SEA 026*, 2001 • C-TYPE

HAN, SUNGPIL • *MY SEA 002*, 1998 • C-TYPE

FOUNTAIN

Bohnchang Koo • *Fountain #7, 1997* • Digitalized Print
Courtesy of Ricco/Maresca Gallery, New York

The Dialectic of the Body and Photography: Bohnchang Koo's Body Archaeology

There is no exact geometrical symmetry in nature. Symmetry has its power only in human speculation. Therefore we should go into the space of thinking to confront the works of Bohnchang Koo. It is impossible to cut off water with a knife. He, however, cuts the shape of water with the eyes or the camera. Then he reproduces it as a symmetrical twin. Though symmetry is a string of destiny that binds photography and the real object, according to the myth it is also the basic pattern of narcissistic self-absorption. It could be the case that the deep question of self-love hidden in the unconscious is exposed in these photographs. It also could be that the unconscious of the photographer, who resists factors to dissociate himself, is uncovered.

Why is the subject here water of all other elements? Bohnchang Koo constructs a form of self-perfection by making a circular ring in water, expecting it to expand itself by making endless waves. The water meets itself and forms the "arche," or the idea of softness. When we touch water, we don't say it is soft, but if something absorbs water, it is softened. The water is the idea of softness. Now the image of the circular ring of self-perfection becomes the image of the womb. The womb comes to us as softness itself. He gives us the womb in which all life is made. He gives us the womb, which is identified as the deepest origin by its softness. Thus the visitors who view his artworks become conspirators with Bohnchang Koo in his attempt to make a universal womb.

Repetition is a feature of the artworks here as well as symmetry. With respect to the fact that he made the various images of the womb by repeating similar work nine times, he might have suggested the productivity of this "womb of water." Why nine times? His mother might have had nine children. Who knows. Philosophically, repetition is characteristic of an essence because an essence makes itself present repeatedly, just as the DNA of the parents is realized repeatedly and variously in their children.

The works of Bohnchang Koo can be interpreted as revealing the circular ring by using symmetry and the essence of productivity by using repetition. Without life, the body is not a body. It becomes dried and hardened like a concrete block. In contrast, Bohnchang Koo has accomplished the shaping of the universal origin of the body with his works.

Cho Kwang-Je
Researcher, The Association for Korean Philosophy and Thoughts

Bohnchang Koo • *Fountain #8*, 1997 • Digitalized Print
Courtesy of Ricco/Maresca Gallery, New York

Bohnchang Koo • *FOUNTAIN #1*, 1997 • DIGITALIZED PRINT
COURTESY OF RICCO/MARESCA GALLERY, NEW YORK

FOTOFEST EXHIBITIONS

OCEAN

Jungjin Lee

JUNGJIN LEE • *OCEAN 99-06,* 1999 • PHOTO-EMULSION ON RICE PAPER

Jungjin Lee • *Ocean 99-42,* 1999 • Photo-Emulsion on Rice Paper

ARTIST: JUNGJIN LEE

The photographs by Jungjin Lee defy the cliché of beauty. When looking at the paper on which her images are printed, the photographic frame, and also the subject matter, one does not see the ideal beauty that is normally thought of as the subject of photography.

I know that Jungjin Lee in front of a so-called "beautiful scene" does not take out her camera; instead she just takes the scene in. In front of a certain scene that captures her, however, she gets stirred up and starts shooting away. "A certain scene" can be some ordinary scenery that one passes by easily because it is so far removed from common beauty or a scene that one is so used to seeing that it is easily ignored.

But such ordinary scenery is what comes alive on Jungjin Lee's Korean paper, called *hanji*, to which she painstakingly applies emulsion. On this *hanji*, silent scenes get a chance to speak out and the familiar gets to tell a very different story. The American desert, the old stone towers of Korea, encounters in the street, ancient Buddhas, or whatever else they may be, these objects do not speak eloquently about themselves using an outdated beauty. Bare but dignified, insignificant but impressive, they are simultaneously reality and illusion, concrete and symbolic.

Here is a group of images of water collected under the title *Ocean*. A word describing a vast body of water—can this title be a joke or have a hidden meaning? The images, unlike their title, don't overwhelm the viewer with a vast stretch of water, the horizon, or threateningly high waves. What is normally considered characteristic of the ocean simply does not show up in Jungjin Lee's images.

The patterns created by the waves, a path leading to a certain place, and something that hangs above the water— such are the things that occupy her surface. Water is filling up or draining away. The path leads to the ocean or land.

This series falls chronologically between her *American Desert* and *On Road* series, and I sense that elements from these two series exist here as well. The abyss of water with its changing light and pattern reminds one of the natural habitat of the desert, and the paths and structures crossing through the water bring to mind the man-made scenery of *On Road*. The artificial interferes with the natural; the flowing liquid meets with the immovable solid, the ocean with land. These scenes are very still, yet at the same time they communicate tension and power.

Jungjin Lee's interest in texture remains here, too. Like the texture of the desert, the texture of water is shown as it is, and the seemingly different textures break down each other's barrier and merge into one. Furthermore, images showing water and cement, the bold line bisecting the picture surface, and the large triangle made by the waves deal with elements that are very abstract; the hanji makes such images look more flat and painterly.

Water is simultaneously pure and dark. I feel that what is reflected on the water is the artist's camera or maybe herself. Only then do I consider that maybe the title *Ocean* points not to the vastness of the water but instead to its invisible depth.

Yoon Huh

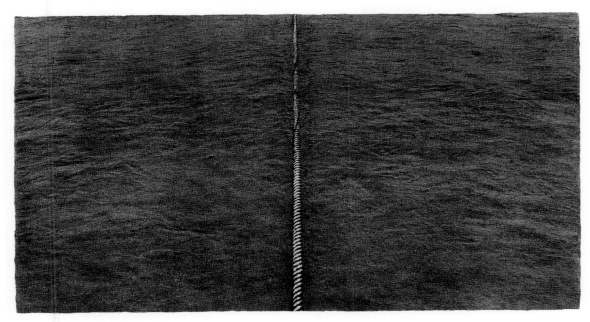

Jungjin Lee • *Ocean 99-37*, 1999 • Photo-Emulsion on Rice Paper

FOTOFEST EXHIBITIONS

THE LAKE PROJECT

Black Maps

DAVID MAISEL • *THE LAKE PROJECT # 9277 – 1*, 2001 • C – PRINT

DAVID MAISEL • *THE LAKE PROJECT # 9285 – 3*, 2001 • C – PRINT

ARTIST: DAVID MAISEL

The *Black Maps* series comprises aerial photographs of environmentally impacted landscapes. These images have as their subject matter the undoing of the natural world by the wide-scale intervention of human action. The depictions of these damaged wastelands, where human efforts have eradicated any natural order, are both spectacular and horrifying. Although these photographs evidence the devastation of these sites, they also transcribe interior psychic landscapes that are profoundly disturbing—for as otherworldly as these images may seem, they depict a shattered reality of our own making.

The photographs in this series are presented as either 30 by 30-inch or 48 by 48-inch color C-prints. The prints extend to encompass the viewer's peripheral vision, and in the process their lushness and strange beauty become psychologically demanding as well as visually exhilarating. The forms of environmental disquiet and degradation are here made to function on both a documentary and a metaphorical level, and the aerial perspective enables one to experience the landscape like a vast map of its own undoing.

These images are meant neither to vilify nor to glorify their content, but rather to expand our notions of what constitutes landscape and landscape art. I am not attempting to make literal records of environmental destruction. Rather I seek to reveal the landscape in something other than purely visual terms, the photograph transcribing it as an archetypal space of destruction and ruin that mirrors the darker corners of our consciousness.

A current chapter in this body of work is *The Lake Project*, begun in 2001. It comprises images from Owens Lake, the site of a formerly 200-square-mile lake in California on the eastern side of the Sierra Mountains. Beginning in 1913, the Owens River was diverted into the Owens Valley Aqueduct to bring water to Los Angeles. By 1926, the lake had been depleted, exposing vast mineral flats. For decades, fierce winds have dislodged microscopic particles from the lakebed, creating carcinogenic dust storms. Indeed, the lakebed has become the highest source of particulate matter pollution in the United States, emitting some 300,000 tons annually of cadmium, chromium, arsenic, and other materials. The concentration of minerals in the remaining water of Owens Lake is so artificially high that blooms of microscopic bacterial organisms result, turning the liquid a deep, bloody red. Viewed from the air, vestiges of the lake appear as a river of blood, a microchip, a bisected vein, or a galaxy's map. It is this contemporary version of the sublime that I find compelling.

In *The Lake Project*, the lake has become the locus of water's absence. The lake is a negation of itself, a void. To grow the city of Los Angeles is to deplete, starve, or implode the body of water that once comprised Owens Lake, so *The Lake Project* images serve, in a sense, as the lake's autopsy. In nearly every image from the entirety of *Black Maps*, water is harnessed for some use, and in the process it is in some manner manipulated or destroyed, its presence denied. This is not to say that it has been stripped of its inherent beauty. But its beauty has been subjugated by its use, and while its physical condition may be thrilling to behold—planes of poison in hues of red, green, amber, and turquoise—it is a beauty born of environmental degradation. There is a sense of both seduction and betrayal with these images, and the viewer is ultimately complicit in their absorption by this toxic liquid.

David Maisel

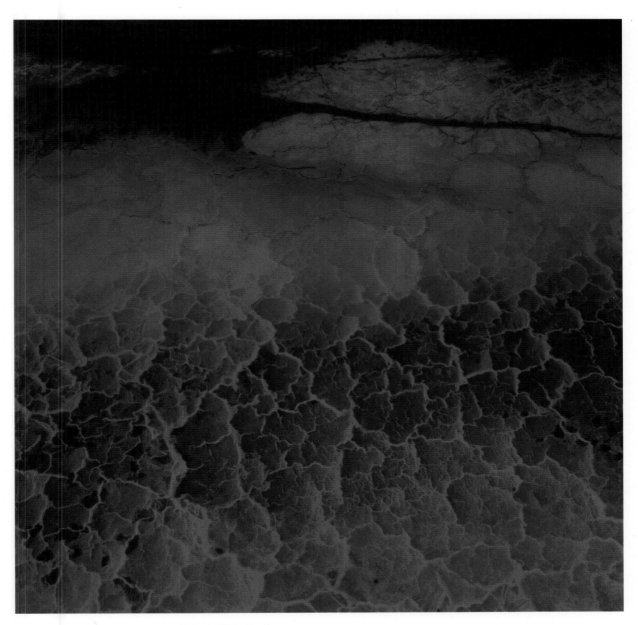

David Maisel • *The Lake Project # 9275 – 8*, 2001 • C – Print

THE COST OF POWER IN CHINA:

The Three Gorges Dam and the Yangtze River Valley

ARTIST: STEVEN BENSON

My purpose in traveling the length of the area to be flooded by the Three Gorges Dam, from Chongqing downstream to the dam's construction site, was to create a lasting photographic document of a part of the planet destined to disappear, and to honor the people of this mythic valley that has inspired poets, artists, and philosophers for countless centuries. It is also my hope that this body of work will function as a warning to future generations.

The desire to build a dam across the Yangtze River, 610 feet high and 1.3 miles long, creating in a densely populated area a reservoir 50 miles longer than Lake Michigan, is an example of how flaws in our perceptual system can cause immeasurable harm. This immense dam, the largest concrete object on the planet, will ultimately force more than two million people to vacate their ancestral homes and will disrupt the lives of the 30 million people living in the reservoir region. In addition to this social cost, the reservoir will cover 8,000 known archaeological sites, 250,000 acres of China's most fertile farmland, and 1,600 factories that have been burying toxic materials in the ground for the past 50 years. Scientists fear that lead, mercury, arsenic, and dozens of other substances, including radioactive waste, will leach out into the reservoir, destroying aquatic life. It is disturbing to consider how quickly human activity can transform fresh water, a source of life, into poison. Seventy-five million people depend on the river for fishing and farming.

The idea to dam the Yangtze River in the vicinity of the Three Gorges has been a point of contention in China for 75 years. It was proposed initially in 1919 by Dr. Sun Yat-Sen, considered to be the father of the Chinese Republic, as part of his "Plan for National Reconstruction." The dam was also of great interest to his successors, including Nationalist leader Chiang Kai-Shek, followed by Mao Zedong and Deng Xiaoping. The project never generated strong support, due to political, financial, and technical obstacles, so it was continually set aside. The project came under consideration yet again in the 1980s. It was one of the issues on the minds of the Democratic Reform demonstrators at Tiananmen Square in 1989. In the wake of the disastrous events of this protest, the Chinese government needed something for the people of China to be proud of and to rally around. With the collapse of the Soviet Union as an additional motivating factor, it was now possible in 1992 for then Premier Li Peng, a Russian-trained hydro-engineer, to push the project through the National People's Congress, with one third of the delegates voting against the dam or abstaining. Whenever a delegate attempted to speak out against the project, the microphone was turned off. Construction of the dam began in 1994.

According to the Chinese government, there are three reasons to build this dam: to generate 11 percent of the country's electricity (the equivalent of 18 nuclear power plants), thus reducing its need for coal-burning facilities; to control the Yangtze's devastating annual floods, which have claimed the lives of more than 300,000 people during the last century; and to improve the standard of living in one of the most impoverished parts of the country by allowing 10,000-ton ships to move goods in and out of the heart of China. As part of a 14-hour television broadcast celebrating the blocking of the Yangtze on November 8, 1997, then President Jiang Zemin made a speech to mark the occasion. He said, "This proves vividly once again that Socialism is superior in being capable of concentrating resources to do big jobs…. Since the twilight of history, the Chinese nation has been engaged in the great feat of conquering, developing, and exploiting nature."

Experts all over the world do not believe this dam will accomplish any of the government's stated goals. Luna Leopold, emeritus professor of geology at the University of California–Berkeley, in a letter to the Export-Import Bank in 1996, pointed out some serious problems with the Three Gorges project. He noted, "The function of storing floodwater is in conflict with the need for sediment to be released from the reservoir," adding that "the sediment-depleted water released from the reservoir would erode the flood control infrastructure downstream." Pollution is another critical subject that was not carefully considered. The Chinese feasibility study did not account for the effect of the dam on water quality. Of the 900 million tons of industrial wastewater and 300 million tons of sewage discharged into the river annually, only 20 percent is treated. In the past, the Yangtze's powerful current has washed this pollution out to the East China Sea. The lake formed behind the dam will have a greatly diminished current, permitting the pollution to collect at a rapid rate. There were reports of increasing levels of E. coli immediately following the formation of the reservoir, but reports on pollution since then have ceased.

On June 10, 2003, at 10:00 p.m., the reservoir began to fill, reaching a depth of 425 feet (135 meters) in spite of the fact that in 1999 100 cracks were discovered running the full height of the upstream face of the dam. The cracks had been repaired, only to reopen. Chinese engineers say this is common in large dams, but others suggest it is the result of improper curing of the concrete. In 2009 the reservoir is planned to reach 575 feet (175 meters), completing the flooding of 13 cities, 140 towns, and 1,352 villages.

What was intended to be a grand proclamation of China's emergence into the modern world is rapidly becoming a monumental problem due to poor planning, inaccurate or falsified estimates and statistics, construction problems, high sedimentation rates, severe residential and industrial pollution, rampant official corruption, and growing civil unrest.

The Mountain Goddess,
if she is still there,
will marvel at a world so changed.
Mao Zedong, from his poem "The Lake Among the Gorges"

Steven Benson

STEVEN BENSON • *YANGTZE RIVER, FULING, CHINA,* 1999 • SILVER GELATIN PRINT

STEVEN BENSON • *THREE GORGES DAM CONSTRUCTION, CHINA,* 1999 • SILVER GELATIN PRINT

STEVEN BENSON • *NEW HARBOR, CHONGQUING, CHINA,* 1999 • SILVER GELATIN PRINT

AQUASCAPE

KAREN GLASER • *TROY SPRING SUWANNEE RIVER*, 2000 • SILVER GELATIN PRINT

Karen Glaser • *Sea Lions, Sea of Cortez*, 2002 • Silver Gelatin Print

ARTIST: KAREN GLASER

Upon receiving a small, yellow Instamatic underwater camera for a birthday gift in 1983, I began photographing children at play in the water. I was fascinated by the magnification and exaggeration of their bodies created by looking at them through water—their lean limbs elongated, their round figures inflated like balloons. Although these images of children—resulting in a series of photographs entitled *Aquanauts*—did not begin as a serious photographic venture, the results of this experimentation changed the direction of my life as a photographer. Twenty years have passed since that initial fascination, and many water-related projects have grown from that beginning.

It was a natural shift to begin shooting the majority of my photographs underwater, as I've been an avid water lover my whole life, enthralled by its force, power, and beauty. I also understand how essential water is to all life on Earth. It is important to note a few facts. Water covers more than 70 percent of the Earth. Water is essential to life on Earth. We are born in water and two-thirds of our bodies are water. We settle by water and use water in all aspects of our lives, from our basic sustenance to recreation. Most life on Earth actually lives in water. When things are put into perspective, the land above water is really such a small percentage of the Earth.

Knowing the above, it has always seemed crazy to me that photographers are grouped as underwater photographers,

as if this category results in one type of photography. We would never dream of grouping all the photographers that shoot on land into one group called "on-land photographers." Be it on land or underwater, photographers have distinct styles: we each work on a variety of projects and our work is different from person to person. However, because humans live on the 30 percent of the Earth that is above water, this is where we place most of our emphasis and attention.

We live on an ocean planet and share it with many creatures. As the distinguished marine biologist Sylvia Earle says in the introduction to her book *Sea Change*, "The living ocean drives planetary chemistry, governs climate and weather, and otherwise provides the cornerstone of the life support system for all creatures on our planet from deep sea starfish to desert sagebrush. That's why the ocean matters. If the sea is sick, we'll feel it. If it dies, we die. Our future and the state of the oceans are one."

I see my photographs as a harmony among art, science, and the spirit. I photograph in many different kinds of water, from the powerful saltwater oceans to the quiet beauty of the pristine freshwater Florida springs. When diving and snorkeling, I am captivated by the exquisite and diverse natural light that graces these environments and use it solely to light my pictures. It doesn't matter if the water is crystal clear or muddy. In fact, the particulate matter—the mud and muck—is the seasoning in the soup that helps creates the magnificent variety in underwater light. Grainy film accentuates the look and "feel" of this environment. The photographs are black and white as well, sometimes toned to add browns to the traditional gray scale to further the "feel" of the atmosphere below. As a point of information, the color spectrum shortens rapidly the deeper you dive. The loss of full color begins to happen as soon as about 10 feet. Photographers who shoot in color underwater often add flash to "regain" color. This addition of flash to my work, however, would disrupt the essence and subtleties of the natural light that I adore. Photographing in these places is a visual, physical, and emotional experience.

I print my photographs on a large scale to envelop the viewer and bring him or her into my world. The pictures are elegant, and their tonal scale reminds many of historic drawings, etchings, or charcoals. They are big, beautiful seductions. The goal is to draw viewers to the pictures by hitting their hearts and guts just long enough to spark their own appreciation, curiosity, and quest for knowledge about these fascinating creatures and places. If my work can do this, then I have some small satisfaction about doing my part toward conservation of these places whose health is essential to us all.

Karen Glaser

The presentation of this exhibition at FotoFest 2004 was made possible through the support of McCord Development Inc. at One City Centre and Kinzelman Art Consulting. Special thanks go to Mark Tompkins and Julie Kinzelman.

KAREN GLASER • *GARFISH, SILVER RIVER*, 2002 • SILVER GELATIN PRINT

MARINE LIFE AND SHIPS

ARTIST: CÁSSIO VASCONCELLOS

SHIPS

Sculptor Richard Serra tells us how the childhood experience of watching a ship being launched made an impression on all his later work. The ship's black hull, disproportionately horizontal, first dipped towards the bow, semisubmerged, but then it rose again until it found its balance. The ship, an enormous dead weight on land, became a free and floating structure in the sea. All the issues of sculpture—weight and lightness, balance and sustainment—are present here.

Cássio Vasconcellos also resorts to ships to reflect on the issue of weight in that most kinetic and impalpable of all means of image production: photography. He brings matter and gravity to light. The presence of the ships' windowless iron bodies, occupying almost the whole picture, is massive. Taken from the viewpoint of someone on the surface of the sea, the photos give the viewer a heightened sense of both the volume of the water and the size of the hull. The print, done with cotton wool, leaves no well-defined margins. Slightly unfocused, without edges, the image acquires the shapeless consistency of clouds. Ship, sky, and water come together in a single material texture. These freighters, apparently stuck in thunderstorms, are imbued with mystery. They give the impression of having emerged from the waves or from 18th-century engravings. Large volumes confront us directly with awesome immensity.

FISH

The newer series, *FISH*, further thickens the texture in which things are wrapped. These are pictures printed to large dimensions, with extremely complex scenes. The images, which are made from a large negative, are collages of parts of various other shots joined with adhesive tape and fire to produce one plate. The result is a print of great density, an atmosphere of heavy materiality. In these turbid landscapes, each one of the collaged figures is in focus, subverting the picture's perspective organization. Because the figures' dimensions do not match the plane they occupy, they also alter the image's conventional proportions. The different planes do not seem to fit into each other naturally. The montage is evident; no attempt has been made to hide the points of junction. The surface of the image is equally full, with schools of fish, a twisted rope, or a mossy stone forming a physical presence that occupies the whole picture. The images are made up of horizontal strips—sky, sea, underwater soil—but the disproportionate dimensions make for spatial ambiguity: our gaze has no viewpoint and moves from top to bottom, as though it could travel along the waterline. These paradoxically low panoramic views are deprived of perspective, presenting an image of the contemporary world that is saturated and opaque: the ocean floor.

Photomontage, which Cássio Vasconcellos has here partially appropriated, was invented to address the impos-

Cássio Vasconcellos • *Paisagens Marinhas #1*, 1993-1994 • Silver Gelatin Print

sibility of photographing the sky and a landscape at the same time, since the color blue imprints itself much faster, saturating the picture. The first photographers would lift the line of the horizon and "photocompose" the sky, making the picture natural. Using one take for each plane, the complete landscape would be composed. In this way, instead of the pale and empty sky we are used to seeing—since the time of exposure necessary for the sea, for instance, would cause the sky to be overexposed—we have cloudy, heavy skies.

Here the photographer resembles the engraver. Instead of flying lightly among the clouds, he treads firmly on high, weighted by matter. He engraves clouds. Mists in these images look more like the maelstrom of seawater, like soil plowed for the sowing. Horizons remind us of underwater seascapes, muddy and disturbed. The engraver gives us earthly clouds: for all their airiness, he caresses them with a stone chisel.

The painter works with landscapes of light. The engraver's landscape is totally different: unable to use color, all he can do is look for movement. Shape alone does not suffice, which is why every stroke of an engraving is a movement in itself, a dislocation of weight, working with matter. The hand speaks to us of shadows and light as matter's truths. So, too, does the photographer. This device invented to capture snapshots of the instant has given way to images full of time and matter. The photograph, a fleeting record made of paper and chemistry, acquires new breadth and consistency. While painting brings light to light, engraving fights limits; it fights against the wall of the landscape. From the stone chisel comes a crafted vision. The chisel desires hostility, the cut, the decision, and every engraving testifies to strength, to effects achieved with an effort, as opposed to the evanescence of immensity.

In Cássio Vasconcellos's pictures, texture becomes a means to an end, building up dense vegetation in which everything else is buried. The space between things—always full, as though taken up by water—works like a glue, connecting objects and planes of varying dimensions. The texture is what provides the link between the image's figures, which are cut and juxtaposed without any retouches, creating the same luminescence of old-fashioned photomontages. It cements the different elements into one image, bringing together landscapes from different starting points. The landscape becomes a massive horizon from which the photographer has torn the contour of things.

Nelson Brissac Peixoto

The presentation of this exhibition at FotoFest 2004 was made possible through the assistance of Century Property Management at Reliant Energy Plaza, 1000 Main.Special thanks go to Joyce Harberson, Vice President, Century Property Management.

Cássio Vasconcellos • *Paisagens Marinhas #12*, 1993-1994 • Silver Gelatin Print

WATERWORKS

ARTIST: STANLEY GREENBERG

The water on Earth today is the same water that was here in the time of the dinosaurs. But water is impermanent and subject to natural cycles. That permanence is an illusion is more apparent today than when I completed this work in the spring of 2001. The emerging awareness that nothing really lasts forever makes us appreciate the faith and effort involved in humanity's constructive efforts to transform a landscape and a society.

When New York City created its water system in the 19th century, it sought to ensure a reliable supply in order to sustain the city's growing population. The water system today is an extraordinary web of places—beautiful landscapes, mysterious structures, and sites where the natural meets the man-made in enigmatic ways. These landscapes, structures, and sites, some old and some still under construction, are monumental and fragile at the same time.

On the surface, it looks very peaceful—the need for a reliable water supply is something we can all agree on. But the reflective beauty of the reservoirs is deceptive, its stillness failing to betray the water rushing underground. Little is what it seems to be. Similarly, New York's water is delivered by a complex system with a contentious history. The system was controversial from the beginning. Aaron Burr used it as a way to start a bank to compete with Alexander Hamilton. The state and city government constantly fought over who would build and control it. New Jersey forbade New York from taking any of its water. Counties outside the city tried to keep the city from taking any water or property. The Tammany political machine used the system to employ its faithful.

We like to think that the things we rely on will always be here. The water supply has faced many threats, from the Confederate Army during the Civil War, later from farm runoff and acid ran, and now from international terrorism. We may continue to take it for granted. Or we may begin to see it with new eyes—an extraordinary moment of confluence, the imperfect and impermanent meeting of nature's power and people's vision and ingenuity.

Stanley Greenberg

The presentation of this exhibition at FotoFest 2004 was made possible with the support of Trizec Office Properties. Special thanks go to Joanna Chain, Director of Tenant Relations at Allen Center/Cullen Center.

STANLEY GREENBERG • *CROTON FALLS DAM, NEW YORK*, 2000 • SILVER GELATIN PRINT

EL AGUA COMO TUMBA

Water as Graveyard — Helen Zout

HELEN ZOUT • *LA PLATA RIVER, ARGENTINA*, 2003 • SILVER GELATIN PRINT
IMAGE REPRESENTING "THE DEATH'S FLIGHTS" WHICH TOOK PLACE DURING THE LAST MILITARY DICTACTORSHIP IN ARGENTINA.
AN UNKNOWN NUMBER OF ALIVE, SEMI-ASLEEP YOUNG PEOPLE WERE THROWN FROM THOSE PLANES INTO THE RÍO DO LA PLATA
(RIVER). TODAY, ALL OF THEM HAVE DISAPPEARED.

HELEN ZOUT • *AERONAUTIC MILITARY MUSEUM, MORON, ARGENTINA*, 2003 • SILVER GELATIN PRINT
AN AEROPLANE SIMILAR TO THOSE PLANES USED FOR THE WELL-KNOWN "DEATH'S FLIGHTS", DURING THE LAST DICTATORSHIP
IN THE REPUBLIC OF ARGENTINA, FLYING OVER THE RÍO DE LA PLATA (RIVER).

ARTIST: HELEN ZOUT

In these photographs, I want to talk about Life.

Yes, I am talking about human beings whose lives that have been cut short. Nevertheless, I prefer to do so in a way that gives emphasis to their lives, the Life that was taken away from them, rather than the means that were used to end their lives.

Moreover, and despite the fact that here I am talking about "water as graveyard," I want it to be clear that I refuse to accept that, what happened in Argentina during the last military dictatorship in the years 1976-1983, can be easily absorbed by humanity or gently dealt with by history.

I want to say that I refuse to take it lightly—the fact that some men, in a cowardly way, threw thousands of other human beings out to sea, after anesthetizing them, in order to eliminate them forever.

I want to say this is terrible, atrocious.

I want to say that our country can never repair this damage, the damage that some inflicted on others.

I want to say that Argentina lost thousands of its best sons and daughters, irreparably damaging the nation and the body politic for generations to come.

I want to say that no human being has attained the right to shorten the lives of thousands of lives barely 20 years old.

I want to say there is no justice, neither human nor divine, that can respond to the eternal gaze of parents and children who stare at the sea waiting for an answer, trying to imagine the last second of life of a beloved one who disappeared or hoping that, by some miracle, the beloved face would come back.

Yes, I am talking about Life, life that wasn't but should have been.

These photographs are part of my work that I have been doing from 1999 to the present — *Footprints of the Disappeared during the Last Military Dictatorship in Argentina 1976-1983.*

Helen Zout

Translated from Spanish

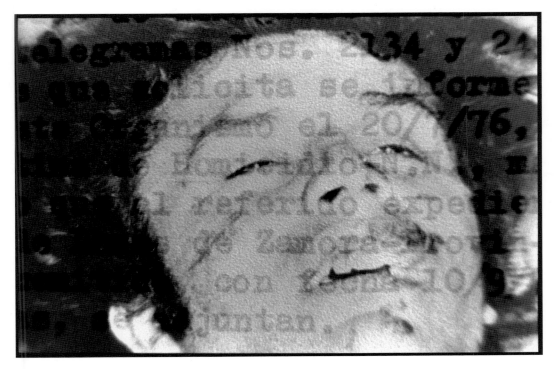

HELEN ZOUT • *LA PLATA CITY, ARGENTINA*, 2003 • SILVER GELATIN PRINT
PHOTOGRAPH OF A PHOTOGRAPH MADE BY JUDICIAL EXPERTS ENTERED IN THE FILE OF A DEAD YOUNG MAN, NOT
IDENTIFIED, WHO IS SUPPOSED TO HAVE BEEN ABDUCTED IN 1976.

WATER AS RITUAL

ARTIST: PHYLLIS GALEMBO

Near Ville Bonheur, thousands of pilgrims annually make the difficult trek to Sodo, a sacred waterfall in the heart of Haiti. Sodo is the Creole spelling of Saut d'Eau, which in French means "waterfall." This holy pilgrimage goes to the place where, it is believed, Vièj Mirak (the Miracle Virgin) dwells. The pilgrimage takes place on or about July 16, when Catholics celebrate the Feast of Our Lady of Mt. Carmel. In Haiti, the period near July 16 also commemorates the time in 1849 when the Virgin Mary appeared in the foliage of a palm tree to a peasant farmer. The blending of these events culminated in the practice of venerating the Vodou spirit of Ezuli Dantò, the warrior mother.

The concept of water as a divine element with cultural ceremonies devoted to its powers is as ancient as recorded history. In the Haitian voodoo culture, water is inhabited by deities who have both spiritual and physical powers, and at Sodo it is believed, there are healing powers as well. This strong belief inspires multitudes to make the arduous journey, on foot or by donkey, to bathe in the sacred waters in hopes of answered prayers. Often pilgrims leave behind a small part of their clothing as a reminder to a deity that they had been there to participate in the ceremonies and to honor Ezuli.

This body of work is part of my continuing interest in, and exploration of, people's desire to interpret and explain the human condition through worship and spiritual communion. Rituals, rights, and regalia are consistent themes that I have explored and documented throughout my career using the photographic medium. At Sodo I was present among many thousands of devotional pilgrims, immersed for hours in the sacred waters. I was granted the privilege of documenting many of the faithful as they were attended to by the priests and priestesses. This proximity afforded me the opportunity to capture revealing images that illuminate the mystical powers of the waters, which turn from darkness to light when the spirit of Vodou reveals itself.

Phyllis Galembo

The presentation of this exhibition at FotoFest 2004 was made possible with the support of Trizec Office Properties. Special thanks go to Joanna Chain, Director of Tenant Relations at Allen Center/Cullen Center.

PHYLLIS GALEMBO • *SAUT D' EAUX,* 1997-2002 • SEPIA TONED SILVER GELATIN PRINT

WATER AS RITUAL

ARTIST: STUART ROME

The inspiration for my pictures comes from diverse sources, including the art of ancient cultures, animism in Indonesia, and voodoo in Haiti. I am deeply influenced by poetry in which the friction of disparate imagery creates a new way of seeing familiar territory. Looking at early Chinese painting, the prints and drawings of Philip Guston, and the photographs of Harry Callahan has guided me toward abstraction as a metaphoric bridge. In my most recent work, I employ this language of abstraction to uproot the objects in my pictures and free them from their familiar domain. These images become a form of guided hallucination, suggestive of curious but recognizable patterns encountered in nature. I use real places to draw out patterns that are analogous to maps of interior emotional and intellectual states.

My intention is to create a bridge between the recognizable world and our thoughts or impressions of other possibilities—even impossibilities. As a photographer, I look for alternative worldviews to counter the materialist culture in which we live. I have followed the example of mythology to unlock hidden worlds, which might hold clues to refute our prevailing cultural ideal. In previous work, I photographed in distant places such as Latin America and Indonesia and examined the relationship between people and their environment: I documented ceremonies that revealed the active dialogue with nature that is achieved through trance and possession. This experience provided me with the alternate viewpoint I was seeking. It allowed me to see the multiplicity of perspectives that might be possible. Through my travels I discovered ways of seeing the natural world as a communicating entity and learned to regard the landscape as a living pattern.

For me, every process in picture making is a vehicle for considering meaning. The choice of black and white materials simplifies chaotic imagery into a form where a new visual order appears, one that better suggests metaphor. While photographing is a fast and intuitive process, printing is a slow and contemplative one. It allows for thought about the nature of light in a stream of consciousness manner, much like my state of mind on a long drive.

Stuart Rome

STUART ROME • *HALONG BAY*, 2000 • SILVER GELATIN PRINT
COURTESY OF SEPIA INTERNATIONAL GALLERY

WATER AS RITUAL

ARTIST: CHRISTIAN CRAVO

No matter who we are, where we are, and what we do, we are all dependent upon water. We need it to hydrate the human body and sustain life, and for purposes as varied as transportation, irrigation, and religion. Despite the importance of water resources in our lives, we have shown an increasing level of disrespect towards this precious liquid. We abuse it. We waste it. We pollute it. We forget how essential it is to our very survival, be it physical or spiritual.

In some cultures, water has long been regarded as part of a sacred life process and not simply as another product for consumption. In modern times, our increased comprehension of the scientific story of evolution gives us a renewed appreciation for the role of water in sustaining life. To see water as a source of life and not merely as a daily resource is the challenge of a new synthesis of science and religion.

From early human history, when the four elements of earth, air, fire, and water were identified as sacred vessels of life processes, to later sacramental uses of water in baptism or purification ceremonies, water has occupied a central place in the human imagination and religious consciousness.

My last completed work, *Irredentos* (2000), portrays the lives of the Sertanejos, a people that lives in one of Brazil's harshest desert landscapes, the Brazilian backlands. This is a place where religion has found its most secure roots, primarily because of the suffering caused by the lack of water.

In the terrible expectation generated by hopes of redemption through the precious and irreplaceable liquid that must fall from heaven, the Brazilian Sertanejos make pilgrimages to sacred sites where they expiates their sins and acquire amulets that will protect them until the next prayer or until rain (the redemption liquid) shall fall.

During the years in which I traveled in the backlands of Brazil, I considered how the religious beliefs of the region found their common element in the lack of water. Since water is the most important life-giving element in the Brazilian backlands, humans are at the mercy of water much as they are at the mercy of God.

I had previously traveled in India, and there, too, water is the epicenter for spiritual life, although not as in the Brazilian backlands because of the difficulties of obtaining it, but because of its abundance in the form of endless rivers and seas. Yet these two distant worlds have in common the veneration of this liquid, which exerts the power of life and death over all.

My primary goal is to recover and unfold a natural and balanced view of our precious waters, one that still exists within these religious creeds, and to challenge viewers of my work to see water as a source of life and divine inspiration and not merely as a resource of daily consumption.

My expected result after 12 months of research is a photographic portfolio of approximately 80 images, which will be part of an art book.

Christian Cravo

CHRISTIAN CRAVO • *PURI, INDIA*, 1992 • Silver Gelatin Print

A PERSONAL VIEW

On the Edge

ARTIST: ERNESTINE RUBEN

My interest in applying photography to other art forms has always led me down exciting paths. When I turned to non-silver techniques several years ago, I plunged into color and landscape. I later became interested in subjects that lack the solidity and clear physical boundaries so often found in my earlier work, which dealt with the nude as well as landscapes. I have been drawn to the work of 19th-century landscape artists and share their fascination with the movement not only of water but of air, fog, and mist, which give the image a mysterious quality. This is quite "unphotographic," but it lets me incorporate some of the strengths of painting, such as the application of brush strokes, and drawing. These effects blur the boundaries between photography and painting in much the same way that water and land blend where they meet. The work that I am doing with water is about the fluidity of thought and technique, as well as about being on the edge, suspended between land and water, and water and sky.

As a photographer looking at water, I realize how much our perception of water depends upon its relationship to the things around it. Malleable and fluid, it becomes a subject by way of other objects, whether it is found in large areas like oceans or small ones, such as a gathering of tiny drops collected in the hollow of a rock. I have explored landscapes in the mountains and ice fields of Antarctica, the rivers of Europe and America, the lakes of Africa, and the volcanic areas in the seas of New Zealand and Hawaii. As I look at water, I envision a composition of layers of transparent colors interacting with each other, the way that land and water do. There is a definite relationship between my perception, my technique, and the meeting of land and water.

Using an old photographic process called gum dichromate, I paint onto the paper a layer of transparent watercolor and then expose the paper, combined with a large negative, to actinic light. The exposed paper is then developed and dried before I add the next layer. The images often have 15 layers. Because I work on each image for weeks, I can see the flow and the effects of time in the transformation of the image's details. The sense is that the water begins to move and become alive, just as it does in nature. Some layers are sharp and others are dreamlike, as if they were seen through a mysterious veil.

The image is often intensified where I apply lines and details using watercolor and other materials directly to the photographic image. In most cases the line where land and water meet becomes imbued with intense color and energy.

Ernestine Ruben

The presentation of *Personal Views* at FotoFest 2004 was made possible with the support of J.P. Morgan Chase. Special thanks go to Yolanda Londoño.

ERNESTINE RUBEN • *THERMAIL NIPPLE*, 2002 • GUM DICHROMATE • COURTESY OF JOHN STEVENSON GALLERY

A PERSONAL VIEW

Venice Series

ARTIST: BARBARA DOWNS

For a number of years, I lived by the sea in Sussex, England, and loved the way that the reflected light from the water changed the atmosphere of the whole place. The same perception informed my response to Venice.

The Venice images demonstrate my working process. I assemble photographs intuitively as a visual notebook, not bounded by accepted formalities, but using experiment and play. In recent works, groups of photographs have become more significant than individual ones.

The photographs and constructed images of the *Venice Series* reflect how traveling on the water dominated my view of Venice and affected the photographs produced. There is a floating quality one feels when looking through the windows of a vaporetti, created by the bounce and the blur and the occasional glimpses of unexpected sharpness.

The images here are not panoramas of public places, but narrow views, closely cropped to give a personal and private response to the city. It perhaps would have been instructive to experience an almost empty Venice—like the city's back streets on Sunday mornings. Instead I shut out the crowds and looked for intimate, iconic details that surprised me, an alternative to the images familiar from a fine arts background.

The fun when developing the work later was in referencing the city in a less traditional, more modern form. I see two contrary aspects to my work on Venice. First, there are images informed by my ongoing affection for the sea and its mirrorlike atmospheric light, for its feeling of infinite possibilities and its affirmation of self and life. And second, there are those images reflecting the secret, inward-looking feel of the interior space, where I explored something elusive and mysterious about the city, something glimpsed through frames, hidden, seen from an outsider's view.

The tension between figurative and abstract forms has always interested me. The resolution of this tension, how these forms are juxtaposed within this series, has taken some time.

Yet the movement of light on water remains essential. While producing images for *Changing Spaces*, my series about the metamorphosis of the city center of inland Birmingham, I realized that they included many indirect references to the coast. I saw how my constructed images so often show a continuing need for the sea.

Barbara Downs

Barbara Downs • *Venice Series: Still Green*, 2003 • C – Type Print

A PERSONAL VIEW

ARTIST: ANNE GABRIELE

Being near the water's edge, within sight and sound of the surf, affects my flow of thought. I find the ocean has a cleansing effect, the ability to draw out images from my memories, dreams, and fears. For me, water is a strong magnetic force, with the power to both attract and repel. I am drawn to the ocean, yet I do not swim in it. The ocean can be fickle, lending its beauty and sharing its vastness one moment, and right after becoming harsh and unrelenting through the pounding of its surf. It is this duality that has both fascinated and frightened me over the years.

Observing the water from the shore, I watch how light alters its personality from calm and serene one minute to dark and forbidding the next. The surf never looks the same way twice, yet it is constant in its ebb and flow.

Water—the wellspring of life—is also the origin of the printmaking process I used in creating this body of work. Using distilled water to soak, remove, and manipulate the Polaroid emulsion, I was aware of how the water altered the emulsion, making it pliable and giving me endless opportunities for combining images and creating an altered reality. The way that the water changes the emulsion mirrors how the surf changes the shoreline.

The meeting of the sea and land, and the sea and the sky, and its ever-shifting moods provide constant inspiration for my artwork

Anne Gabriele

Anne Gabriele • *Listing*, 2003 • Emulsion Transfer on Paper

A PERSONAL VIEW

ARTIST: GINA GLOVER

Sea at Rest
It is my destiny
To fracture time
And climb to silence
Through the breach
To touch a memory

        – Cecil Hemley

This series of pinhole photographs reveals the sea at rest in a variety of climatic conditions and times of day: before and after a snowstorm, at dawn, or in the evening light. These shots were taken on Lewis, a remote Hebridean Island off the coast of Scotland, on the north coast of Wales, and on the shoreline of Long Island, New York.

My interest is in making pictures that evoke our relationship to nature. I aim to produce seascapes with a restorative quality, a means of calming the mind. Using a camera without a lens, I capture the sea through a tiny hole of light that creates a different relationship to reality, allowing me to stretch the boundaries of the photographic moment.

Our eyes capture information at approximately one-sixtieth of a second. A pinhole exposure can last hours, even days. Such long exposures have the potential to embed a synchronic narrative within an image in a way that fast-focus photography can never do. In some of these pictures, the sea appears frozen solid, imparting to it our sense of being there on a chilly day.

By nature the sea is unpredictable. We can try to understand it, reveal it, and revel in it, but we are always conscious of its force and we are humbled by its vastness. Just as the sea represents our primordial beginnings, so, too, through its changing and repeating tides, it remains a source of renewal, linking many of us to our childhood memories and providing us with moments of total absorption where time is transcended.

Gina Glover

GINA GLOVER • *EXAMINER SOUTH SHORE LONG ISLAND SOUND NEW YORK*, 2001 • C-TYPE PRINT

A PERSONAL VIEW

ARTIST: JULIA HOERNER

My thoughts on water tumble onto paper like rain on my pond, as difficult to rein in as it would be to confine a thunderstorm. Water is with you, as it is with me, always, a part of us by its presence as well as its absence or scarcity. My awareness of the aesthetic qualities of water extends from infancy, recalling the child's pure, sunlit joy at standing in Florida's boiling surf, to the deepest grief felt looking across a blue-black night sea toward home from Australia on the evening of my mother's death.

Many years ago I sat in a rowboat on a New England lake for hours, trying to paint the shifting positive/negative ripple forms, and when I was back on dry land, the world rocked and swayed for as many hours, my penance for having tried to fix the mutable. Stopping motion is perhaps a human instinct to save what we love, what moves us, and what connects us. This may be a betrayal of the mutability that water exemplifies, but art is full of such betrayals.

That is the magic for me: bringing a flat and fixed image to the wall of other such betrayals—to the wall of something that is constant change in its essential nature.

I love the turquoise of a glacier's ancient compressed water and the mean gray of water that the camera has turned to molten metal. I love the brazen slithering of swimming pool reflections. I love the sky upturned as the clouds run under the surface of my pond.

Julia Hoerner

JULIA HOERNER • *THERE IS NO RESOLUTION (WATER LESSON)*, 2001 • LAMBDA METALLIC PRINT

A PERSONAL VIEW

ARTIST: CORINNE MERCADIER

What does one see in Corinne Mercadier's photographs? Sky and water, the line of the horizon, fragile landing stages with loose planks, one or two boats hauled up on the shore, almost nothing. Objects were scarcely more numerous in the purist paintings by Italian artist Giorgio Morandi with their vases, jugs, bottles. Corinne Mercadier demonstrates an equal perseverance in laconism: an art of little, where the lifeless and the second-rate become the most radiant reality, and an illustration of forlornness that metamorphoses in the ecstasy of solitude.

Against all that which obliterates our vision, Corinne Mercadier opens the path of the void. And this void strangely arouses a presence in the world. It is the structure and rigging of the gaze. Bit by bit, this state of abandon that impregnates the countryside insinuates itself in us. Little by little, everything that is not light takes refuge. The rare objects that we see live in the vacancy of their use. There is in them something that is infinitely available, which communicates its calm and its peace to the very edges of the heart.

The places photographed are always the same. Never named, they are impossible to pin down, as if they were the margins of the world. But they are not nowhere to be found: they seem rather to already have been present in us before we saw them.

Jean-Baptiste Para, 2000

Corinne Mercadier • Untitled from the *Paysages* Series, 1994 • Enlarged Poaroid SX70
Courtesy of Galerie Les filles du calvaire

LOOKING AT WATER

ARTISTS: DAVID GOLDES

Riding the 1950s post-Sputnik wave of science education enthusiasm, I majored in chemistry and biology in college, and afterwards enrolled in a graduate molecular genetics program. But before all that, back in the sixth grade, I had built a giant light meter. Later, in an eighth-grade science project, I modulated the brightness of a light beam with my voice and used this to communicate across the length of my hallway to a photo-cell receiver. This involvement with light would propel me into the world of picture-making and photography, and I eventually left professional science.

But my interest in physical phenomena did not diminish. During the early 1990s, I was drawn to water for the same reasons that many are. It is wondrous stuff—ubiquitous in our daily lives and consciousnesses, yet possessing unique and strange properties.

At the same time, I had been reconsidering how science becomes involved in an individual's life, determining whether or not one is to become a scientist. Pictures of experiments seem critical not only to illustrate a principle, as is often the case in textbooks, but also to suggest a larger rational ordering of the world. When I viewed such pictures as a child, they suggested the potential for future understanding—how observed experimental events might be fitted with an elucidating theory. As an adult, I find the challenge is different. When I look at science pictures now, I think about how much I have yet to comprehend to come to a full and rich understanding of even the simplest, most straightforward phenomena. I could, after all, generate equations to describe the direction and velocity of a ball falling toward me—but what about the nature of gravity, or my very real fear of being hit?

One way of thinking about the history of photography is to approach it as the history of where one places the camera, and by consequence of how the resultant picture situates the viewer in physical, cultural, and personal terms. The subject of the camera's scrutiny is always physical, but in the best pictures this attention takes on meanings that reflect concerns outside the small rectangle. Art loosens and embellishes the linkage between what is observed and an explanatory hypothesis. What is experienced by the viewer when a phenomenon is observed? What memories are evoked, what emotions triggered, and what stories formulated? Art's great seduction is that it offers and shapes these questions for its audience. Indeed it embraces the audience as part of the observed event.

This work grew out of a revisiting of simple experiments with water. I am particularly interested in situations where the physicality of water can be linked to cultural function. Human history is a story of relationships with water, so it is no wonder that water holds various meanings. Many of the pictures resulted from a clear programmatic approach to a specific property of water. Others resulted from time spent being attentive, patient with myself and the water, and willing to see where my efforts might lead. The best pictures, like the best equations, are elegant and implicitly argue that they offer the only solution.

David Goldes

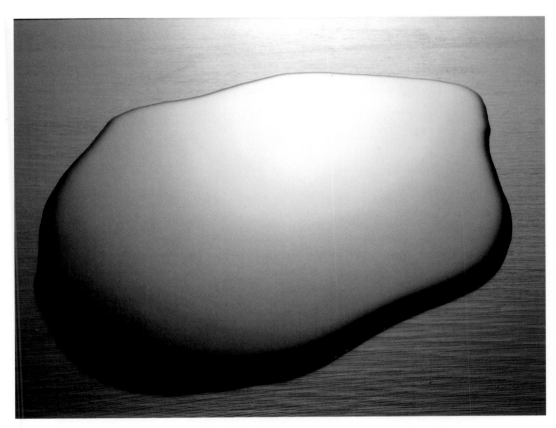

David Goldes • *Puddle*, 2003 • Silver Gelatin Print
Courtesy Yossi Milo Gallery, New York

David Goldes • *Five Spoons*, 1996 • Silver Gelatin Print
Courtesy Yossi Milo Gallery, New York

Perhaps the word "bottle" already gives too much away, so it might be better to "read" these images without any kind of prompt. I have taken familiar objects—ordinary, throwaway, and numerous—and re-placed them in the environment so as to effect a transformation.

The humble plastic water bottle is a transparent vessel, symbolic of our quest for health, to be cleansed, to flush out the "dirt" from our bodies, to keep our blood flowing without clot or hitch. We want life extensions and vigor, and we're in a hurry! Quench that thirst, gratify that urge, and move on.

We consume in seconds and discard dregs quickly to degrade slowly. An empty vessel rolls, wind-blown, along the beach, scumbled and scuffed by the rocks; it lodges for a moment, then is caught by the tide, turned over and over as in a jeweller's polishing box. This is not just a history of abuse but a legacy in the making…

Water has somehow wended its way through and around my work. After I completed a major project at the Royal College of Surgeons, London, I became preoccupied with the notions of preservation and suspension. I saw them extend well beyond the 200-year-old specimen jars that I was photographing. Through preservation, we hold something in a fixed state because we value it or want to say something about it. The object is often isolated from its original environment and bestowed with new status. Suspended in a watery world, it seems neither fully alive nor properly dead; it's an attempt at cheating death…

For me, photography has become an "act of preservation," and the objects I focus on have become the locators or igniters of memory. The traces and remnants we find in any landscape can spark recognition or what might be called "momentary resurrections."[1] They can even invoke a presence, and this is the reason why I am starting to investigate the role of relics in our own time. The act of photographing gives "shape" to a moment, and in so doing, we fix time. We create a memento: something to keep which future generations may analyze and regard in order to seek meaning.

Water has to be contained, otherwise it is anarchic. Some of the experiments, which followed on from working with specimen jars, involved water in a very tangible way. I devised a technique that enabled me to suspend images in a tank of water, circulate them, and rephotograph them. This in itself felt anarchic, as the tendency is to protect photographs from water. Interestingly, it seemed that my photographs were becoming the specimen, suspended and protected.

Implicit within the examination of preservation is the acknowledgment of decay as the ultimate breaking down of both physical and mental certainties. The thought of decay and bodily corruption is generally held to be unsavory and actually is why we ply our systems with the water that we hope will keep our aging bodies alive for longer. The body is a vessel, that which is both "a container and the contained." With its awe-inspiring navigation system, life courses through the veins and arteries. Without pump and circulation, life ebbs away and the body becomes as dry as dust…

So, make of these dazzling "monuments" what you will— objects in a landscape, personal or universal metaphors, or aide-mémoire…

Elaine Duigenan

[1] Celeste Olalquiaga, *The Artificial Kingdom: On the Kitsch Experience* (Minneapolis: Univ. of Minnesota Press, 2002).

LATITUDES AND LONGING

ARTIST: DON GLENTZER

Fishermen and birdwatchers love the Texas Gulf Coast for its abundant wildlife. The area around Rockport, in particular, is among the most popular in the world for coastal birding. During the winter months, migratory waterfowl skim the region's shallow bays and marshes, which are filled with redfish, trout and flounder. I am inspired, paradoxically, by the sense of emptiness and quietude that surrounds all this human and animal activity.

Sport fishermen are continually in pursuit of the next catch at the end of their lines, always hoping to add larger specimens to their record books. Birders, through their binoculars, are likewise regularly on a quest to add new or rarely spotted avian treasures to their "life lists." Year after year, it's the thrill of the hunt and the joy of conquest that keep fishermen and birders absorbed: No two catches or sightings are alike. It's much the same for me when I'm photographing moments that derive from these activities.

My work is a personal narrative. It evolves from my reaction to a place or a moment in time and what I find mysterious or magical about that moment. An element of tension usually comes into play. It might be the relationship of a person or an object to the space, or the space itself. To capture my subjects, perspective is critical, because I want to engage the viewer's imagination beyond a literal viewpoint. I strive to produce images that conceal as much as they reveal. They are purposefully enigmatic.

Achieving this quality in photographs can be as challenging as finding that elusive shorebird. It often means returning again and again to a location and experimenting until the light quality is finally right. This is not so much a technical process as a perceptive one; I like to explore intuitively rather than deductively. I try to respect technique, but it is only a tool: Too much emphasis on it stunts progress and can actually interfere with creating an image.

I prefer to concentrate on composition, seeking single visual elements that serve the essence of the whole. I compose and crop images in the camera, on film, rather than relying on cropping options while printing. This method keeps me more focused and in the moment when I'm shooting.

Don Glentzer

DON GLENTZER • *#3 N 28° 06' 83"/W 97° 01' 54" (PHOBIA)*, 2003
• SILVER GELATIN PRINT

DON GLENTZER • *#21 N 29° 17' 00"/W 94° 50' 12" (EPIPHANY)*, 2003
• SILVER GELATIN PRINT

FOTOFEST COLLABORATIONS—WATER

FOTOFEST COLLABORATIONS   2

MEMORÍAS DEL AGUA, EL ORINOCO

[Memoirs of Water, The Orinoco] —*Edgar Moreno*

EDGAR MORENO • *ZIAJE AL CORIZÓN DE LAS TINIEBLAS [JOURNEY TO THE HEART OF DARKNESS]*, 2001 • TONED SILVER GELATIN PRINT

EDGAR MORENO • FROM *VIAJE AL INTERIOR DE LAS ANTÍPODAS [JOURNEY TO THE HEART OF THE ANTIPODES]*, N/D • TONED SILVER GELATIN PRINT

ARTIST: EDGAR MORENO

Pantón Neké, Iná Ekarayi
Esto no es cuento, es un relato
This is not a fairytale, it is an account.

1983–2002

The Yekuanas, our bold Indian navigators, were the Phoenicians of the forest. In their voyages, they discovered the union of the Negro River with the Amazon River. They led the famous 1951 French-Venezuelan expedition to the source of the Orinoco River. From an elevated spot in the forest, a small spring arose among some rocks. Right there, the Orinoco, one of the world's largest rivers, was born.

....

On October 12, 1992, I had the good fortune of being on the island of Amboina, Indonesia, the same one that Columbus was in search of before finding America: the Island of Spices. I asked a Chinese taxi driver if there was in Indonesia any commemoration of the 500th anniversary of the discovery of the New World, Columbus Day or whatever it is called there. "I don't know what you are talking about, sir," he replied. As I was getting out, I asked him to give me the front leaf of the tear-off calendar he had in his car: "Monday, October 12."

....

On my return to Europe, I stopped in Spain, where there were grand celebrations in commemoration of the 500th anniversary, including a new 1,000 peseta note with the portraits of Pizarro and Cortés, the psychopath and the hippomanic, two renowned Extremadurans who were efficient promoters of the Incan and Aztec exterminations.

....

Jimmie Angel was the first "jungle pilot" and the first white man to see the Churún Merú or Angel Falls. From then on there followed a hierarchy of the most important toponken (the dressed people) in the Pemón world: First came the cajichana, or aircraft captain, then came the doctor, equally or even more powerful than a piasán or a chamán. And since our worlds are dominated by the mass media and tourism has permeated everything with its money, we, the photographers, ranked third among the travelers to the West Indies—beloved for our desire to keep the pristine and romantic side of the forest, and hated for reporting outrageous behavior and stealing the Indians' soul when photographing them.

....

I arrived with some Roman tourists at a Pemón village. They said they were eager to see genuine, half-naked Indians like those portrayed in la Nationale Geografiche. The place was deserted. Did they go hunting with their blowpipes? Were they farming? Were they fishing in the river with barbasco*? There was only a wrinkled old man, whom I asked in my very poor Pemón, "?Ada tun se to etepuese? [Did they go fishing with barbasco?] *He replied, "No mijo, los indios están en el supermercado comprando sardinas enlatadas* [No, my son, the Indians are buying canned sardines in the supermarket]."*

Edgar Moreno

From "Anotaciones /A Personal Record," in *Memorías del agua: Obras de Edgar Moreno [Memoirs of Water: Works by Edgar Moreno]* (Caracas: Museo de Bellas Artes, 2003), pp. 104–119.

This presentation at FotoFest 2004 is the first exhibition of these works in the U.S. It is made possible with the support and collaboration of The Station, James and Ann Harithas. Special thanks go Tex Kerschen, curator, The Station.

The publication of *Memorías del agua: Obras de Edgar Moreno [Memoirs of Water: Works by Edgar Moreno]* was supported by ChevronTexaco. The exhibition was produced and curated by Tomás Rodríguez and Edgar Moreno for the Museo de Bellas Artes (MBA) in Caracas.

*A poisonous plant used in water for fishing purposes.

EDGAR MORENO • *EN LAS INDIAS OCCIDENTALES [IN THE WEST INDIES]*, 2000 • TONED SILVER GELATIN PRINT

Viaje al interior de las antípodas

Memory and imagination have gone hand in hand since ancient times. Prompted by an urgent need, people sieve their memories through their own retrospective viewpoints. This is how they grow and develop. Seen through the eyes of art, this sieving gives way to a flow of images molded by time. This is the subject of this work. By means of his photographs, Venezuelan artist Edgar Moreno has initiated a dialogue with work done centuries ago in his homeland by Theodore Von Bry, the famous Flemish engraver and artist who in the 16th century wrote, illustrated, and published, along with his family, 14 volumes of stories narrated by invaders and pioneers who traveled to America from Europe.

Memoirs of Water is the diary of a journey to the heart of the antipodes: a voyage to the seas and rivers, real or imaginary, undertaken by those early explorers who went to the West Indies on the very edge of the unknown. The core of this work is the book *La quarta parte del mundo. La conquista en imágenes, Theodoro de Bry 1528–1598 [The Fourth Part of the World. The Conquest in Images, Theodoro de Bry 1528–1598]* by Lieselotte Venter (Caracas: Editions Galería Félix, 1992) with interventions by Edgar Moreno's own photographs and travel memoirs.

Tomás Rodríguez Soto
Curator, Museo de Bellas Artes, Caracas

From the essay *Journey to the Heart of the Antipodes in Memorías del agua: Obras de Edgar Moreno [Memoirs of Water: Works by Edgar Moreno]* (Caracas: Museo de Bellas Artes, 2003), pp. 13–24.

Theodore Von Bry: Grands Voyages-Americae

…..The work having the most enduring influence on the European view of the islands and lands on the other side of the Atlantic was the series of compilations of accounts of various journeys that Theodore Von Bry and his family published in Frankfurt between 1590 and 1644. Known as the *Grands Voyages-Americae*, it includes more than 300 illustrations and 40 maps…. The series' numerous plates were reproduced and copied for centuries…. For three generations the Von Bry family devoted itself to this enterprise…. The first volumes were published at a time when the Protestant powers had begun to take part in the colonization of America, so they served a political and religious purpose in addition to their informative aim…. The interpretations of the indigenous people's customs and habits came from the imaginations of Von Bry and his craftsmen, who never met an Indian and so based their work on other people's summaries, graphic materials, and writings, thus carrying out an authentic "staging"….

Lieselotte Venter

From her essay *Theodore Von Bry: Grands Voyages-Americae, in Memorías del agua: Obras de Edgar Moreno* [Memoirs of Water: Works by Edgar Moreno] (Caracas: Museo de Bellas Artes, 2003), pp. 28–32.

EDGAR MORENO • *LA FUAGA DE LOS TOLISAURIOS ASESINOS [THE FLIGHT OF THE MURDEROUS POLYSAURS]*, 1989 • TONED SILVER GELATIN PRINT

EDGAR MORENO • *EL ORIGEN DE LAS FORMAS [THE ORIGIN OF FORMS]*, 2002 • TONED SILVER GELATIN PRINT

OCEANS APART

ARTIST: INGRID POLLARD

The starting point for *Oceans Apart* (1989) and *Boy who watches ships go by* (2002) was both autobiographical and historical narratives involving the sea. Using the sea as a way of exploring the themes of separation and the diaspora experience of migration, I looked at journeys that have crisscrossed the Atlantic Ocean both east and west.

These voyages echo the sea's own relentless movement of waves and tides: journeys out toward the sea's horizon and journeys of arrival from the same horizon. What traces are left of the past accumulate in contemporary coastal locations.

For some time the concerns of my visual work have centered on the question of historical development and how to frame the changing nature of the "English environment" within the context of storytelling and narrative. The work has appropriated many photographic forms, from postcards and tinted photographs to panoramic images, using photographic emulsion on a range of surfaces, as well as digital processes and processes from the 19th century. The work has engaged with the photographic genre of constructed imagery and what could be called the "historical presence of black people." In the past it has used the "urbanized black body" within the English countryside, questioning common sense assumptions about what makes up definitions of "Englishness" and exploring how race and gender can define individual lives and identity within the form of photographic narratives.

Form and content meet within the two works presented here.

Ingrid Pollard, Untitled from the series *The Boy Who Watches Ships Go By*, 2002 • Photographic Emulsion on Stretched Canvas

Boy who watches ships go by

This series of photographic canvases describes the shifting landscapes and histories of a quiet coastal village. The viewer enters into a world of imagination, memory, and narrative created by images of land and sea.

Sunderland Point, through its involvement in shipbuilding for the slave trade in the Americas and the Caribbean, was for some 40 years in the 18th century one of the busiest ports in northern England. Today the quiet coastal village of Sunderland Point is the site of "Sambo's" 1739 grave. According to one of the local traditions, a sea captain returning from the Caribbean brought him as a boy to the village.

Oceans Apart

The Atlantic as a physical and psychic space forms the basis of this work. During the last 600 years, stretches of the eastern shore in the Caribbean and Americas and the western shores of England and Europe have been the sites of important arrivals and departures.

Using the juxtaposition of various voices, this work examines how the legacy of black families in the Caribbean connects with the stories of European maritime heroes such as Elizabethan naval captains and adventurers Sir Frances Drake and Sir Walter Raleigh, and the explorers Christopher Columbus and James Cook.

Ingrid Pollard

Special support for the presentation of this exhibition at FotoFest 2004 came from the British Art Council and Project Row Houses.

INGRID POLLARD, UNTITLED FROM THE SERIES *OCEANS APART*, 1995 • HAND TINTED SILVER
PRINT

TOWARDS NATURE

Nils-Udo

NILS-UDO • *BIRCH STICKS, FERN LEAVES, RIBWORT STEMS, PINE NEEDLES, PETALS OF THE DOG ROSE ROSA RUGOSA "THUNBERG"*, GERMANY, 1986 •
ILFORCHROME ON ALUMINUM

FOTOFEST COLLABORATIONS

NILS-UDO • *WATERNEST, REEDS, SUMMER-WINTER*, DIPTYCH, GERMANY, 1986 • ILFORCHROME ON ALUMINUM

NILS-UDO • *WATERNEST, REEDS, SUMMER-WINTER*, DIPTYCH, GERMANY, 1986 • ILFORCHROME ON ALUMINUM

ARTIST: NILS-UDO

Sketching with flowers. Painting with clouds. Writing with water. Tracing the May wind, the path of a falling leaf. Working for a thunderstorm. Awaiting a glacier. Bending the wind. Directing water and light. The spring-green call of the cuckoo and the invisible trace of its flight. Space.

The cry of an animal. The bitter taste of daphne. Burying the pond and the dragonfly. Setting fire to the fog and the perfume of the yellow barberry.

Marrying sounds, colors, and smells. The green grass. Counting a forest and a meadow.

1972: The sensations are omnipresent. Being a realist, I just need to pick them up and release them from their anonymity. Utopias are under every rock, on every leaf, behind every tree, in the clouds and in the wind. The sun's course on the days of the equinox; the tiny habitat of a beetle on a lime leaf; the pointed maple's red fire; the scent of herbs in a wooded gorge; a frog's croak in the water lentils; the primrose's perfume on the banks of a mountain creek; animal traces in the snow; the remaining trajectory of a bird darting through the woods; a gust of wind in a tree; the dancing of light on leaves; the endlessly complex relationship of branch to branch, twig to twig, leaf to leaf…

Everything perceivable through the human senses takes part. Natural space is experienced through hearing, seeing, smelling, tasting, and touching. By means of the smallest possible interventions, living, three-dimensional natural space is reorganized, unlocked, and put under tension—a reorganization, of course, for a finite period of time. One day the intervention is wiped away, undone by nature without leaving a trace.

Clearly it is only in her very last refuges that nature is still intact, inexhaustible. It is only there that enchantment is

still reality: on any day of the year, in every season, in any light, in any weather; in the Largest and Smallest.

These days, however, people are not interested in this. Nature is no longer an issue, except to a few Greens, who mostly can no longer tell a lime tree from a beech tree.

Of course, there are many who pretend to love nature, like the ones who claim to want peace. The fact is, they lost nature long ago. They don't see it any more, let alone hear it, smell it, taste it, or touch it. When they do in fact take a look, they still don't see: they lost the prerequisites long ago for a larger, expansive, and transitory overall view.

Documentation of a world experience becoming extinct. Providing evidence at the last possible moment of a seemingly anachronistic life-awareness. An attitude hardly conceivable, even to the well intentioned.

A basic idea is to achieve absolute purity: nature performs a demonstration of itself. Every non-natural element is ruled out as impure; no other materials are used than those found in each natural space. The characteristics, the respective possibilities for processing, and the character of the natural space itself play the major roles in determining the shape of the work. In botany, collecting, preserving, and displaying, the overwhelming abundance of natural phenomena can often only be catagorized under the most minute fragments of their inherent structures.

The element of time: In 1972, my first work in the Chiemgau Alps consisted of a planting. By installing plantings or by integrating them into more complex installations, I literally implant the work into nature. As a part of nature, the work lives and passes away in the rhythm of the seasons.

Even though I work in parallel with nature and create my interventions with all possible caution, they will always remain a fundamental contradiction in themselves. It is this contradiction on which all my work is based . Even this work cannot avoid one fundamental disaster of our existence: it injures what it draws attention to, what it touches, the virginity of nature.

My work exists to unite, condense, and amalgamate the specific possibilities of a landscape at a given season to form a unique pinnacle, the apotheosis of that season in that landscape. Implementing what is potentially possible, what latently exists in nature, is to literally allow what never existed but was always there to become reality: the ever-present Utopia. Even one second of a lifetime is enough. The event has happened. I have awakened it and made it visible.

Make natural space into art space? Where is the limit on the narrow line between nature and art? Art? Life! What counts is the utopian character, the life- and art-blending character of my actions. My response to the events that mark my existence. My life.

Are there art lovers interested in my life?

A picture. A leaf, laden with flowers, drifting down a brook. Life.

Nils-Udo

Translated by Kieran McVey 3.2.02

The installation by Nils Udo at FotoFest 2004 was made possible by the Buffalo Bayou ArtPark with the assistance of the Buffalo Bayou Partnership (BBP). Special thanks go to Kevin Phillips, Director, Buffalo Bayou ArtPark; Anne Olson, Director of the Buffalo Bayou Partnership, and Toni Beauchamp, Chairperson of the BBP Art Board.

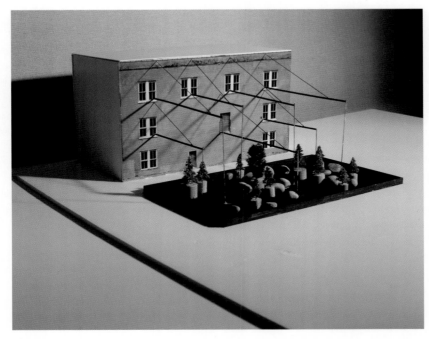

NIL-UDO • *LANDSCAPE WITH WATERFALL*, 2004 • MODEL OF INSTALLATIOIN AT SUNSET COFFEE BUILDING ALLENS'S LANDING, HOUSTON

FISH FLAG MOURANT

ARTIST: MALACHI FARRELL

[M]alachi] Farrell's most recent exhibition ... opened with a spectacle that was more distressing than violent: *Fish Flag Mourant [Dying Fish Flag]*, 1998–2000. On the ground floor of the gallery, in a polluted pond filled with scummy water and trash, several mechanized fish appeared to die a slow, agonizing death. Others hung above the stagnation as though just caught, making their last frantic movements. There toy-like robotic sculptures each bore the colors of a nation and symbolized, according to the artist...the abolition of frontiers in terms of pollution . [Malachi] Farrell doesn't beat around the bush or take refuge in metaphors but rather plots out the realities of the contemporary world's brutal bluntness....

There is a bit of Public Enemy in [Malachi] Farrell, then. And, in fact, it is not beside the point to note that he has particular affinities with French and American rap. Brother of the musician Liam Farrell, aka Doctor L., who made his debut with the band Assassin before making his way into electronic music, Malachi Farrell also designed the album cover Hip-Hop Against Racism in 1988. But while he has distanced himself from the hip-hop aesthetic to develop this furious art of the machine, mixing noise and sounds, bricolage and high technology, Farrell has nevertheless maintained all of rap's violence, its aesthetic of literalness and assault.

From an essay by Jean Max Colard, *Review, Artforum 39*, no. 8 (April 2001): 146–47.

Contemporary artists are often criticized for not seeking to move people. Anyone who holds that opinion ought to check out the work of Malachi Farrell, in particular Fish Flag Mourant...In this emotionally powerful piece set on the floor, a dozen articulated metal fish flop around frantically in a puddle of dirty water while one of their number seems to give its last gasp in the middle. The work, of course, refers to the sorry spectacle of polluted rivers. Bundles of trash, empty bottles, steel drums, and aspirin containers spread all around add an extra dramatic touch. The soundtrack reinforces this poignancy—the ominous arrhythmic beat of a heart moniter about to flatline.

Like Thomas Hirshhorn, Malachi Farrell has discarded the aesthetic approach in favor of an immediate impact on the spectator. His project is to make art that gets right to the point and provides direct access to the reality that inspired it. The violent language he has developed seems to be an almost instinctive reaction to the violence of mankind, whether it be unleashed against other men (*Hooliganisme*, 1997) or [directed] here against ecological equilibrium and the environment.

From an essay by Catherine Francblin, Artpresse, no. 252 (December 1999): 82–84. Translated from French by L-S Torgoff.

This exhibition was done in collaboration with the Buffalo Bayou Partnership (BBP). Special support was provided by the Cultural Services of the French Embassy in the United States and the Cultural Services of the French Consulate in Houston. Special thanks go to Denis Simmoneau, Consul General of France in Houston; Joel Savary, Cultural Representative of the French Consulate in Houston; Anne Olson; Toni Beauchamp; and Winifred Riser, BB P; and Jane Kim, Gallerie Xippas, Paris.

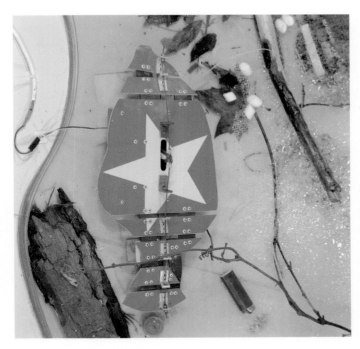

MALACHI FARRELL • *FISH FLAG MOURANT*, 1997-2000 • INSTALLATION
COURTESY OF GALERIE XIPPAS

MALACHI FARRELL • *FISH FLAG MOURANT*, 1997-2000 • INSTALLATION
COURTESY OF GALERIE XIPPAS

THE RIVER PEOPLE

ARTIST: ALVARO LEIVA

Major rivers provide thousands of kilometers of lifeblood to millions of people on a daily basis. For these people, rivers are more than squiggly blue lines on a map. They are thermometers of environmental change, economic highways, power generators, ablutions for the national consciousness, battlegrounds of political wrangling, or a spot to wash their clothes.

My project documents the daily life of the people who live and work along four of the world's major rivers: the Amazon, the Ganges, the Mississippi, and the Niger. These rivers comprise staggering geographical statistics, running through some of the most populated countries on earth—India, the United States, Africa, and Bangladesh, one of the world's most densely populated countries. Whether their waters are clean or polluted, industrialized or virgin, dammed or free flowing, these rivers impact enormous swaths of humanity with common offerings.

Farmers in the midwestern United States depend on the Mississippi for their crops and mills as much as the oil refineries and shrimping industries depend on it down in the Gulf of Mexico. What happens at the head of the river affects what gushes out at the foot.

The whole world is watching the rampant logging and deforestation ripping up the Amazon rainforest. Much like those prospectors who flocked to the U.S. West during the Gold Rush, gold miners and loggers in the Amazon are flocking to the river to try to make a living, perhaps blind to the whole painting of destruction because they are too close to the canvas.

And then there is poor low-lying Bangladesh, half underwater most of the time. The country has almost no control over the Ganges, its rainy season, or rising ocean levels. If the floodgates of the Megawatti Dam at the India/Bangladesh border open too fast or not at all, the consequences can be catastrophic for everyone in Bangladesh, from rice paddy farmers to homeowners. Ferries in Bangladesh are so overloaded that they seem ready to sink with the addition of only one more person or the movement of a stray wave.

Great rivers are embedded into the psyches of the people who live along them and the nations through which they wind. The Ganges is a spiritual place for Hindus: they are supposed to bathe in its waters at least once before they die. Witness a sadhu, or holy man, praying on a block of ice near the Ganges's source in the Himalayas or the vast confluence of the masses at Kumbh Mela in holy cities like Varanasi.

More than myth or food for the soul, a river like the Niger is essential to countries like Mali, Niger, and Nigeria, all on the edge of the Sahara. In the country of Niger, where the north and middle of the country are succumbing to spreading desertification, the population huddles in the green sliver in the south that the Niger fertilizes and cools. Children carry chopped firewood and woman carry clay pots of water on their heads in villages made out of mud that can be washed away with the next storm or river rising.

Conflicting forces of modernization and tradition continue to clash and swirl in these rivers. An Indian in the Amazon still wears his mask and war paint as the loggers roar their chainsaws in his swath of jungle. Peruvians high up in the Andes, thousands of kilometers away from the Atlantic, think little about deforestation when their sheep need to drink from a tributary of the Amazon. Along China's Yangtze River, local villagers and academics mourn the fact that 3,000 temples and ancestral homelands will go under water as the Three Gorges Dam is constructed; others count their compensation money.

I have been taking photos of people along these rivers over the past four years, traveling up and down their banks, traversing their bridges, riding in ferries and canoes, and seeing dead bodies, lily pads, and chains of barges a mile long float down them. The river people who survive, profit, exploit, and endure continue to amaze me.

Alvaro Leiva

Special support came from Abrams, Scott & Bickley LLP, Houston, for the presentation of this exhibition at FotoFest 2004 and the collaboration with Rice University Department of Visual Arts.

ALVARO LEIVA • UNTITLED FROM THE SERIES *THE MISSISSIPPI*, 2000-03 • SILVER GELATIN PRINT

ALVARO LEIVA • UNTITLED FROM THE SERIES *THE NIGER,* 2000-03 • SILVER GELATIN PRINT

Alvaro Leiva • Untitled from the series *The Ganges*, 2000-03 • Silver Gelatin Print

ALVARO LEIVA • UNTITLED FROM THE SERIES *THE AMAZON*, 2000-03 • SILVER GELATIN PRINT

Alvaro Leiva • Untitled from the series *The Mississippi*, 2000-03 • Silver Gelatin Print

EDGE OF WATER

ARTIST: BARRY ANDERSON

Death and sex. Without a terrible amount of interpretive prodding, most art falls neatly into those categories. But run the numbers. Certainly all of us die, and most of us at some point have sex, but each of us holds a life-affirming relationship with water. Claiming 71 percent of our planet, approximately 60 percent of our bodies, status as one of the four medieval elements and one of the 12 zodiac signs, and even a couple of ages (Ice and Aquarius) unto itself, water saturates our existence, even if it seems only to decorate our urban experience.

Tour a city's center—like the subtly urban locales in Barry Anderson's exhibition *Edge of Water*—and water is relegated to the scenic set dressing of a quaint koi pond or a gurgling fountain that seasons our experience, but rarely informs it. However, Barry Anderson takes those peripheral aquatics and makes them the focus of his three video pieces, reshaping and redefining our experience of the urban and the everyday.

Pain of Poison (a linguistic allusion—*pain, poisson*—to the bread and fish at the Sermon on the Mount) pushes the decorative koi pond of the Tuilleries in Paris to the center, where it becomes a symbol of psychological, spiritual, and evolutionary transformation. Projected on the floor at double and sometimes triple life size, the video installation reveals a silent, almost epic struggle between these monstrous fish and a tattered baguette. No longer the

unassuming frame to tourists' photos or a receptacle for table scraps, the blood-red pond and its voracious, seemingly cannibalistic fish take on a mythic inevitability—illustrating the battle and reconciliation within ourselves and between humans and nature.

Likewise, Barry Anderson's *Pigeon* (year) waxes mythic, transforming an urban nuisance into a poetic protagonist. In the Piazza del Campo in Siena, Italy, the pigeon sits for his close-up under an arch of water. It occasionally takes in a beakful, but mostly it engages the viewer with a sometimes contemplative, sometimes taunting look. Shifting the voyeuristic gaze back at the viewer, the pigeon seems to challenge us to take that same kind of contemplative look at ourselves, a suggestion the artist further encourages by requiring the viewer to wear headphones that isolate the auditory experience and move the public context of piazza and gallery into private introspection.

In the three-channel video installation *Fountain* (year), Barry Anderson chooses the simplicity of a single jet of water shown in triplicate over the elaborate water architecture that decorates Kansas City's Country Club Plaza. Here, he once again pushes the peripheral to mythic proportions, magnifying the six-inch jet to nearly a 10-foot projection, and reveals the beauty and sensuality that can be found in a spurt of water that would usually escape our notice.

All three pieces—*Pain of Poison, Pigeon, and Fountain*—appropriate art that takes water out of its context. The fountain art that Barry Anderson borrows shapes, contains, and transforms the fluid, amorphous quality of water into an ornamental sculpture that distorts, if not wholly ignores, its origin, function, and even archetypal meaning.

Barry Anderson makes the decorative essential. Forcing us to focus on a koi pond, a single pigeon in a piazza, and a water jet, he transforms the mundane to the mythic and asks us to search for poetry, beauty, sensuality, and ulti-mately ourselves in those things that we let slip past from the corner of our eye. He rescues water from the decora-tive, infusing it with new meanings—mythic struggle, rec-onciliation, a call to introspection, the universal mirrored in the particular. And, of course, death and sex.

Sarah Mote
Indiana University, Comparative Arts

BARRY ANDERSON • *PIGEON*, 2001 • STILL FROM A SINGLE-CHANNEL VIDEO

PALE RIDER

ARTISTS: BARRY ANDERSON, BRENDON BUSHMAN, DANA SPERRY

Formed in the summer of 2000, the Gray Sandbox collaborative explores new ways of expressing ideas and metaphors using sound, video, and the surrounding environment. Utilizing a wide range of conceptual and formal approaches, *Pale Water* represents the collaborative's fourth completed project.

In its latest interactive video installation, *Pale Water*, the Gray Sandbox explores the connections between ideas about water, flow, entropy, and death while immersing individuals in a small horizontal video chamber.

Gray Sandbox Collaborative

The Barry Anderson and *Pale Rider* exhibition at FotoFest 2004 were made possible with support from Houston Community College, Central Art Gallery. Special thanks go to Michael Golden.

GRAY SANDBOX • *PALE WATER*, YEAR? • INSTALLATION

3

DISCOVERIES OF THE MEETING PLACE

Sian Bonnell, United Kingdom

Vincent Cianni, United States

Brian Finke, United States

Bill Jorden, United States

Thomas Kellner, Germany

Elaine Ling, Canada

Boris Missirkov and Georgi Bogdanov, Bulgaria

A.Leo Nash, United States

Simon Norfolk, United Kingdom

Dominic Rouse, United Kingdom

DISCOVERIES OF THE MEETING PLACE 3

DISCOVERIES OF THE MEETING PLACE

ARTISTS:

SIAN BONNELL, UNITED KINGDOM
(SELECTED BY CLINT WILLOUR, DIRECTOR, GALVESTON
ARTS CENTER, GALVESTON, TEXAS)

VINCENT CIANNI, UNITED STATES
(SELECTED BY BARBARA TANNENBAUM, CURATOR,
AKRON ART MUSEUM, AKRON, OHIO)

BRIAN FINKE, UNITED STATES
(SELECTED BY VACLAV MACEK, DIRECTOR,
MONTH OF PHOTOGRAPHY, BRATISLAVA, SLOVAKIA)

BILL JORDEN, UNITED STATES
(SELECTED BY JOAQUIM PAIVA, PRIVATE COLLECTOR
AND CURATOR, BRAZIL)

THOMAS KELLNER, GERMANY
(SELECTED BY MELISSA HARRIS, EDITORIAL DIRECTOR,
APERTURE, NEW YORK, NEW YORK)

ELAINE LING, CANADA
(SELECTED BY FRANK GIMPAYA, PHOTOGRAPHER AND
ART DIRECTOR, NUEVA LUZ, NEW YORK, NEW YORK)

BORIS MISSIRKOV AND GEORGI BOGDANOV, BULGARIA
(SELECTED BY STEPHEN BULGER, DIRECTOR,
STEPHEN BULGERGALLERY, TORONTO, CANADA)

A.LEO NASH, UNITED STATES
(SELECTED BY KATE MENCONERI, CENTER FOR PHOTOGRAPHY,
WOODSTOCK, NEW YORK, NEW YORK)

SIMON NORFOLK, UNITED KINGDOM
(SELECTED BY MANFRED ZOLLNER, EDITOR, *FOTO MAGAZIN*,
MUNICH)

DOMINIC ROUSE, UNITED KINGDOM
(SELECTED BY GARY HESSE, LIGHT WORK, SYRACUSE, NEW YORK)

FotoFest's international portfolio review program, the International Meeting Place, gives photographers the opportunity to meet personally with influential people in photography and have their portfolios reviewed by curators, editors, publishers, and collectors from throughout the world. Held alongside FotoFest's exhibitions, the Meeting Place is an important avenue for the discovery of new and interesting photographic work.

Curators and collectors return each Biennial to the Meeting Place knowing that they will find some of the best work that is available in the photographic field. In turn, many registrants have gone on to successful artistic careers as a result of their participation in the Meeting Place.

To give the Meeting Place and its registrants even greater visibility, FotoFest has established a Biennial showcase for 10 photographers from each portfolio review. At the end of each Biennial, a diverse group of 10 international curators/reviewers is asked to individually choose one artist that he/she "discovered" and considered particularly outstanding or interesting among those they reviewed. The 10 artists are then invited to show their work as part of the next Biennial's *Discoveries of the Meeting Place* exhibition.

FotoFest inaugurated the *Discoveries of the Meeting Place* exhibition in 1996 as part of the Biennial's regular exhibition programming. The 2004 Discoveries of the Meeting Place is the fifth such exhibition.

Half the artists selected for the 2004 Discoveries exhibition are from countries outside the U.S. The artists again demonstrate a broad range of styles, from black and white documentary work to staged still-lifes and deconstructed architectural environments. Digital processes are included in the exhibition alongside images made from traditional film, silver gelatin, and color printing techniques. In the exhibition, a curatorial statement by each of the selecting curators appears alongside the work he/she has chosen.

FotoFest's International Meeting Place continues to grow in size and popularity. The two-week program is fully subscribed very soon after the initial brochure is mailed, nationally and internationally, nine months in advance. It remains the largest, most international program of its kind in the world. Photography events in Argentina, Great Britain, Slovakia, Colombia, Denmark, Canada, and the U.S. (Portland, Oregon) have now started their own versions of the FotoFest Meeting Place.

In 2003, FotoFest selected 10 artists from previous Discoveries exhibitions to be part of FotoFest—*Discoveries of the Meeting Place 1996–2002*, an exhibition presented at the Museum of Fine Arts in Samara, Russia, and ROSIZO State Centre for Museums & Exhibitions of the Ministry of Culture of the Russian Federation. The exhibition took place June–July 2003 at the Samara regional Museum of Fine Arts and may go to Moscow in 2004.

FotoFest dedicates the 2004 *Discoveries of the Meeting Place* exhibition to the memory of a longtime Meeting Place |participant and one of the artists selected for this year's exhibition, Bill Jorden. He died of cancer in August 2003.

FotoFest

Support for the installation of this exhibition came from The Wealth Group, Eunice Fong, owner of Erie City Ironworks.

Thomas Kellner • *London, Take Modern*, 2001 • Chromogenic Print • Courtesy of Schneider Gallery Inc., Chicago

ELAINE LING • *CASA HAVANA, CUBA #25*, 2000 • SILVER GELATIN PRINT

VINCENT CIANNI • *ANTHONY HITTING ON GISELLE, VIVIEN WAITING, LORIMER STREET, WILLIAMSBURG, BROOKLYN,* 1996 • SILVER GELATIN PRINT
COURTESY OF EDWARD OSOWSKI

BRIAN FINKE • UNTITILED CHEERLEADER, 2002 • CHROMOGENIC PRINT ° COURTESY OF THE ARTIST AND CLAMPART, NEW YORK

SIAN BONNELL • *SILVER SEA*, 2000 • PINHOLE PAPER NEGATIVE, DIGITAL PRINT
COURTESY OF HIRSCHL CONTEMPORARY ART, LONDON

BILL JORDEN • *MEDITATION IN THE DESERT, LA QUINTA, CALIFORNIA,* FROM THE SERIES *MODERN NATURE,* 2002 • COLOR PHOTOGRAPH

Boris Missirkov and Georgi Bogdanov • *Bold and the Beautiful #16* • Color Photograph

A. Leo Nash • *Chris Campbell's Orbicular Construction*, 1999 • Iris Print on Paper

DOMINIC ROUSE • *DANCE FOR NO-ONE (UNSEEN OBEISANCE),* 2001 • SILVER TONED GELATIN PRINT

Simon Norfolk • *The Northgate of Baghdad*, 2003 • Digital C-type

4

FILM AND VIDEO—WATER

Angelika Flim Center

Aurora Picture Show

KUHT–Houston Channel 8

Microcinema International

Rice Media Center

Southwest Alternate Media Project

Voices Breaking Boundaries

FILM AND VIDEO 4

FILM AND VIDEO SERIES—WATER

The 2004 Film and Video Series Water continues FotoFest's inquiry into issues raised by FotoFest 2002—The Photographic Eye and Beyond. The FotoFest 2004 Biennial renews that earlier commitment to the expanding photographic image by presenting an independent film and video series. Broadening the scope of the installations and exhibitions that it parallels, the six-week series is the result of collaboration with over a dozen Houston-based media arts organizations and venues. This citywide partnership is representative of a growing Texas media arts renaissance. Anchored by now established institutions, formed in the 1970s with the sponsorship and enthusiasm of John and Dominique de Menil, media arts moved into less charted territory by burgeoning young organizations.

This series represents the diversity of contemporary film and video discourse as well as the extent of water's impact on creative expression. The programs also address the influence of water globally, nationally, and locally. In exploring the simultaneously universal and idiosyncratic subject of water, the works in this series range from the development of personal metaphor to a study of geopolitics and the environment. Included are activist documentaries, poetic narratives, avant-garde short films and videos, independent features, a collaborative music performance, and a panel discussion. Each program seeks to challenge and utilize established and experimental practices within the language of the moving image.

In February, the series opens with a screening of *Drowned Out: We Can't Wish Them Away*, a documentary investigating the consequences of the controversial Narmada Dam in India. The film is presented by Voices Breaking Boundaries, a cross-cultural organization whose mission is to incite cultural change through living art. The group will also close the series in April with a screening of *Area K: A Political Fishing Documentary*, which records an unlikely partnership between members of a Palestinian fishing clan and their Israeli counterparts.

On a local scale, KUHT–Houston (PBS), the nation's first public television station, is broadcasting regional and local documentaries, including a profile of Houstonian Beth Miller: *Clearwater, One Woman's Prayer*. Drawing from natural wetlands for her design, Miller devised a way to naturally cleanse water, which has gained her international attention and inspired Nevada to develop a similar site to recycle and reuse rainwater.

Reinforcing the investigation of human interaction with the Earth's surface, Aurora Picture Show, Houston's internationally recognized microcinema, is presenting an experimental interpretation of similar subject matter, curated by Mathew Coolidge, director of the Center for Land Use Interpretation. Containing less traditional works, this program screens contemporary industrial, documentary, government, and ephemeral films about land. Aurora Picture Show is also presenting *The Garden in the Machine*, an examination of the depiction of place in alternative cinema, curated by Scott MacDonald.

FRANNY ARMSTRONG • *DROWNED OUT*, 2002 • STILL FROM VIDEO • PRESENTED BY VOICES BREAKING BOUNDARIES

Included are works by moving-image makers who use mechanical, chemical, and electronic technologies as a means of transforming the screening space into a psychic or spiritual "garden" within the "machine" of modern life.

More experimental media programs are being shown by Microcinema International, based in San Francisco and Houston, which is premiering a series of new short videoworks at Lawndale Art Center dealing with water. This is a special edition of Microcinema's *Independent Exposure* series, based on a call for works for short form media that in some way represent the subject of water. Since 1996, Microcinema International has curated a monthly touring program of independent film and video to be screened at microcinemas, alternative venues, and festivals around the world. After the Biennial, the FotoFest 2004 series will travel to microcinemas worldwide and a DVD of the program will be produced

Addressing the growing local film and video community, Southwest Alternate Media Project (SWAMP) will present a program of short pieces inspired by Texas water. A prominent presence in Texas film and video making since the 1970s, SWAMP has fueled the development of Texas media art with its education, information, and broadcast programs.

Using water as a metaphor and backdrop, classical and contemporary work in the narrative vein is being showcased at Rice University Media Center and the Angelika Film Center. Rice University Media Center, one of Houston's first experimental media arts centers, is screening the recently restored *L'Atlante* (1934) and *Taris* (1931), respectively a classic film and an experimental short by legendary French filmmaker Jean Vigo. Angelika Film Center, known for its screenings of fine independent and foreign films, is presenting a special water-related showing of Japanese director Shohei Imamura's exploration of sexuality and desire in *Warm Water Under a Red Bridge*.

As a special part of the Film and Video Series, FotoFest is the co-sponsor of a media arts panel, *Exit the Waiting Room: Contemporary Media Art in Houston*, which looks at Houston's media arts past, where it is today, and what the future promises. Organized by video artists Serena Lin Bush at DiverseWorks Art Space, this panel of nine prominent Houston artists, curators, and collectors discuss the history and future of media arts in Houston.

Eileen Maxson
FotoFest

CHEL WHITE • *PASSAGE*, 2001 • STILL FROM VIDEO

PETER HUTTON • *TWO RIVERS HUDSON/YANGTZE,* 2001-03• STILL FROM VIDEO

LITERACY THROUGH PHOTOGRAPHY®

SPONSORS:

FotoFest's Literacy Through Photography® program is supported by foundations, government agencies, corporations, and individuals. Institutional supporters have included:

Foundations: The William Stamps Farish Fund, The Cullen Foundation, The Bernard and Audre Rapoport Foundation, The Vale-Asche Foundation, The Simmons Foundation, The Powell Foundation, The Bruni Foundation, The Favrot Fund, The Clayton Fund, Houston Endowment, Inc., Susan Vaughan Foundation, The George and Mary Josephine Hamman Foundation, The Jack H. and William M. Light Charitable Trust, The Felvis Fund, Harris and Eliza Kempner Fund, Marion and Speros Martel Foundation, Education Foundation of America, The Charles Engelhard Foundation, The Kettering Family Foundation, Ettinger Foundation, Scurlock Foundation, Margaret Cullinan Wray Charitable Lead Annuity Trust, The Samuels Foundation of the Jewish Community of Houston, and The Gordon and Mary Cain Foundation.

Government: The City of Houston and the Texas Commission for the Arts through the Cultural Arts Council of Houston/Harris County

Corporations: Manzanita Alliance-GoBase2, CANON USA, Fuji Photo Film USA, Inc., J. P. Morgan Chase Foundation, HEB Pantry Foods, Olympus Corporation, American General Corporation, Southwestern Bell, and Charter Bank.

LITERACY THROUGH PHOTOGRAPHY 5

LITERACY THROUGH PHOTOGRAPHY

FotoFest 2004 - Literacy Through Photography and Water

Literacy Through Photography (LTP) is the year-round educational component of FotoFest International that uses photography to improve students' writing abilities, cognitive thinking, and classroom communication skills. LTP provides teachers with a 27-lesson project-based writing and photography curriculum in addition to comprehensive program training, classroom support, and teaching resources. Currently, LTP is in 44 schools, serving more than 81 teachers and 2,000 students. With program support from school administrators, teachers, and education organizations, LTP provides quality programming that is aligned with Texas state-mandated curriculum requirements for students in third to 12th grades.

FOTOFEST 2004—LITERACY THROUGH PHOTOGRAPHY AND WATER

JUST A DROP — WATER CURRICULUM

As individuals, we can make changes in our water consumption. Together as a community, we can make major changes that can provide positive solutions to our great need for water and its limited availability. Some environmentalists believe that without solving global water issues, all other efforts to protect our Earth's ecosystems and resources will fail. Each of us decides daily how we will use, interact with, protect, abuse, or sustain the quantity and quality of fresh water available to our community, our planet, and ourselves. The decisions we make daily hinge on our view, understanding, and use of fresh water.

Introduction to the *Just a Drop* water curriculum, 2003–2004

FotoFest developed the *Just a Drop* water curriculum for the 2004 Biennial as part of its Literacy Through Photography (LTP) program to teach elementary and middle school students about water issues and water conservation. In fall 2003, the four-lesson *Just a Drop* water curriculum was distributed to more than 100 classrooms in Houston/Harris County and Galveston public schools. Through factual information about water, maps, photographic images, experiments, creative writing exercises, and photography assignments, students are introduced to new perspectives on personal, regional, and global water issues.

Stewardship is an important part of the water curriculum. Students do hands-on activities and document home water usage to involve family members in the story of water — and how water issues at home are linked to community and global water issues. In most parts of the United States, we are only beginning to feel the impact of water shortages and the abuse of water, The purpose of this special curriculum is to provide students with information about water issues and strengthen their visual and verbal communication skills. *Just a Drop* is just a beginning. It gives them tools they will need to help preserve the earth's water supply for their future.

For FotoFest 2004, the Education Foundation of Harris County is sponsoring at the Harris County Department of Education Headquarters an exhibition of more than 100 posters created by students using the FotoFest *Just A Drop* curriculum. In May 2004, the posters will be displayed in FotoFest's student *FotoFence* exhibition at Union Station in the Houston Astros Minute Maid Park.

MARK NELSON • *JUST A DROP*, 2004 • WATER CURRICULUM CLASS, GRADY MIDDLE SCHOOL

FotoFest has also collaborated with the Galveston Independent School District and The Artist Boat to provide the water curriculum to public school classrooms in Galveston, TX, 50 miles southeast of Houston on the Gulf of Mexico. Reaching students that are affected every day by the water that surrounds them has been an important part of FotoFest's 2004 Biennial Programming. Poster displays of student photography, writing and fieldwork results will be displayed in Galveston and in Houston. To insure that every student had a working camera to complete the *Just A Drop* photo assignments, Fuji Photo Film USA, Inc. provided QuickSnap 35mm one-time use cameras for the Galveston students.

To connect students to Houston's bayou system, FotoFest has collaborated with the Harris County Department of Education and the Buffalo Bayou Partnership to host Kid's Day, an annual event sponsored by The Education Foundation of Harris County, at historic Allen's Landing on Buffalo Bayou. Seventy-five students from the Cooperative for After School Enrichment (CASE) spend the day visiting FotoFest exhibitions on water. They then end the day with a picnic and photo scavenger hunt at Allen's Landing. The Buffalo Bayou Partnership's peppermint pink, garbage-guzzling *Mighty Tidy* skimmer boat will make a special appearance on the Bayou for the students.

FotoFest's *Just A Drop* curriculum was written by marine biologist and artist Karla Klay and environmental scientist Tina Proctor, co-directors of The Artist Boat, Galveston, Texas. The Artist Boat is a non-profit organization that promotes awareness and preservation of coastal areas through guided kayak and canoe trips that combine environmental education and art activities.

Mary Doyle Glover
Director, Literacy Through Photography
FotoFest

MARK NELSON • *JUST A DROP*, 2004 • WATER CURRICULUM CLASS, GRADY MIDDLE SCHOOL

LITERACY THROUGH PHOTOGRAPHY

The Literacy Through Photography (LTP) curriculum asks students to write about themselves, their families, their community, and their dreams. By using a camera to record their everyday lives, students create images that inspire their writing. Using one's imagination, composing a subject, and incorporating details and backgrounds are important elements in both photography and creative writing. By integrating writing and photography, students build cognitive skills and develop new learning strategies.

Jean Barber, a former LTP teacher at Milby High School, says, "Literacy Through Photography allows students to connect writing with their lives. It leads them to a deeper understanding of themselves, their family, and their world." By sharing their own experiences, students gain a greater sense of their importance as individuals. Teachers also gain insight into students' personal lives that they rarely achieve in the day-to-day classroom environment. One fourth-grade student, for example, wrote in her LTP journal that she is the one who has to do all the grocery shopping for her household.

Throughout the year, LTP operates in the classroom. In the summer, LTP does workshops. Currently, FotoFest is working with the Harris County Department of Education's Cooperative for After School Enrichment (CASE) to provide after-school programming by certified teachers for at-risk students in 10 Harris County school districts. Research has proven that after-school programming like CASE improves academic achievement and healthy development. Tara Faulds, teaching fellow for "After Blast" Citizen Schools at Killough Middle School, states, "It is essential to have flexible, enriching material when teaching after the students have been in a classroom all day, and FotoFest provides the structure to engage the students."

The 2003–2004 school year is FotoFest's third year of collaboration with Project GRAD (Graduation Really Achieves Dreams). Project GRAD's objective is to increase the test scores of students above national norms and reduce dropout rates. The Project GRAD Fine Arts Program is an innovative pilot program providing basic skills and knowledge in arts disciplines in an effort to enhance overall student performance. FotoFest is now developing two new curricula in partnership with the Project GRAD Fine Arts Program.

The new *LTP DIGITAL* curriculum adapts LTP's current 27 lessons to digital technology and adds digital information resources and PhotoShop assignments. It is designed to fill the demand for new technology in the classroom. It is being written and tested by teacher and artist Ted Estrada with his art and media classes at Jefferson Davis High School in Houston. With the new curriculum, students use digital cameras, a digital photo printer, and computers, if available, to create and alter imagery that they then use in LTP creative writing assignments.

The *LTP English as a Second Language (ESL)* curriculum began development last spring in Obed Franco's ESL class at Thomas Jefferson Elementary School. It addresses a growing need for lessons specifically designed to teach second-language learners to achieve proficiency in English. The new *LTP ESL* curriculum includes four new lessons, teaching strategies, and resources in addition to the current LTP lessons. By 2006, FotoFest's two new LTP curricula will be implemented in all Harris County Independent School Districts.

The final lesson of the LTP curriculum is a collage assignment that gives students the opportunity to assemble their favorite writing and photographs into a collage. These collages are displayed at *FotoFence*, a spring exhibition sponsored by FotoFest. In 2004, Union Station at the Houston Astros Minute Maid Park is the FotoFence site. The exhibition gives the student work exposure to thousands of viewers. Every year, FotoFest honors LTP teachers and students with a special reception during the exhibition. FotoFest has sponsored the annual *FotoFence* exhibition in very visible downtown locations since 1994.

ARTURO SANCHEZ • *FOTOFENCE*, 2003 • UNION STATION LOBBY, HOUSTON ASTROS MINUTE MAID PARK

HISTORY

In 1987, FotoFest brought teacher/photographer Wendy Ewald and her innovative photography education project to the Children's Museum in Houston. Wendy Ewald had achieved great success using photography to stimulate children to take pictures and write about their lives and dreams. In 1990, FotoFest expanded the project to public schools and 1,000 Houston Independent School District children. Teacher and student response was enthusiastic and led to establishing Literacy Through Photography as a permanent program. In 1991, FotoFest hired teacher and poet David Brown as full-time education director to create a full-year curriculum that modified the Ewald program. LTP has grown from a pilot project to a rapidly expanding literacy program used by the Harris County Department of Education, Project GRAD (Graduation Really Achieves Dreams), and the Houston Independent School District. It has reached school districts in Texas, Colorado, Oklahoma, and North Carolina. In 2005, LTP will be implemented in Taos, New Mexico. Around 15,000 students have used the LTP program since 1990.

Mary Doyle Glover
Director, Literacy Through Photography
FotoFest

MARGARITA YLANA, 12TH GRADE, JEFFERSON DAVIS HIGH SCHOOL, 2003 • LTP DIGITAL PILOT PROGRAM • COLLAGE

Community

I live near the Heights in a small community called Cottage Grove. This Community revolves around my culture and shows others a little bit more about who I am. In my collage I wanted to show others what makes the community so special.

Everywhere you go many are involved in different activities with friends or family. The local park is one location in which many get together to relax, play basketball, and watch the future of tomorrow run and play.

The one thing that stands out in the community the most is the Latino Culture. Throughout the several convenient stores are murals. The murals are drawings of Aztecs, religion and the future. These drawings took lots of dedication and talent by several artists.

A famous building in the neighborhood is the Santana Funeral home. Even though it is very depressing to see the parking lot full, many in the community attend this building to pay respect for others.

I appreciate all this community does in times of need. I hope, one day, to pay back to my community for all the things they have done for me.

Margarita Ylana

CHRISTIAN MARTINEZ, 10TH GRADE, JEFFERSON DAVIS HIGH SCHOOL, 2003 • LTP DIGITAL PILOT PROGRAM • COLLAGE

My Childhood

This collage represents my childhood. I was a lovely boy that grew up without any brothers or sisters. I was a naughty little boy. I always got into trouble and never will be mature. I wasn't a normal kid. Around other people I was shy because I didn't know them. With people I knew, I was normal. My mom always loved me with all her heart. I was her little boy.

Christian Martinez

Había una vez unos pescaditos nadando y jugando en el agua. De pronto, voltearon y ahí estaba una ballena malvada. Ella los persiguió alrededor del mar. En ese momento, la ballena miró hacia arriba y había unos señores que querían pescar unos pescaditos. Su barco se movió porque la ballena le pegó y los señores se calleron al mar. Los pescaditos rescataron a los señores rápidamente porque la ballena se los quería comer pero la ballena en vez de seguirlos se fué a otro lugar para encontrar pescados y comerlos.

MELISSA MENDEZ, 3RD GRADE BILINGUAL, THOMAS JEFFERSON ELEMENTARY, 2003• LTP ESL PILOT PROGRAM • COLLAGE

La Ballena

Había una vez unos pescaditos nadando y jugando en el agua. De pronto, voltearon y ahí estaba una ballena malvada. Ella los persiguió alrededor del mar. En ese momento, la ballena miró hacia arriba y habia unos señores que querían pescar unos pescaditos. Su barco se movió porque la ballena le pegó y los señores se calleron al mar. Los pescaditos rescataron a los señores rápidamente porque la ballena se los quería comer, pero la ballena en vez de seguirlos se fué a otro lugar para encontrar pescados y comerlos.

The Whale

Once upon a time, there were some small fish and they played in the water. Suddenly, they see a mean whale. The whale chased them in the ocean. At that moment, the whale looked up and saw fisherman that wanted to catch some fish. The whale knocked the boat and the fisherman fell into the sea. The little fish saved the fisherman from the whale that wanted to eat them. The whale went somewhere else to eat fish.

Melissa Mendez

EDWIN CASTILLO, 7TH GRADE BILINGUAL, ALBRIGHT MIDDLE SCHOOL, 2003 • LTP ESL PILOT PROGRAM

Tough Times

In the year of 1983, my dad took an eleven day trip that would change his life forever. My dad has been through many experiences in his life. Some experiences have been good, some bad, some heart breaking, some heart warming, but he has overcome all of these things to be where he is now. He grew up in a small town located in the country of El Salvador, located in Central America. My dad was born into a large family with two brothers and three sisters.

My dad and his family came to Houston from El Salvador on foot and entered as illegals. They passed through various countries, slept in fields, and did not eat for hours maybe even days to get here.

When my father arrived here in Houston and settled in a new house, he began going to school without knowing how to speak English. The rest of his family also had a hard time in Houston. My grandpa began working for a landscaping company from seven in the morning until five in the afternoon.

After living in Houston for a couple of months, a tragic event happened which hurt my entire family. It affected the course of their lives forever. One day when my grandma was crossing one of the busiest roadways in Houston, Westheimer, she got hit by a bus. The paramedics then arrived and rushed her to the hospital, where she later died. When my dad found out what had happened, he felt devastated. In the interview with my father he told me that after the accident his family (including him) did not know where to go with their lives or what to do.

With what happened to my grandma, my dad had to work with my grandpa in the landscaping businesses at the young age of twenty years old. It was tough on my father to work for nearly twelve hours, outside in the hot, humid temperatures of Houston, but he did it to support his family. To this very day, my dad and grandpa still work for the same landscaping company and because of their hard work over the years their jobs are easier, and my dad is even the Vice-President of the company. As you can see, my father has been through tough times in his life and he made sacrifices to be where he is today.

Edwin Castillo

ARTIST BIOGRAPHIES

FotoFest Exhibitions

STEVEN BENSON

Steven Benson received his BFA from the College for Creative Studies in Detroit and an MFA from Cranbrook Academy of Art in Bloomfield Hills, Michigan. His work has been exhibited internationally, including a solo exhibition at the Centre Georges Pompidou in Paris. He is the recipient of three Creative Artist Grants from the Michigan Council for the Arts and an NEA/ArtsMidwest Regional Fellowship. His photographs are represented in numerous permanent collections including the Detroit Institute of Arts, Bibliothèque Nationale and the Centre Georges Pompidou. He has done many lectures, including the Peoples University of China School for Journalism in Beijing and the 1998 and 2000 National Conferences of the Society for Photographic Education. In November 2004, his work will be the subject of a 30-year retrospective in Paris during Le Mois de la Photo, *Steven Benson: Thirty Years in Black and White*. He has been a freelance photographer and teacher for 25 years. Currently, he is an Associate Professor in the photography department at the College for Creative Studies where he has been teaching since 1994.

EDWARD BURTYNSKY

Born in 1955 in St. Catherines, Ontario, Edward Burtynsky graduated from Ryerson University's photographic arts program in 1982. Three years later, he founded Toronto Image Works, a media education center, darkroom rental facility, custom photo lab, and digital imaging facility. His subjects include mines, quarries, recycling, oil fields, refineries, and ship-breaking yards. Full color and large scale, his detailed and precisely rendered works document the changing relationships of humankind to nature through the industries that we have built. Neither celebrating nor condemning industry, Burtynsky strives through photography to mediate between the life we lead and the places that allow us to lead life. *Manufactured Landscapes*, a major mid-career traveling retrospective organized in 2003 by the National Gallery of Canada in Ottawa, was shown at the Art Gallery of Ontario, Toronto, from January-April 2004. Edward Burtynsky's works have been widely exhibited in North America and abroad. He is represented in numerous public and private collections. The artist lives and works in Toronto and was elected to the Royal Academy of Arts in 2003.

ANDREW BUURMAN

Born in Liverpool in 1966, Andrew Buurman was educated in the north of England and studied politics at University College Swansea. He bought his first camera while living in Japan. Returning to the U.K., he studied photojournalism at the London College of Printing, after which he became a photographer with *The Independent*, a newspaper in London. His editorial work has appeared in such publications as *The Observer Magazine* [London], *Der Spiegel*, and *The Sunday Times* [London]. *The Serpentine Swimming Club* won a prize in the 2003 World Press Awards, and Andrew Buurman was featured in the April 2003 issue of *Photo District News*.

ANDREY CHEZHIN (ALSO AT ANYA TISH GALLERY, HOUSTON)

Born in 1960 in St. Petersburg, Andrey Chezhin graduated from the Leningrad Institute of Cinema Engineers, St. Petersburg, in 1967-1982. He became a member of the Photo-society Mirror in 1985 and the TAK group in 1987. The curator for PhotoImage Gallery, St. Petersburg, and a member of the board of directors of the Festival of Photography *Autumn PhotoMarathon* in St. Petersburg, Andrey Chezhin has participated in more than 120 group shows in Russia and abroad. His more than 50 one-person shows include an exhibition at Anya Tish Gallery at FotoFest 1998. His works are part of the collections of 19 museums, including the State Russian Museum, St. Petersburg; Ministry of Culture of the Russian Federation, Moscow; Corcoran Gallery of Art, Washington, D.C.; and Museum of Fine Arts, Houston. The author of two published books and several artist handmade books, Andrey Chezhin is represented in the United States by Nailya Alexander Gallery, Washington, D.C.

CHRISTIAN CRAVO

Born of a Danish mother and a Brazilian father in 1974, Christian Cravo grew up in the Brazilian port city of Salvador de Bahia. Son of a photographer and grandson of a sculptor, Christian was introduced to the art world at a very early age. When he was 13 and living in Denmark, where he spent his adolescence, he began to experiment with photographic techniques. He then returned to Brazil, where he became seriously involved in working with his camera. In 1993 he interrupted his photography research to do military service in Denmark. Once he returned to Brazil, his work began to achieve national and international recognition in a number of exhibitions (both one-person shows and group exhibitions): Museum of Modern Art of Bahia, Brazil, 1996; Billedhusets Galleri, Copenhagen, 1999; Throckmorton Fine Arts, New York, 2000; Ashmolean Museum, Oxford, England, 2001; Ministério da Cultura, Foyer da Sala Guimarães Rosa, Brasília, Brazil, 2003; Galeria Fidanza, Museu de Arte Sacra do Pará, Belém, Brazil, 2003; and *The First Decade: Masters of Latin American Photography*, Throckmorton Fine Arts, New York, 2003.

VALDIR CRUZ

Although Brazilian photographer Valdir Cruz has lived in the United States for more than 20 years, much of his work in photography has focused on the people, architecture, and landscape of Brazil. In 1994 he started photographing Faces of the Rainforest, an ongoing project documenting the life of indigenous people in the Brazilian rainforest for which he was awarded a Guggenheim Fellowship in 1996. His publications include *Catedral Basilica de Nossa Senhora da Luz dos Pinhais* (New York: Brave Wolf Publishing, 1996), Patrick Tierney's acclaimed *Darkness in El Dorado* (New York: W.W. Norton, 2000), and *Faces of the Rainforest—The Yanomami* (New York: powerHouse, 2002); the last received the support of an award from the Guggenheim Foundation in 2000. Valdir Cruz is represented in the permanent collections of the Museu de Arte de São Paulo; The Museum of Modern Art, New York, and the Smithsonian Institution, Washington, D.C., among others. He lives in New York.

SUSAN DERGES

Born in 1955, Susan Derges has established an international reputation over the past 15 years with one-person exhibitions in London, Cambridge [England], Edinburgh, New York, San Francisco, and Tokyo. Her artistic practice has involved cameraless, lens-based, digital, and reinvented photographic processes as well as video. Her work has been concerned with subject matter informed by the physical and biological sciences as well as landscape and abstraction. Susan Derges's art is an ongoing inquiry into the relationship of the self to the observed. She has generated images that combine aesthetic beauty with thought-provoking content. Her published work includes *Woman Thinking River* (Fraenkel Gallery, San Francisco, 1999); *Liquid Form* (Michael Hue-Williams Fine Art, UK, 1999), with an essay by Martin Kemp; and *Kingswood* (Stour Valley Arts Project, Photoworks, UK, 2002).

BARBARA DOWNS

Barbara Downs is a fine art photographer. She creates painterly photographs and constructed images that convey her subjective response to particular physical situations, showing the unexpectedly incongruous colors and shapes within them; her work moves from realism to abstraction. She trained in fine art at the University of Durham, England, where her early photographic influences were lecturer Richard Hamilton and artists like Lázló Moholy-Nagy and the Russian Constructivists. Her work as a lecturer in art and her interest in fine art processes have informed her photographic practice. Barbara Downs's exploration of the way that people inhabit and experience spaces, arising from issues of social and cultural ownership of concern in the 1980s, has continued to develop and take on different forms. Recent work, *Changing Spaces*, a series reflecting the metamorphosis of the Bull Ring development in Birmingham, England, was included in the group exhibition *narrascape* at New Art Gallery Walsall, England, in May 2003, curated by Rhonda Wilson of Seeing the Light. The *Venice* series can been seen as a contrast to, and continuation of, Barbara Downs's previous work.

ELAINE DUIGENAN

Elaine Duigenan's first camera was a Kodak Instamatic and she was introduced to the magic of printing in a tiny darkroom under the stairs at school. She studied art and art history at Goldsmiths College, London, and persisted with photography despite the lack of encouragement. Her early years were spent helping to run the photographic section of a large overseas development agency and traveling extensively as a photojournalist. Since the late nineties, she has worked as an artist, one who is always open to new avenues of exploration. In 1999, on the strength of work published in *TANK* magazine, she was approached by an agent who got her an advertising campaign with Saatchi and Saatchi. In 2000 she had several pieces in the Psycho show alongside works by Damien Hirst, Helen Chadwick, and Mark Quinn. Recently she has had a solo portrait show and become a core artist with Scicult.com. She is working on an architectural collaboration that includes an exhibition in London's Soho.

ANNE GABRIELE

Anne Gabriele's passion for photography began more than 25 years ago, but she only recently began exhibiting her work. In addition to various private collections, her work is in the Polaroid Corporation Collection, Waltham, Massachusetts. Some of her awards and honors include the C-Scape fellowship and residency in a dune shack at the Cape Cod National Seashore; honorable mention in the Santa Fe Assignment Earth Vision Awards; and most recently a residency awarded by the Seaside Institute in Florida. Born in Brooklyn, New York, in 1961, Anne Gabriele studied photography at the School of Visual Arts, New York. Despite never living anywhere other than in New York, she spends extended time at shorelines every chance she gets.

PHYLLIS GALEMBO

Phyllis Galembo has had one-person exhibitions at the International Center for Photography, New York, and the American Museum of Natural History, New York. She has also exhibited at the African Voices Gallery, Smithsonian Institution, Washington, D.C.; American Museum of Natural History, New York; and Newark Museum, Newark, New Jersey. She is the author of *Divine Inspiration from Benin to Bahia* (Albuquerque: Univ. of New Mexico Press, 1993) and *Vodou: Visions and Voices of Haiti* (Berkeley, Calif.: Ten Speed Press, 1998). Her most recent one-person exhibition, Dressed for Thrills, was shown in Fall 2003 at the Museum At FIT, New York, and celebrated the publishing of her book *Dressed for Thrills, 100 Years of Halloween Costumes and Masquerade* (New York: Harry N. Abrams Inc., 2003). Upcoming exhibitions include *Visions of Haiti: Vodou* and *Carnaval* at the Mead Art Museum, Amherst, Massachusetts. Phyllis Galembo is the recipient of a Fulbright Scholar Senior Research Award to Nigeria and has also received grants from the New York Council for the Arts and the New York Foundation for the Arts. Her work is included in numerous public and private collections including those of the Museum of Fine Arts, Houston, and the Schomburg Center for Research in Black Culture, New York Public Library. In connection to her work and exhibitions, she has appeared on CNN, NPR Radio, and NBC Today in New York. Phyllis Galembo is a photographer and a professor of art at the State University of New York at Albany. The artist resides in New York, where she maintains her studio.

KAREN GLASER

Karen Glaser was born and raised in Pittsburgh. She resides in Chicago and has been an independent photographer, teaching photography at Columbia College, Chicago, since 1980. Her photographs are in the permanent collections of the Art Institute of Chicago; Museum of Fine Arts, Houston; Museum of Contemporary Photography, Chicago; Harry Ransom Center at The University of Texas at Austin; and LaSalle Bank, Chicago, among many others. Glaser co-authored with John E. Reynolds III the book *Mysterious Manatees* (Gainesville, Fla.: Univ. Press of Florida, 2003). She recently completed a commission in Florida, a 226-foot aquatic photographic mural installed permanently at the Seaport in Miami.

Among her grants are a Ford Foundation fellowship and a National Endowment for the Arts regional fellowship. She has exhibited her photographs at more than 30 museums and galleries. These include the National Museum of Natural History, Smithsonian Institution, Washington, D.C.; Centro Colombo Americano, Medellin, Colombia; Aperture's Burden Gallery, New York; and The Museum of Contemporary Photography, Chicago, among others.

DON GLENTZER

Texas-based photographer Don Glentzer was born in Franklin, Indiana, in 1949 and received his associate degree in photography at the Atlanta Art Institute, Atlanta. His work is represented in the permanent collections of the Museum of Fine Arts, Houston; El Paso Museum of Art, El Paso; and Wittliff Gallery of Southwestern and Mexican Photography, San Marcos, Texas. Glentzer's group exhibitions include "The Pictures of Texas Monthly" (Museum of Fine Arts, Houston, 2002), "New Acquisitions" (Museum of Fine Arts, Houston, 2000), "Shot in El Paso" (El Paso Museum of Art, El Paso, 1994), and "Texas Invitational Group Exhibit" (Benteler Morgan Gallery, Houston, 1992). His solo exhibition, "Historical Cemeteries," has been on permanent display since 1997 at the Texas State Cemetery in Austin. Other solo shows include "Land, Sea and Sky" (Ocotillo Gallery, Houston, 1996) and "El Paso Missions" (Galleria las Vigas, El Paso, 1993). Don Glentzer's *Latitudes and Longing* series received the Maine Photographic Workshop's 2003 Golden Light Award for Personal and Fine Art. His award-winning commercial and editorial images have appeared in *Communication Arts Photography Annual* and *Graphis Photo*, and in shows organized by the New York Art Directors Club, Dallas Society of Visual Communications, and Art Directors Club of Houston.

GINA GLOVER

Gina Glover is a photographic artist and educator. She became a professional photographer in the early 1980s and is one of the founders of the Photofusions Photography Centre in London. Glover's early work ranged from documentary photography to the exploration of family life. Today she focuses on the relationship between human beings and nature. Her imagery explores the complex inner struggle to make sense of the world and the place of human beings within it. Glover runs photography workshops in psychiatric hospitals and lectures on themes such as *Creativity, Photography and the Mind*. Her work *About Time* has recently been shown at Gables Yard Gallery Norfolk. Other shows have been: *Round Trip* at the Tom Blau gallery in London; *Obsessions 2* at Huddersfield Art Gallery; *Shaking the Tail Feather* with Mary Hooper at Bexhill Costume and Natural Hospital in London. She is currently Photographic Artist in Residence in the Genetics Department of Guys Hospital in London. *Sea Scape* has been curated as a permanent exhibition for the new Day Procedures Unit at George Eliot Hospital in Nuneaton. Portfolios of her work have been published in *AG* magazine (#29) and *Portfolio* magazine (#36).

DAVID GOLDES

Educated first as a scientist, David Goldes received a M.A. in molecular genetics from Harvard University, Cambridge, Massachusetts. Later he received a M.F.A. in photography from the Visual Studies Workshop/State University of New York, Buffalo. Currently he is a professor of media arts at Minneapolis College of Art and Design, Minneapolis. His photographs are in many major museum collections including the Museum of Modern Art, New York; Walker Art Center, Minneapolis; Whitney Museum of American Art, New York; Museum of Fine Arts, Houston; Art Institute of Chicago; and Bibliotheque Nationale, Paris. His work has recently appeared in *2wice*, *American Scientist*, *Science*, *Natural History*, *Leonardo*, and *Speakeasy*. David Goldes has received fellowships from the National Endowment for the Arts, Guggenheim Foundation, Bush Foundation, and McKnight Foundation. In 2002 and 2003, he completed residencies at the MacDowell Colony, Peterborough, New Hampshire. His work is represented by Yossi Milo Gallery, New York (www.yossimilogallery.com).

STANLEY GREENBERG

Stanley Greenberg has published two books of photographs of New York City's infrastructure: *Invisible New York: The Hidden Infrastructure of the City* (Baltimore: Johns Hopkins University Press, 1998) and *Waterworks: A Photographic Journey Through New York's Hidden Water System* (Princeton, N.J.: Princeton Architectural Press, 2003). His work is in the collections of the Metropolitan Museum of Art, New York, and the Whitney Museum of American Art, New York. He has been awarded grants from the New York Foundation for the Arts, New York State Council on the Arts, and Graham Foundation. Stanley Greenberg was born in Brooklyn, New York, in 1956. He attended Stuyvesant High School, received a B.A. in art history from the State University of New York at Stony Brook, and earned a master's degree in public administration from the Maxwell School at Syracuse University, Syracuse, New York. He lives in Brooklyn with his wife and daughter.

KEVIN GRIFFIN

Born in London in 1964, Kevin Griffin was introduced to photography at an early age by the works of his grandfather, a photographer with the R.A.F. during World War II. He left school at 16, and it was not until the age of 20 that he started taking pictures. After three months of a two-year photography course at Watford College, England, he left to become an assistant in a London studio. It was here that he gained the invaluable technical experience he had found lacking at college. After assisting Paul Wakefield and Don McCullin, the latter a big influence on his work, Kevin Griffin started working regularly for the *Sunday Times Magazine* in London. The editors commissioned him to shoot many photo essays, among them "The River Thames" and "The Coastline of Britain." Subsequent advertising commissions would take him all over the world. In 1996, after spending all his life in London, Kevin Griffin and his family decided to relocate to Ireland so he could concentrate on his personal photographic projects. One of these projects is the *Wave* series.

JULIA HOERNER

Julia Hoerner was born in Chicago in 1940. She has lived in Georgia, New York, Montréal, and Colorado, and now resides in Texas. She studied ceramic sculpture with Dirk Hubers at Tulane University, New Orleans, and painting with Jack Tworkov at Yale University, New Haven, Connecticut. She taught briefly at the Maryland Institute and College of Art, Baltimore, and was a member of the original resident faculty at Dawson College's New School in Montreal. Returning to the United States in 1982, she was an artist-in-residence at Texas A&M College of Architecture, College Station, where she later returned for a time as a visiting professor in digital media, on leave from the University of Colorado, Colorado Springs. Julia Hoerner was a recipient of a film and video fellowship from Colorado's Council on the Arts and a fellowship in digital media from Australia's University of Western Sydney. She has a national and international exhibition record, and has traveled widely in Mexico, Asia, and Australia. She lives and works near Houston, surrounded by woods, water, and sky.

INSTITUTE FOR FLOW SCIENCES
THEODOR SCHWENK

Theodor Schwenk (1910–1986) lived in Germany. Throughout his life he observed the physical world and was particularly interested in how water motion directly revealed qualitative aspects of its nature. For many years he worked as an engineer for Weleda, researching the role of water in the pharmaceutical processes. In 1961, he founded the Institut für Strömungswissenschaften [Institute for Flow Sciences], Herrischried, Germany, to conduct research into understanding water's more hidden qualities and its importance as a mediator of life. In 1962, his book *Sensitive Chaos: The Creation of Flowing Forms in Water and Air* was published. Jacques Cousteau called it the "first phenomenological treatise on water." The book has remained a classic in its field and has been translated into eight languages. The Drop-Picture Method was developed in the 1960s by Theodor Schwenk in order to visually depict water quality.

INSTITUTE FOR FLOW SCIENCES
WOLFRAM SCHWENK

Wolfram Schwenk was born in 1942 in Germany. He studied biology, specializing in limnology, at Freiburg University, Freiburg, Germany. After his studies, he spent three years at the German Federal Institute of Hydrology, Koblenz, as a researcher. In 1972, he joined the Institut für Strömungswissenshaften [Institute for Flow Sciences] in Herrischried, Germany, as a junior scientist and assistant to Theodor Schwenk, who founded the Institute in 1961. Since 1976, Wolfram Schwenk has served as a member of the leading group of the Institute. In water flow research, Wolfram Schwenk's principal goal is to understand and characterize the life-giving aspects of water, especially good drinking water, by means of the Drop-Picture Method, which reveals water's shape-creating behavior of motion as an indication of its positive qualities. He lectures at symposia throughout Europe on the positive qualities of water. He is married and has two grown sons. With FotoFest, Wolfram Schwenk, Andreas Wilkens, and Jennifer Greene are co-curators of the exhibition from the Institute for Flow Sciences.

INSTITUTE FOR FLOW SCIENCES
ANDREAS WILKENS

Andreas Wilkens was born in 1955 in Bremen, Germany. His interest in water began early, exploring the coast of the North Sea by ship with his parents. The oppportunity to work in mechanics and technology in his father's workshop and his later development of photographic skills have aided Wilkens' work to determine how to observe exactly and to record how a drop of water falls. His interest in water grew at the University of Bremen where he built a computer apparatus for cell biology research. Detailed scientific and photographic studies of water drops led him to the Institut für Strömungswissenschaften [Institute for Flow Sciences], Herrischried, Germany, where he became a co-worker in 1989. His area of expertise and work involve basic research in flow phenomena pertaining to the Drop-Picture Method and the development of laboratory equipment to study minute water phenomena. He has mounted several exhibitions, the most comprehensive of which is *Wasser verstehen lernen [Understanding Water]*, and he has written extensively on research techniques and phenomena pertaining to the Drop-Picture Method. He is on the board of trustees for the Institute. With FotoFest, Andreas Wilkens, Wolfram Schwenk, and Jennifer Greene are co-curators of the exhibition from the Institute for Flow Sciences.

INSTITUTE FOR FLOW SCIENCES
JENNIFER GREENE

Jennifer Greene, born in 1945 in New York, grew up on the family farm where the sap runs during maple sugaring time and the spring mud puddles stirred an early fascination with water. Questions about form, form development, and metamorphoses that manifest in nature already interested her during her high school years. These interests were pursued at Sarah Lawrence College, Bronxville, New York, and later at Adelphi University, Garden City, New York, where she received a masters in education. An early edition of Theodor Schwenk's book *Sensitive Chaos: The Creation of Flowing Forms in Water and Air* led her to his work at the Institut für Strömungswissenschaften [Institute for Flow Sciences], Herrischried, Germany. Since the 1980s she has lectured and given water phenomena workshops in the U.S., South Africa, India, Japan, and Europe. In 1991, she founded the Water Research Institute of Blue Hill in Maine. In the 1980s and 1990s, she trained in the Drop-Picture Method. She is currently working on a four-part film series *Water: The Language of Nature*. With FotoFest, Andreas Wilkens, Wolfram Schwenk, and Jennifer Greene are co-curators of the exhibition from the Institute for Flow Sciences.

BOHNCHANG KOO

Bohnchang Koo was born in 1953 in Seoul, Korea . His work has always dealt with the passage of time; he captures still and fragile moments, attempting to reveal the unseen breath of life. He is a highly regarded teacher who earned his diploma in photography at Fachhochschule, Hamburg, Germany, in 1985. He has had 22 solo exhibitions in Korea, Japan, Germany, Denmark, and the United States, where he is represented by Ricco/Maresca Gallery, New York. Recent shows in the United States were at the San Diego Museum of Photographic Arts, San Diego, and Peabody Essex Museum, Salem, Massachusetts. During FotoFest 2000, he organized with FotoFest the exhibition *Contemporary Korean Photographers*, which was the first important photographic group show of Korean photographers in the United States. His work is in the collections of the San Francisco Museum of Modern Art, San Francisco; Museum of Fine Arts, Houston; Museum of Art and Craft, Hamburg, Germany; Queensland Art Gallery, Brisbane, Australia: Reykjavik Museum of Photography, Reykjavik, Iceland; Shadai Gallery, Tokyo; National Museum of Contemporary Art, Gwacheon, Korea; and Samsung Museum and Sonje Museum of Contemporary Art, Gyongju, Korea. Bohnchang Koo currently works and lives in Seoul.

JUNGJIN LEE

Jungjin Lee was born in 1961 in Taegu, Korea. She studied ceramics at Hong-Ik University, Seoul, and received a M.A. degree in photography from New York University, New York, in 1991. While living in New York from 1989 to 1996, she frequently traveled in the Southwest to photograph desert scenes, and she produced various series on the American desert. She developed her own print technique, which involved coating Liquid Light on handmade rice paper and printing on a large scale. Since returning to Seoul in 1997, she has completed her *Pagoda* series, *Water* series, *On Road* series, and *Buddha* series, and now is working on a *Thing/Wall* series. Jungjin Lee has participated in more than 20 one-person shows as well as many group exhibitions, including shows at Pace/MacGill Gallery, New York; Bellas Artes Gallery, Santa Fe; Kukje Gallery, Seoul; Asian Art Museum, San Francisco; Whitney Museum of American Art, New York; and FotoFest 2000, Houston. Her work is in the collections of the Metropolitan Museum of Art, New York; Los Angeles County Museum of Art, Los Angeles; Museum of Fine Arts, Houston; Portland Museum, Oregon; Santa Fe Museum of Art, Santa Fe; and National Museum of Contemporary Art, Seoul.

DAVID MAISEL

David Maisel has been photographing landscapes that have undergone radical transformations for the past 20 years. Much of his work is aerial photography, looking down on sites that have been utterly changed by human activity. This cycle of work, known as *Black Maps*, has unfolded in chapters, focusing on such subjects as strip mines, clear-cuts, cyanide leaching fields, tailings ponds, firestorms, the drainage remnants of Owens Lake in California, the periphery of the Great Salt Lake, and other manipulations of the natural world. David Maisel began his studies in photography at Princeton University, Princeton, New Jersey, working with the photographer Emmet Gowin at Mount St. Helens, and he continued his studies at Harvard University's Graduate School of Design, Cambridge, Massachusetts. *The Lake Project*, a monograph of surreal aerial images documenting the vestiges of Owens Lake, will be published by Nazraeli Press of Tucson in 2004 with an introduction by Robert Sobieszek of the Los Angeles County Museum of Art, Los Angeles.

CORINNE MERCADIER

Corinne Mercadier was born in 1955. She lives in Paris and is represented by Galerie Les Filles du Calvaire, Paris and Brussels. In her photographic work, she uses SX 70 Polaroid film, from which she makes print enlargements for exhibition. In her series *Paysages* [*Landscapes*] (1992) and *Ou commence le ciel? [Where does the sky begin?]* (1996), she focused on empty places, water, and skies. Her 1998 series *Glasstypes* comprises photographs of paintings on glass that reveal the aura of the objects. Since 2000, she has been doing sculptures, including *Une fois et pas plus [Once and no more]* and *La Suite d'Arles* (both 2003). Corinne Mercadier has shown her work at Foire Internationale d'Art Contemporain (FIAC), Paris; Paris–Photo, Paris; La Primavera FotoGrafica, Barcelona; and ARCO, Madrid. In 2001, she won the Altadis Prize from Galerie Durand-Dessert, Paris, and Galerie Helga de Alvear, Madrid. In 2003, the French Ministry of Culture commissioned her to do a series of works for the Rencontres Internationales de la Photographie (RIP) in Arles, France. Corinne Mercadier's work is in the collections of La Maison Européene de la Photographie, Paris; FNAC, Paris; Bibliothèque Nationale, Paris; and Polaroid Corporation Collection, Cambridge, Massachusetts. She has published four books with Filigranes Editions and Actes Sud, Paris.

DODO JIN MING

DoDo Jin Ming was born in Beijing in 1955. She began her life as a musician, studying the violin from the age of four. In 1978 she moved from Beijing to Hong Kong, where she continued her studies at the Hong Kong Academy for the Performing Arts. When a selection of her landscape photographs was chosen by the Italian Embassy in Hong Kong for an exhibition sponsored by Fuji Film, her photographic career began in earnest. In 1994, works from her *Sunflower* series were included in an exhibition at the Museum of Fine Arts, Hong Kong, and at Takashimaya Gallery, New York, where they were met with critical and popular acclaim. Her work was featured in 1996 in *Back to Egypt* at Laurence Miller Gallery, New York, followed by *Free Element* in 2002 at the same gallery. The photographs in *Free Element* were also included in *Regarding Seas and Skies: Photographic Seascapes of Gustave LeGray, Hiroshi Sugimoto, and DoDo Jin Ming* at the Art Institute of Chicago. DoDo Jin Ming emigrated to the United States in 1994 and at present resides in New York. She is represented exclusively by Laurence Miller Gallery, New York, which will premiere new seascapes and sunflowers in *Earth Air Fire Water* to open in May 2004.

MANUEL PIÑA

Manuel Piña was born in 1958 in Cuba. He lives and works in Vancouver, Canada, and Havana. Piña finished university in the Vladimir Polytechnic institute, Russia in 1983. After a number of years of practicing engineering, he started working as an artist in the early 1990s. His work has been included in FotoFest, Houston, 1994; in the Fifth, Sixth and Seventh Havana Bienals, 1994-1998; the Fifth Istanbul Biennale, 1997; *Maps of Desires*, Kunsthalle Wien, Vienna, Austria 1999; *Shifting Tides*, Grey Art Gallery, Los Angeles Museum of Art, 2001; *La Mirada*, DAROS collection, Switzerland; *Cuba on the Verge*, International Center of Photography, New York; *Stretch*, The Power Plant, Canada 2003. His solo shows include *Manipulaciones Verdades y Otras Ilusiones*, Centro de Arte Contemporáneo Wifredo Lam, Havana, 1995; *De-Constructing Utopias I* at Art Speak Gallery and Belkin Gallery, Vancouver 1997, 1998; *Slowly, not too deep*, Galería Habana, Cuba 2001; *Displacements and Encounters*, Canadian Museum of Contemporary Photography, National Gallery of Canada and the Presentation House, Canada, 2002- 2003. Piña's work has been reviewed and/or published in *Art and Auction, Flash Art, Art Nexus, Black Flash, Lo Que Venga, CV Photo, Tema Celeste*, the *New York Times*. He is represented by Marvelli Gallery, New York and Nina Menocal Gallery, Mexico City.

STUART ROME

Born in 1953 in Bridgeport, Connecticut, Stuart Rome received his bachelor of fine arts degree in photography in 1977 from Rochester Institute of Technology, Rochester, New York, and a master of fine arts degree in photography from Arizona State University, Tempe, in 1980. He moved to Philadelphia in 1985 to form a new photography department at Drexel University, where he currently is an associate professor of photography. Among his grants and awards are Pennsylvania Council on the Arts grants in 1999 and 1992, artist-in-residence at Blue Mountain in 1997, and artist-in-residence at Light Work, Syracuse University, Syracuse, New York, in 1978. Stuart Rome has exhibited extensively in the United States, including shows at the Philadelphia Museum of Art, Philadelphia; Center for Creative Photography, Tucson; International Museum of Photography, George Eastman House, Rochester, New York; New Orleans Museum of Fine Art, New Orleans; and Santa Barbara Museum of Modern Art, Santa Barbara, California. Recent exhibitions of his work have been presented by Craig Krull Gallery, Los Angeles, and Sepia International, New York. Along with the public collections noted above, his work has been collected by the San Francisco Museum of Modern Art, San Francisco; Yale Art Museum, New Haven, Connecticut; and Los Angeles County Museum of Art, Los Angeles. Stuart Rome's work has been published in numerous magazines and books, including *Maya, Treasures of an Ancient Civilization* (Albuquerque: Abrams, 1985), *Balinese Dance in Transition, Kaja and Kelod* (Oxford, England: Oxford University Press, 1995), and "Haiti," *Aperture Magazine*, Spring 1992. He is currently working on a book

project, entitled *Language of the Land*. A concurrent exhibition of these photographs will travel nationally to commercial galleries and museum venues in a tour scheduled to begin in 2005.

ERNESTINE RUBEN (ALSO IN GROUP SHOW AT TRAVIS TOWER)

Ernestine Ruben is internationally known through her extensive exhibitions, books, photo performance, and workshops. She grew up surrounded by art and has devoted the past 25 years to the study of the human body in photography and how it relates to other media and subjects. She now applies her love of life and the human spirit to waterscapes, landscapes, architecture, and archeological sites. Her work can be found in eight monographs as well as many other publications. The most recent, *In Human Touch* (Tucson: Nazraeli, 2001), won the award for Best Photography Book of 2002 presented by the International Publishers Association. Her work is in many private and public collections, including the Museum of Modern Art, Philadelphia; Museum of Fine Arts, Houston; Museum of Modern Art, Detroit; Museum of Modern Art, New York; and La Maison Européene de la Photographie and Bibliothèque Nationale, Paris. She has had recent solo shows at John Stevenson Gallery, New York, and Baudoin Lebon Gallery, Paris. She will have a retrospective at La Maison Européene, Paris, in June 2004. She is an active teacher, associated with the University of the Arts in Philadelphia, and lives in Princeton, New Jersey, and New York.

HAN SUNGPIL

Han Sungpil was born in Korea in 1972. He began his career in photography while studying fine arts photography at Chung-Ang University in Seoul. After his graduation, he joined Korea Fuji Film Co., Ltd., where he worked for professional photographers in the professional photography department. While working there, he was featured in several exhibitions, and Kiyosato Museum of Photographic Arts, Kiyosato, Japan, included his photographs in its collection. Through discussions with Asian and international curators at exhibitions, he learned of the need for better artistic interchange between Asian and Western countries. Currently, he is completing a M.A. in curating contemporary design at Kingston University, London, for the purpose of introducing Asian arts to Western countries. In the future he would like not only to become a good artist but also to play an important role in the cultural and artistic interchange between Western countries and Asia.

ALEXEY TITARENKO

Alexey Titarenko was born in St. Petersburg, Russia in 1962. He graduated from the Department of Cinematic and Photographic Art at the Leningrad Academy of Culture in 1983. In 1989, he joined Ligovka art-group in St. Petersburg. He founded and joined the Board of Directors of the Charitable Trust for Development of Classical Music and Culture in St. Petersburg in 1994. Titarenko is a member of the Russian Union of Artists since 1997. He has received awards from the Musée de L'Elysée, Museum for Photography

(Lausanne, Switzerland) in 1993; the Soros Center for Contemporary Art in 1995; the Mosaic Program of the Luxembourg National Center for Audio/Visual, Ministry of Culture (Luxembourg) in 1998; and the Kulture Kontakt (Vienna, Austria) in 1998. He has participated in well-known programs and projects as *Aufbruch – Die neue Russiche Fotografie* at Internationalen Photoszene (Cologne, Germany) in 1998; *Chronicles of Change* at the Southwest Museum of Photography (Daytona Beach, USA) in 1996; *Photostroyka: New Soviet Photography* at the Aperture Foundation (New York, NY) in1990. Titarenko has had 28 one-man shows, including *St. Petersburg: La cité des ombres* at Camera Obscura Gallery in Paris, France, 2003; *Alexey Titarenko: Four Movements of St. Petersburg* in the us Musée Réattu (Arles International Photography Festival, France) in 2002; *Ville des ombres. La magie noire et blanche de St. Petersburg* at the Musée de Nice, Galerie des Pochettes (Nice, France) in 1999. His works are in the collections of the State Russian Museum (St. Petersburg, Russia) and 13 European and U.S. museums, including the Museum of Fine Arts, Houston and Boston Museum of Fine Arts, the maison Europèene de la Photographie, in Paris and the Musée de l'Elysée in Lausanne. His works are published in the monographs *Alexey Titarenko. Photographs, Essay by Gabriel Bauret* and *City of Shadows. Alexey Titarenko, Essay by Irinia Tchmyreva*. He is represented by Nailya Alexander Gallery, Washington D.C. and New york.

CÁSSIO VASCONCELLOS
Cássio Vasconcellos was born in São Paulo on September 29, 1965. He started his journey in photography in 1981, at the Imagem-Ação school. He had his first exhibition at age 17, sponsored by the Museo de Arte de São Paulo. During his career, his personal work, which he always directed to artistic projects, has been shown in many galleries and museums in Brazil and abroad. He is frequently invited to develop new projects, such as *Arte/Cidade* in 1994 and 2002.

WATER IN THE WEST
LAURIE BROWN
Photographer Laurie Brown grew up in Los Angeles and currently resides in Newport Beach, California. She was awarded a National Endowment for the Arts fellowship in 1978 and more recently, in 2002, was chosen Outstanding Individual Artist in the Visual Arts by ARTS Orange County. A book of her photographs entitled *RECENT TERRAINS: Terraforming the American West* was published by Johns Hopkins University Press, Baltimore, in cooperation with the Center for American Places, in late 2000. The following year, these photographs were exhibited in a one-person show at the Laguna Art Museum, Laguna Beach, California, and at Craig Krull Gallery, Santa Monica, California. Her photographs have also been exhibited at the Seon Museum, Tokyo; Los Angeles County Museum of Art, Los Angeles; San Francisco Museum of Modern Art, San Francisco; Museum of Fine Arts, Houston; Oakland Museum, Oakland, California; Center for Creative Photography, Tucson; Santa Barbara Museum of Art, Santa Barbara, California; Minneapolis Institute of Arts, Minneapolis; New Orleans Museum of Art, New Orleans; UCR

California Museum of Photography, Riverside; and Orange County Museum of Art, Newport Beach, California, among others.

WATER IN THE WEST
ROBERT DAWSON
Robert Dawson's photographs have been recognized by a fellowship from the National Endowment for the Arts, and with Gray Brechin, he received the Dorothea Lange–Paul Taylor Prize from the Center for Documentary Studies at Duke University, Durham, North Carolina. His books include *Robert Dawson Photographs* (Tokyo: Gallery MIN, 1988); with Steve Johnson and Gerald Haslam, *The Great Central Valley: California's Heartland* (Berkeley: Univ. of California Press, 1993); with Gray Brechin, *Farewell, Promised Land: Waking From the California Dream* (Berkeley: Univ. of California Press, 1999); and with Peter Goin and Mary Webb, *A Doubtful River* (Reno: Univ. of Nevada Press, 2000). He is founder and co-director with his wife, Ellen Manchester, of the Water in the West Project. His photographs are in the collections of the Museum of Modern Art, New York; San Francisco Museum of Modern Art, San Francisco; National Museum of American Art, Smithsonian Institution, Washington, D.C.; Center for Creative Photography at the University of Arizona, Tucson; Oakland Museum, Oakland, California; and Library of Congress, Washington, D.C. He received his B.A. from the University of California at Santa Cruz and his M.A. from San Francisco State University, San Francisco. He has been an instructor of photography at San Jose State University, San Jose, California, since 1986 and an instructor of photography at Stanford University, Stanford, California, since 1996.

WATER IN THE WEST
TERRY EVANS
Terry Evans is a photographer whose work is an inquiry into the nature of the prairie from its native state to its subsequent use, abandonment, and care. She photographs from both ground and aerial perspectives, and lately she has worked within the confines of natural history herbaria, and bird and mammal museum storage areas, where she has recently photographed 19th-century prairie specimens. Her intention is to tell the prairie's stories, past and present, through visible facts and the layers of time and memory detectable on the landscape. Her current work explores the complexities of the urban prairie as she photographs Chicago and the surrounding region from the air. She has exhibited widely, including one-person shows at the Art Institute of Chicago; National Museum of Natural History, Smithsonian Institution, Washington, D.C.; and Field Museum of Natural History, Chicago. She is a Guggenheim fellow, and her work is in major museum collections including those of the Art Institute of Chicago; Museum of Modern Art, New York; San Francisco Museum of Modern Art, San Francisco; National Museum of American Art, Smithsonian Institution, Washington, D.C.; Los Angeles County Museum of Art, Los Angeles; and Whitney Museum of American Art, New York.

WATER IN THE WEST
GEOFFREY FRICKER

Geoffrey Fricker lives in Chico, California, where he chairs the photography program at Butte College and has taught for the past 30 years. Throughout his teaching career, he has exhibited prints reflecting his interest in the cultural context of water. Much of the work represents his concern for sustainable uses of water in both the Sacramento and San Joaquin valleys. His most recent exhibitions include *Wanderers, Travelers, and Adventurers*, Gallery at Munn Napa, Rutherford, CA; *Sylva: A Tree Show*, Ariel Meyerowitz Gallery, New York; and *The Ing Show*, Ariel Meyerowitz Gallery, New York. In October 2003, he exhibited his work at the Resources Agency in Sacramento as part of a state-level effort to integrate the arts with the conservation of natural resources. Geoffrey Fricker's photographs have appeared in *Capturing Light: Masterpieces of California Photography, 1850–2000* (New York: W.W. Norton, 2001), *Black and White Magazine* (2001), *High Performance* (Summer 1993), *Darkroom Magazine* (1980), *Camera Maininchi* (1980), and Science (cover, 1974). In 1993, he received a National Science Foundation grant for a dinosaur mapping project. More recently, he received a National Endowment for the Arts grant for his watershed work in northern California. He has worked with the Department of Water Resources, Nature Conservancy, River Partners, Sacramento River Preservation Trust, Friends of the River, Four Winds (a school for Native Americans), and others. He has photographs in the permanent collections of the Oakland Museum, Oakland, California; San Francisco Museum of Modern Art, San Francisco; National Museum of American Art, Smithsonian Institution, Washington, D.C.; Library of Congress, Washington, D.C.; Center for Creative Photography at the University of Arizona, Tucson; Museum of Photographic Arts, San Diego; Hawaii State Art Museum, Honolulu; and Nevada Museum of Art, Reno. He received his M.F.A. from the San Francisco Art Institute, San Francisco, in 1972.

WATER IN THE WEST
PETER GOIN

Peter Goin is the author of *Tracing the Line: A Photographic Survey of the Mexican-American Border* (limited edition artist book, 1987), *Nuclear Landscapes* (Baltimore: Johns Hopkins Univ. Press, 1991), *Stopping Time: A Rephotographic Survey of Lake Tahoe*, essays by C. Elizabeth Raymond and Robert E. Blesse (Albuquerque: Univ. of New Mexico Press, 1992), and *Humanature* (Austin: Univ. of Texas Press, 1996). He served as editor of a fifth book, *Arid Waters: Photographs From the Water in the West Project* (Reno: Univ. of Nevada Press, 1992). Peter is also co-author of numerous books, including *Atlas of the New West*, a collaborative effort with members of the Center of the American West at the University of Colorado at Boulder (New York: W.W. Norton, 1997); *A Doubtful River* (Reno: Univ. of Nevada Press, 1996), a project that examines the complex watershed of the first federal irrigation dam, the Newlands Project; and *Changing Mines in America*

(Harrisonburg, Va.: Center for American Places, 2003), reinterpreting the legacy and importance of mining landscapes throughout the United States. Peter Goin's photographs have been exhibited in more than 50 museums nationally and internationally, and he is the recipient of two National Endowment for the Arts fellowships. His video work has earned him an Emmy nomination, and he was awarded the Governor's Millennium Arts Award for Excellence in the Arts. He lives with his family in Reno, Nevada. He is a Foundation Professor of Art in photography and video at the University of Nevada, Reno.

WATER IN THE WEST
WANDA HAMMERBECK

Wanda Hammerbeck is an internationally exhibited photographer. A graduate of the University of North Carolina–Chapel Hill and the San Francisco Art Institute, San Francisco, she has received two prestigious National Endowment for the Arts grants. She was a Tiffany Fellow and the 2003 recipient of the Haynes Fellowship at the Huntington Library and Norton Simon Museum, San Marino, California. Her work has appeared nationally and internationally in more than 100 exhibitions. These include shows at the San Francisco Museum of Modern Art, San Francisco; Princeton Art Museum, Princeton, New Jersey; Center for Creative Photography, Tucson; Museum of Photographic Arts, San Diego; National Gallery of Australia, Canberre; Santa Barbara Museum of Art, Santa Barbara, California; Spencer Museum of Art, Lawrence, Kansas; Fogg Art Museum, Harvard University, Cambridge, Massachusetts; and Metropolitan Museum of Art, New York. Her most recent exhibitions were at the Pomona College Art Museum, Claremont,, California, and the Museum of Fotographi, Denmark.

WATER IN THE WEST
SANT KHALSA

Sant Khalsa has received prestigious awards and support for her water projects from the National Endowment for the Arts, California Arts Council, California Council for the Humanities, U.S. Environmental Protection Agency, and Center for Photographic Art in Carmel. Her artworks have been shown in close to 100 exhibitions throughout the United States and in Europe, and they are housed in public and private collections including the Center for Creative Photography at the University of Arizona, Tucson; UCR California Museum of Photography, Riverside; and Nevada Museum of Art, Reno. She is a professor of art and chair of the art department at California State University, San Bernardino, where she is one of the founding faculty of the Water Resources Institute. Her artwork is represented by Acuna-Hansen Gallery in Los Angeles and Etherton Gallery in Tucson.

WATER IN THE WEST
MARK KLETT

Mark Klett's work focuses on time, landscape, and culture. He has been making photographs for 25 years, with one-person and group shows at national and international venues ranging from large museums, to regional and local nonprofits, to university spaces. His work is in the permanent collections of more than 60 museums and public institutions. He has authored or co-authored nine books including *Second View*, *The Rephotographic Survey Project* (Albuquerque: Univ. of Mexico Press, 1984); *Revealing Territory* (Albuquerque: Univ. of Mexico Press, 1992); *Desert Legends* (New York: Henry Holt, 1994); and most recently *The Black Rock Desert* (Tucson: Univ. of Arizona Press, 2002). Klett's work was the subject of the book *View Finder: Mark Klett, Photography, and the Reinvention of Landscape* (Albuquerque: Univ. of New Mexico Press, 2001). His awards include three National Endowment for the Arts fellowships, the Buhl Foundation Award, and Photographer of the Year from the Friends of Photography. He is currently working on three separate books that address (1) time and historic images from Yosemite, (2) the western survey era, and (3) the 1906 San Francisco earthquake and fire. Mark Klett teaches at Arizona State University, Tempe, where he is the Regents' Professor of Art.

WATER IN THE WEST
ELLEN LAND-WEBER

Ellen Land-Weber is a photographer and professor of art at Humboldt State University, Arcata, California, where she teaches photography and digital imaging. She has exhibited her work in solo or group exhibitions every year since 1968. Her photographs are in the permanent collections of museums in 12 states and in France, Japan, Canada, and Australia. She has received various grants over the years including National Endowment for the Arts photography fellowships, Polaroid Artist's Support, and a Fulbright senior fellowship. Her photographic work has appeared in many books and other photography publications. She is the author of, and photographer for, two books: *The Passionate Collector* (New York: Simon and Schuster, 1980) and *To Save a Life: Stories of Holocaust Rescue* (Champaign: Univ. of Illinois Press, 2000).

WATER IN THE WEST
SHARON STEWART

Born in Edinburg, Texas, on the southern borderlands with Mexico, and educated in finance and economics at the University of Texas, Austin, and Harvard University, Cambridge, Massachusetts, Sharon Stewart now resides at the confluence of the Great Plains and the Sangre de Christo Mountains in the northern New Mexican village of Chacón. A cultural landscape photographer, she a is founding vice president of the Houston Center for Photography, a member of the Water in the West Project and Archive, and a member of the progressive photo agency Impact Digitals. In addition to being exhibited at the Center for Creative Photography, Tucson; Museum of Fine Arts, Houston; Musée de la Photographie áCharleroi, Belgium; Capitol Art Foundation, Santa Fe; and Nevada Museum of Art, Reno, her photographs are found in those institutions' collections. Her work has also been exhibited at the Frankfurter Kunstverein, Frankfurt am Main, Germany; Wessel + O'Connor Gallery, New York; DiverseWorks, Houston; New Orleans Museum of Art, New Orleans; Houston Center for Photography, Houston; and Visual Studies Workshop, Rochester, New York. Selected publications

include her monograph *Toxic Tour of Texas* (Sharon Stewart, Houston, 1992), *Frauen Sehen Männer* (Verlag Photographie Koln, Germany, 1998), *Texas Land Ethics* (University of Texas Press, Austin, 1997), *and The Altered Landscape* (University of Nevada Press, Reno, 1999). Sharon Stewart has been the recipient of an Artist's Residency from Light Work and a grant from the Mid-America Arts Alliance through the National Endowment for the Arts.

WATER IN THE WEST
MARTIN STUPICH

Martin Stupich was trained in painting and sculpture, which he gave up for photography in 1970. His earliest serious work, documenting the construction of the MARTA subway system in Atlanta, led to his first National Endowment for the Arts grants in the late 1970s. Those years mark the beginning of his professional life photographing the engineered landscape. In 1980 he moved to Nevada to photograph the Comstock Mining District for the Library of Congress collection. Since then, his clients and his personal interests have led to documentary projects on the Panama Canal, at Cape Canaveral, and in Japan, Vietnam, and China—as well as his current work in the western United States. He maintains a small gallery, studio, and darkroom in Wyoming, where he is currently working with writer Annie Proulx and anthropologist Dudley Gardner on researching and documenting the Great Divide Basin region of the Central Rockies. He divides his time between there and Albuquerque.

ANDREJ ZDRAVIC

Andrej Zdravic, independent filmmaker, cameraman, editor, and sound composer, was born in Ljubljana, Slovenia, in 1952 to a musician mother and surgeon father. He received his education in Ljubljana, Algiers, and the U.S., and began filmmaking in 1973, inspired by music and nature. He studied film and sound at the State University of New York, Buffalo, then lived and worked in first New York (1975–1980) and later San Francisco (1980–1995). He has created over 30 independent films and soundtracks, mostly focusing on the energies and spiritual aspects of natural phenomena. He has also been greatly influenced by his medical filmmaking and has produced numerous scientific documentaries for the San Francisco Exploratorium and others. Andrej Zdravic's films have been featured in over 200 one-person shows, retrospectives, festivals, and seminars in the U.S. and Europe, and broadcast on Television ARTE, ZDF, KCET Los Angeles, and elsewhere. He is also the author of a multichannel video installation concept—Time Horizon—showcased at the 1999 Venice Biennale and at EXPO '98 in Lisbon, and now a permanent feature in science and art museums in the U.S., Taiwan, and Slovenia. He has lectured on filmmaking and sound at various U.S. universities and has received grants and awards from, among others, the National Science Foundation, the National Endowment for the Arts, and the Preseren Fund in Slovenia. At present, he is working on *The Forest* (2004-06), a feature-length essay on the spirit of the forest aimed for theatrical distribution. *Riverglass* was produced and directed by Andrej Zdravic, who also did the camerawork, editing, and music and sound composition. It has won awards from the Preseren

Fund in Slovenia (1999), the Grand Prix of the Third International Festival of Film & Video in Split, Croatia (1998), and the Best Art Video at the Festival of Slovene Film in Portoroz, Slovenia (1998). His work is distributed by ANTARA Soundfilm in Ljubljana, Slovenia, and Canyon Cinema in the U.S.

HELEN ZOUT

Helen Zout was born in Argentina and studied cultural anthropology at the National University in La Plata. At 19, pregnant with her first son and the target of political persecution, she had to abandon her studies. She remained in hiding for three years under another identity. At the end of this time, she began to study photography. In 1983, with the emergence of a democratic regime in the city of La Plata, she decided to dedicate herself to photography. She was a photojournalist for *Diario la Razón* from 1983 to 1986. Since 1983, Zout has realized a number of photographic projects. She has also been a teacher of photography. In 1983, she did a photographic registry of indigenous and migrant communities in the province of Misiones for the National University of La Plata. In 1989, she received a scholarship from the Fondo Nacional de las Artes. From 1989 to 1993, she produced a photographic essay on mental health for which she was awarded the Fist Prize of National Photography in 1989. In 1989–2004, she worked on a photographic investigation of HIV-positive children. She received the Miguel Gordman Prize for this work. From 1990 to 2004, Zout worked as a photographer for the Chamber of Senators of the Province of Buenos Aires. During this time, she also worked on her series *Traces of the Disappeared during the Last Military Dictatorship in Argentina 1976–1983*. She received a Guggenheim Foundation fellowship for this work in 2002. She has exhibited in one-person and group exhibitions in major cities in Latin America, Europe, and Asia. Her works are in the collections of the Museum of Fine Arts, Houston; Museos Nacional de Bellas Artes, Buenos Aires; and Museo de Arte Moderno de Buenos Aires.

FotoFest Collaborations

BARRY ANDERSON
HOUSTON COMMUNITY COLLEGE – CENTRAL ART GALLERY

Born in 1969 in North Texas, Barry Anderson currently lives in Kansas City, Missouri, where he teaches electronic media at the University of Missouri–Kansas City. He received his B.F.A. in photography in 1991 from The University of Texas at Austin and his M.F.A. in photography and digital media in 2002 from Indiana University, Bloomington. He has shown his photography and video work at numerous locations in the United States and abroad, with recent exhibitions in New York, Chicago, Kansas City, Madrid, Havana, and Rio de Janeiro. His video work was also shown during FotoFest 2002.

MALACHI FARRELL
BUFFALO BAYOU PARTNERSHIP, SUNSET COFFEE BUILDING

Malachi Farrell was born in Dublin, Ireland in 1970. He lives and works in Paris, France. He attended the Ecole de Beaux-Art, Rouen, France, the prestigious Rijskakademie in Amsterdam, and the exper-

imental Institut Supérieur des Hautes Etudes, Paris in 1993, created by Pontus Hulten. After his studies, Farrell was first seen in the 1994 group exhibition *Atelier 94* at the L'ARC (Musée d'Art Moderne de la Ville de Paris) and then went on to participate in shows in major institutions such as Le Magasin, Grenoble, France, The Succession, Vienna, Kunsthalle Bremen, Germany, capc, Bordeaux, France, The San Francisco Art Institute, San Francisco, Sprengel Museum Hannover, Germany, and The Gemeete museum Denhaag, The Hague, Holland. In 2002, he was included in Taschen's publicatio *ART NOW, 137 Artists at the Rise of the Millennium*. Farrell's moving and sound installations can be seen in 2004–2005 at the Kunsthaus Graz, Austria, PS1 Contemporary Art Center, New York, Centre Georges Pompidou, Paris, and The Jean Tinguely Museum, Basel. He is represented by Galerie Xippas in Paris.

ALVARO LEIVA
RICE UNIVERSITY MEDIA CENTER

Alvaro Leiva was born in 1970 in Madrid. He shoots photography for a variety of publicity agencies and travel magazines. Apart from a single course in photography, he is largely self-taught. From 1986 to 1988, he worked as an assistant to various commercial and fashion photographers. In 1989 he started shooting travel photography. Since then he has traveled to more than 80 countries on assignment. He has published his work in a variety of magazines including *El País*, *Geo Germany*, *Visa Gold*, *Cosmopolitan*, *ELLE*, *GQ*, and *Vogue*. His current projects include one on child labor and another on Indian tribes around the world. His work is represented by Grazia Neri and Panos Pictures.

EDGAR MORENO
THE STATION

Edgar Moreno was born in Caracas in 1958. In 1977, he studied at New Mexico State University, Las Cruces, where he began his photographic education and received a degree in music and visual arts. He returned to the U.S. in 1986 to take art courses at the Pratt Institute and National Academy of Arts in New York. In 1989, Edgar Moreno received a fellowship to study art in Florence, Italy, and he began a series of trips that would take him to more than 50 countries. He has had numerous exhibitions in Venezuela and abroad, and has been the recipient of prestigious art awards in Venezuela: the Premio de Fotografía del Salón Arturo Michelena [Photography Prize from the Salón Arturo Michelena] three times and the Premio de Fotografía Luis Felipe Toro, CONAC [Luis Felipe Toro Photography Prize]. In 2002, he received a prize from the Asociación Nacional de Críticos de Arte [National Association of Art Critics] in Venezuela, a study fellowship from Gasworks in London, and a study grant from the Italian government. Edgar Moreno has had a continuing preocupation with social and geological subjects as well as the origin of forms. From the beginning of his long artistic career, he has taken a personal approach in his work on nature and landscapes transformed by humankind. Among his most significant works are *Las sillas cagadas* (1985), a series that deals with chairs as symbols of power; *Iniciación y final y Calcuta de seis a doce* (1991), two photographic essays on India, Pakistan, and Nepal; *El peso de un imaginario* (1992), diverse essays on the work of bearers, such as the Sherpas, reflecting ancestral professions and cultures; *Entre* (1993), an essay on the aboriginal peoples of Papua and New Guinea; *Body & Soul y los Taxidermistas; Zooilógico* (1996), work on the relationship of modern man to animals; *El malandro mágico* (1997), works on the poor, marginal neighborhoods of Caracas; and *Naturaleza con trastos* (1999), a series revealing the refuse of economic progress left in the middle of the natural landscape. He lives in Caracas, where he teaches and pursues photographic and musical research. He is a passionate collector of flutes, which he has found on his many trips.

NILS-UDO
BUFFALO BAYOU ARTPARK AND BUFFALO BAYOU PARTNERSHIP

Nils-Udo was born in Germany in 1937. He began his career as a painter, before discovering his true artistic vocation in nature—an adventure that has taken him to all four corners of the planet: from India to Mexico, from Namibia to Japan. He sculpts within nature, using whatever he finds on site. He rearranges elements of nature, not with a bulldozer, but with a delicacy and deftness of touch before capturing the microcosm he has created in a photograph. Nils-Udo's photographs are exhibited in museums all over the world, and he has been invited to create installations on five continents. Sculptures that burst into flower, grow foliage, and change color with the seasons; sculptures that are buried in snow and metamorphosized by vegetation refkect the originality of Nils-Udo's work. He harnesses the vital spark of nature itself as an integral part of his creative activity. Nature is no longer simply a model, but instead the very object of the artistic process. He began working with nature in 1972, transcending borders and categorization. His creations are rooted in a quest shared by all human societies that look for themselves in nature, while nature makes us look at ourselves. In his installations and arrangements, Nils-Udo works in a series of undestructive gestures, making simple changes and subtle realignments that bring colors, plants, and other natural elements together. The most ordinary of materials becomes the focal point of artistic composition, crystallizing in miniature the whole spectrum of natural forms that inspired architecture and ornament throughout civilization. The artist acts as mediator. In his work, creativity is the fruit of solitary reflection and activity, an exclusively personal journey. To record this journey, Nils-Udo uses photography to document the various phases of the living process of change in his work. Through his photographs, one observes the growth, life, and occasionally the death of a work of art.

INGRID POLLARD
PROJECT ROW HOUSES

Born in Guyana, Ingrid Pollard moved to England at age four. She received a B.A. in film and video, and a M.A. in photographic studies. Beginning her photographic career in the 1980s with documentary and theatre photography, she has also taught screen-printing and photographyin Community Arts. Ingrid Pollard has exhibited widely in Europe and the Americas. At present, she is a research fellow on the faculty of Arts & Human Science at London South Bank University, London. *Postcards Home*, a major survey of her photographic work from 1989–2003, was published by Chris Boot in 2004.

DANA SPERRY (GRAY SANDBOX COLLABORATIVE)
HOUSTON COMMUNITY COLLEGE, CENTRAL ART GALLERY

Dana Sperry is a video/conceptual artist living in Bloomington, Indiana. He has exhibited his work nationally, including shows in Chicago, Atlanta, Kansas City, and New York. He recently completed the video installation *Water Under The Bridge* at the Society for Contemporary Photography in Kansas City and participated in the exhibition "Uncovered" at the Museum of Contemporary Art in Chicago. He is currently the associate director of the Fine Arts Gallery at Indiana University and director of Fuller Projects. His video work was also shown during FotoFest 2002.

FotoFest Exhibition
Discoveries of the Meeting Place

SIAN BONNELL

Sian Bonnell lives and works in Dorset on the south coast of England. Her background is in sculpture and theatre design: she worked in fringe theatres on leaving art school and before studying for a M.F.A. in 1983. She has exhibited widely and is represented by Hirschi Contemporary Art in London. A selection of her photographs is held in the collection at the Victoria and Albert Museum, London. One of these, from the series *Putting Hills in Holland*, was included in *Seeing Things: Photographing Objects 1850–2001*, held at Canon Photography Gallery, City, in 2002. Sian Bonnell's photograph was used on the poster to promote the exhibition. Her work is also in the collection of the Museum of Fine Arts, Houston.She works in series, using found objects and household articles, placing them out of context within her local rural and coastal environment or constructing imagined landscapes in the studio. She then photographs these interventions with conventional and pinhole cameras; the choice depends on the piece of work being produced. The images are documents not just of the objects but also of an event made specifically for the camera. Working within the landscape tradition, one of the oldest and most baggage-laden of genres, Sian Bonnell seeks to undercut the rhetoric of Romanticism to comment on and create other fictions—landscapes of the imagination. For the last two years, Sian Bonnell has been running Trace, a not-for-profit arts organization. Trace exhibitions mounted in her home at Weymouth have featured international art and photography; the first showing of new photograms by Susan Derges was held at Trace in June 2002. Other Trace projects include an International Photography Festival to be held in Poole and Bournemouth, England, during May 2004.

VINCENT CIANNI

Vincent Cianni works in Brooklyn, New York. He is a documentary/fine art photographer and has been exhibited nationally and internationally at venues that include the Museum of Fine Arts, Houston; Museum of the City of New York; and The Photographers' Gallery, London. His work explores community and memory, and the human condition, as well as the use of image and text stemming from personal experience and discovery. Vincent Cianni teaches at Parsons School of Design, New York, and is represented by the Sarah Morthland Gallery, New York. His photographs have been widely published in photo journals and anthologies (i.e., *Double Take* and *Aperture*), and his first book, *We Skate Hardcore*, will be published by New York University Press and the Center for Documentary Studies, New York, in September 2004, with an accompanying exhibition at the Museum of the City of New York. His work is represented in numerous public and private collections. His recent work focuses on our relationship to the landscape.

BRIAN FINKE

Brian Finke grew up in a suburb of Houston and attended the School of Visual Arts in New York. He has won awards from the World Press Photo Masterclass, a Photography for Social Change grant, and an award from The Alexia Foundation for World Peace. After receiving his bachelor of fine arts in 1998, he became a well-known editorial and commercial photographer, working with such publications as *GQ*, *Details*, *Entertainment Weekly*, *Discover*, and *The New York Times Magazine*. Brian Fink has also continued to work on several personal documentary projects, including his cheerleader and football player series. This series, entitled *2-4-6-8: American Cheerleaders & Football Players*, was featured in his first monograph and New York exhibition, and has received much attention in New York and abroad. His work is included in museums in Houston, St. Louis, Paris, and Japan. His photographs will be on display in a group show at the Royal Hibernian Academy in Dublin this spring.

BILL JORDEN

Bill Jorden was an award-winning photographer, a TV producer and writer, and a lecturer on the role of art, science, and holistic knowledge in society. His photographic work won three grand prizes in nationwide competitions, including first place in the 1997 "Assignment Earth" contest. His work was reviewed and published in *The New York Times*, as well as many other leading magazines, including *Popular Photography*, *ZOOM*, *Travel & Leisure*, the *Village Voice*, and *Lapis*. *Camera Arts* will publish a major article on his *Mystical Landscapes* series in an upcoming issue. His work has also been exhibited extensively in the U.S. and around the world, and is in several major public and private collections, including that of the Museum of Fine Arts, Houston. He won a National Endowment for Arts award for *LUMINA: Reports on the Arts*, which was broadcast nationwide by PBS-TV. His seminal articles on contemporary photography have appeared in *AfterIMage*, Camera Lucida, and Photograph, which he helped found. He teaches photography at the International Center of Photography, and the Westchester Art Workshops. His *Mystical Landscapes* series, inspired by Stanley Kubrick's *Barry Lyndon*, explores the presence of ancient memory and knowledge in the landscapes of western Ireland and other places. His *Portraits in Paradise* series deals with tourists seeking external as well as internal Edens. And his *Modern Nature* series, based on Henry James's writings, uses paired images to compare how the U.S. and Europe tame nature.

THOMAS KELLNER

Thomas Kellner was born in Bonn, Germany, in 1966. In 1996 he finished his studies in teaching art and social sciences at the University of Siegen, Germany. Right from the beginning of his studies, his basic interest was in experimental photography. He worked with different pinhole series, photograms, and printing in alternative techniques like cyanotype. His final project received the prize for young professionals given by Kodak Germany. In 1997 he decided to concentrate on photography. In 2003–2004 he was a visiting professor for photography in art at the Justus-Liebig-University of Giessen, Germany. He works today as a free-lance artist and lives in Siegen, Germany. By the time he completed his university degree, his work had been nationally and internationally exhibited and published. Since 1997, with his series on European monuments, he has experienced a wider international recognition, furthered by his participation in FotoFest 2002 and several exhibitions in New York, Chicago, and other cities around the U.S. He has been published as well in international magazines like *Aperture* (New York). Today he is well represented by galleries in Europe and the United States. His work has been collected by private collectors and museums, such as the Museum of Fine Arts, Houston, and The Art Institute of Chicago. His photos are defined by a wide range of complexity in both content and form, reflected in his multiple-exposure pinhole work and deconstructive architectural images. In his treatment of nature, architecture, and the human figure, his works have the quality of still-lifes, contemplative works on contemporary themes. His treatment of monuments is more humorous even as they explore cultural values, their meanings and vulnerability.

ELAINE LING

Seeking the solitude of deserts and the abandoned architecture of ancient cultures, Elaine Ling is exploring the shifting equilibrium between nature and what is man-made. Photographing in the deserts of Namibia, North Africa, Chile, the Middle East, and the American Southwest, and in the citadels of Persepolis, Petra, Angkor Wat, and Great Zimbabwe, she has furthered that dialogue. In Havana, a city caught between the decay of the immediate epoch and the grandeur of past glory, she found an urban landscape that reflects a similar struggle between daily life and the slow forces of nature. Havana is filled with the architecture of a decadent past, but there is a tangible new energy of reconstruction and restoration signaling the city's rebirth. The abandoned pleasure gardens and the intimate interiors of Cuban homes are in a flux of metamorphosis. She has exhibited extensively in North America and Europe. Her photographs are in the permanent collections of the Museum of Fine Arts Houston; Henry Buhl Foundation, New York; Brooklyn Museum, Brooklyn, New York; Musée de la Photographie, Charleroi, Belgium; and Museet for Fotokunst, Odense, Denmark. Her work is also in the collections of the Royal Ontario Museum, Toronto, and the Canadian Museum of Contemporary Photography, Ottawa. Born in Hong Kong, Elaine Ling has lived in Canada since the age of nine. She is based in Toronto.

GEORGI BOGDANOV AND BORIS MISSIRKOV

Georgi Bogdanov and Boris Missirkov were born in 1971 in Bulgaria. Both graduated from the National Academy of Theatre and Film Arts, Sofia, with a masters degree in cinematography. They co-founded the Bulgarian House of Photography in Sofia, supporting and presenting new media and traditional photography. They have received several European fellowships, including one from Benetton in La Fabrica, Italy. Georgi Bogdanov and Boris Missirkov have worked together for many years and have collaborated on many projects. Their own work includes photography, film documentaries, and video. Their work has been exhibited extensively throughout Europe and appeared in FotoFest 2002.

A. LEO NASH

A. Leo Nash was born in the Berkshire Mountains of western Massachusetts in 1964. A college career that began with a major in geography at Clark University, Worcester, Massachusetts, in 1982 ended with a degree in photography from the Rochester Institute of Technology, Rochester, New York, in 1989. During these years, A. Leo Nash traveled extensively in the U.S., Europe, and Middle East, working as a chef, bike messenger, and carpenter. Starting in 1990, he linked his persistent interest in the psychology of human interactions with clinical coursework at both the Berkeley Psychic Institute and the Aesclepion Healing Center. He integrates this continuing development of awareness in his use of space in his work. Images of machines, artistic objects, and their remnants lead to a broader understanding of what it means to be human. He continues to document people who live at the edges of mainstream culture, photographing temporary artistic communities and endeavors, often in remote areas. He makes his living as a gaffer/lighting director in the film industry in both the San Francisco Bay Area and Los Angeles, and he calls a studio in West Oakland, California, home.

SIMON NORFOLK

Simon Norfolk learned journalism by working for the far left press through the early 1990s. He was staff photographer for *Living Marxism* magazine in 1990–94. He did extensive work on fascism and the far right, especially the British National Party, whose edges he infiltrated in 1993–94. He also worked over a long period as a photojournalist on anti-racism issues, the poll tax, and Northern Ireland. He was assigned to Eastern Europe at the fall of the Berlin Wall and he covered the Gulf War. His work has been published in all the U.K. broadsheets and many European magazines. He later became inter-

ested in anti-Semitism and was introduced to Holocaust revisionism by David Irving, et al., while meeting and photographing Holocaust survivors. He then abandoned photojournalism to do landscape work. In 1994, he began the project *For Most of It I Have No Words* about the landscapes of places that have seen genocide. The work is based heavily on Joseph Conrad's *Heart of Darkness* and Romance philosophy. This work was published by Dewi Lewis Publishing (U.K.) in 1998 with an introduction by Michael Ignatieff. Simon Norfolk visited Afghanistan during the war in 2001, using a wooden 5 by 4 camera to make the work *Afghanistan: chronotopia*, which was inspired by 17th-century landscape painting, 19th-century war photography, and Donald Rumsfeld. The title is taken from an idea put forward by Mikhail Bakhtin. The work won the European Publishers' Award in 2002 and was published by Dewi Lewis Publishing (U.K.) in English, French, German, Spanish, and Italian editions in September 2002. The Afghanistan work is the beginning of a larger project, to be completed by 2004, about how war and conflict create landscape.

DOMINIC ROUSE

Dominic Rouse was born in England in 1959 and started his career as a press photographer at the age of 16 working for local and national newspapers. Finding himself constrained by the technical limitations of photojournalism, he returned to college in 1982 to study commercial and advertising photography. While in college, he developed a particular interest in multiple exposure techniques using large format cameras. After a brief spell in London assisting advertising photographer Phil Jude, he opened his own studio in 1986. No longer reliant upon commercial commissions for his livelihood, Dominic Rouse is now free to devote his time to producing personal work, using a blend of traditional and modern techniques.

Film and Video — Water

AURORA PICTURE SHOW

Aurora Picture Show was founded in 1998 by two Houston-based media artists, Andrea Grover and Patrick Walsh. The two founders had noticed an increase in the number of artist-made films and videos, and identified a need for exhibition opportunities for these works in Houston.. Through volunteer labor and equipment donation, they converted a 1924 church building in a multiethnic neighborhood into a 100-seat film and video theater. In June 1999, Aurora Picture Show received its 501(c)(3) non-profit status, and it has since been awarded grants from the Cultural Arts Council of Houston/Harris County, Texas Commission on the Arts, Houston Endowment, National Endowment for the Arts, and The Andy Warhol Foundation for the Visual Arts. Aurora regularly collaborates with renowned arts organizations including the Contemporary Arts Museum Houston; Museum of Fine Arts, Houston; DiverseWorks Art Space; Blaffer Gallery; and FotoFest. Aurora hosts the most distinguished media artists in the U.S.

KUHT-HOUSTON (PBS)

In May 1953, the University of Houston launched the world's first educational television station. Initiated in Houston as a bold experiment in broadcasting, America's first public television station is now a nationally respected community resource. Houston PBS (Channel 8) uses the power of noncommercial television, the Internet, and other media to present quality programs and education services to the Houston public. Almost 50 years later, in 2001, Houston PBS continued to carry its founders' innovative vision forward by moving beyond analog television into the digital broadcast spectrum.

RICE MEDIA CENTER

The Rice University Media Center was founded in 1969 by international art patrons John and Dominique de Menil, with the assistance of Colin Young, then chair of the UCLA theater arts department, and Roberto Rossellini, the premier Italian filmmaker of the postwar period. As the home of film and photography at Rice University, Houston, the Center has fulfilled its founders' vision of providing a channel through which different peoples of the world can communicate. In recent years, the addition of video production, media studies, and the digital arts to the curriculum has further expanded the Center's offerings and increased its impact in an increasingly interconnected world. The Center is home to the photography department of Rice University and of the Rice Cinema.

SOUTHWEST ALTERNATE MEDIA PROJECT

As the oldest nonprofit media arts center in Texas, Southwest Alternate Media Project (SWAMP) has facilitated the production of independent film for 27 years. Its mission remains an enduring commitment to the creation and appreciation of film, video, and new media as art forms for a multicultural public. To this end, SWAMP provides filmmakers, in all their diversity, with opportunities for exhibition, education, and information. SWAMP, which evolved from the film program at Rice University Media Center, realized the vision of filmmaker and educator James Blue (1930–1980), who taught there in 1970–1977. A media arts center, Blue believed, was a tool for democracy: a vehicle for access to, and control and distribution of, film and video information. The community programs initiated at Rice were transformed into a new entity, the Southwest Alternate Media Project, which was incorporated as a nonprofit in 1977. Over the years SWAMP has continued Blue's democratic ideals of community involvement, education, and access in an unbroken record of service to independent media artists and their audiences. The oldest of SWAMP's programs is *The Territory*, a showcase for short films and videos by independent makers, which will begin its 29th season in 2004. It is the longest-running series of independent media art on public television in the United States. *The Territory*, available for broadcast on all the PBS stations in Texas, features work in all genres by Texas, national, and international film and video makers. The series is a unique collaboration between a media arts center (SWAMP), a public broadcasting station (KUHT), and two museums (The Austin Museum of Art and the Museum of Fine Arts, Houston). Through The Territory, SWAMP has built statewide public awareness in the millions for independent filmmakers.

VOICES BREAKING BOUNDARIES

Voices Breaking Boundaries (VBB) was founded four years ago by five women poets and writers. Today VBB hosts multimedia performances, at-risk student art workshops, and adult writing workshops. Since the organization's inception, VBB has created programming that addresses its mission to cross borders, sustain dialogue, and incite change through living art. A strong goal of the organization is to bring together Houston's rich cultures under one roof so people can begin a dialogue through art to better understand each other. Many of VBB's performances and programs are collaborations with local organizations. VBB's programs include multidisciplinary performances—events that allow artists of all ages, backgrounds, and disciplines to perform their work and speak out on local, national, and global issues. Over the years VBB has shown documentary films from Palestine, South Asia, and the U.S., held telephone readings by writers such as Arundhati Roy and Naomi Shihab Nye, and showcased music from the Philippines and Brazil, as well as by local jazz artists. Some of the issues addressed include antiwar protest, the growing HIV pandemic, and women's rights. VBB's MultiMedia Workshops for at-risk students in partnership with local high schools and universities give at-risk students opportunities to express themselves through art. VBB's High School Workshops aim to connect students to Houston's higher education campuses and to arts organizations so students have a greater understanding of their options after graduating from high school. At the college level, VBB offers internship-mentorship programs and trains students in arts administration, arts education, and personal artistic development. Its Writing Workshops for immigrant writers—VBB's partnership with Project Row Houses—provides a sliding scale workshop, "Voices of the Displaced: Exploring Personal Voice Through Writing," that reaches out to Houston's adult immigrant community and links them to writers from the Third Ward. Each session, VBB offers one full scholarship to a college student. VBB's Web site is www.voicesbreakingboundaries.org.

SERENA LIN BUSH

Serena Lin Bush is a video installation artist who has been working in Houston since 1998. Her art practice focuses on sculptural media environments, but also includes screened works as well as a series of ongoing collaborative projects with dance and performing arts groups. She has received artist grants from both the Cultural Arts Council of Houston/Harris County (2003) and the Maryland State Arts Council (1998). Bush has mounted her installations at sites such as Women and Their Work Gallery, Austin, Texas; DiverseWorks Artspace, Houston; Lawndale Art Center, Houston; and Maryland Art Place, Baltimore. Her work has also been screened in international venues including the International Symposium on Electronic Art, the New York Digital Salon, and "imagelarchitetura in movimento," an annual conference on architecture and the moving image held in Florence, Italy. Bush holds an M.F.A. from the University of Maryland, Baltimore County, and a B.F.A. from Washington University, St. Louis.

PATRICK KWIATKOWSKI
MICROCINEMA INTERNATIONAL

Patrick Kwiatkowski co-founded Blackchair Productions in 1996 and Microcinema International in 2000. He developed *Independent Exposure*, an international short moving image screening program that has presented the works of over 1,000 artists in 43 countries plus Palestine and Antarctica. The series received the award for Best New Microcinema in 2002 from the *Houston Press* and has been the recipient of numerous grants, including those from the Texas Commission on the Arts, The LEF Foundation, and the William and Flora Hewlett Foundation. In 2003 Microcinema created its Blackchair DVD label, which features compilations of international independent artists. Patrick Kwiatkowski has recently participated in panels at the FIFI Internet Film Festival in Lille, France, the SWAMP (Southwest Alternative Media Project) Texas Media Arts Conference in Houston, the conference of the National Association of Latino Independent Producers, the Amarillo KickFest, the Global Media and Entertainment Network Conference in New York, and South by Southwest 2004 in Austin, Texas. He was a jurist on the 2003 Texas Show of the Dallas Video Festival.

EILEEN MAXSON
FILM AND VIDEO COORDINATOR, FOTOFEST 2004

Eileen Maxson began curating film and video programs for FotoFest in the summer of 2002 as part of an exhibition program commemorating the events of September 11, 2001. She is currently coordinating the film and video programs on water for FotoFest's 2004 Biennial. In May 2002, Eileen Maxson graduated magna cum laude with a B.F.A. in photography and digital media from the University of Houston. Since her graduation, she has been gaining recognition and visibility as an award-winning video artist and photographer. Her work has screened at the Dallas Museum of Art, Dallas; New York Underground Film Festival, New York; The Aurora Picture Show, Houston; and Smogdance Film Festival, Pomona, California, where her entry received the distinction of Best Experimental Film. Her work has toured nationally as a part of "The Best of The Aurora Picture Show: Volume I" exhibition, curated by Andrea Grover. Born August 27, 1980, in Long Island, New York, Eileen Maxson spent her childhood moving with her family from state to state, from one suburb to the next. She currently lives and works in Houston. She continues to exhibit her own video work and photography.

Literacy Through Photography

MARY DOYLE GLOVER
DIRECTOR, LITERACY THROUGH PHOTOGRAPHY, FOTOFEST

Mary Doyle Glover joined FotoFest's staff in the fall of 2000 as exhibitions coordinator. In the summer of 2002, she became the full-time Literacy Through Photography director. Mary Glover has 20 years of experience in arts education, beginning in Florida as the art coordinator and teacher for a Tampa enrichment program for at-risk youth.

She also created and taught a multidisciplinary summer program for the Ruth Eckerd Hall Center for the Performing Arts in Clearwater, Florida. In 1986 she moved to Houston and worked for the Children's Museum of Houston as program coordinator. Mary Glover has taught classes and developed programming for the Contemporary Arts Museum Houston and the Glassell School of Art Junior Program, Museum of Fine Arts, Houston. She was the project director for the Museum of Fine Arts, Houston exhibition *Getting Into Focus* at FotoFest 1994, held at the George R. Brown Convention Center. This exhibition featured hands-on projects and educational components about photography for visitors of all ages. In 1998 Glover co-founded and directed Houston Sculpture 2000. This two-year project culminated in the mounting of 80 sculpture exhibitions citywide, educational programs on the high school and college levels, a catalogue, and programs and events for the 18th International Sculpture Conference in the spring of 2000. Glover has managed an artist's ceramics studio and has consulted on large-scale projects for sculpture installations. She has broad knowledge of educational institutions, artists, galleries, and non-profits throughout Texas and the United States.

Curators

FREDERICK BALDWIN
CHAIRMAN AND CO-FOUNDER, FOTOFEST

Frederick Baldwin is a co-founder of FotoFest and has served as the organization's president and chairman since 1984. He was responsible for the organizational and financial development of FotoFest® in 1984–1991. In 1988–1990, he organized FotoFest's education program, Literacy Through Photography. Since 1991, he has shared responsibility for FotoFest's artistic programming as well as administration and finances with FotoFest® Artistic Director Wendy Watriss. In 1994, he initiated an international collaboration of 22 photography festivals, resulting in the Festival of Light 2000, and an ongoing international network of photography events. He has had an extensive career in photography, both as a professional photographer and as a professor. From 1957 to 1982, he worked as a photographer on international commissions for publications such as *LIFE, National Geographic, GEO, STERN, Time,* and *The New York Times.* His award-wining work covers subjects such as the civil rights movement in Georgia, rural poverty in the Carolinas, Arctic fishermen in the Lofoten Islands, the Peace Corps in India, and wildlife in the Arctic. In 1971, he began a photographic documentary and oral history project in Texas with Wendy Watriss. The project resulted in numerous exhibitions, fellowships (from the National Endowment for the Humanities and The Rockefeller Foundation), and the book *Coming To Terms, The German Hill Country of Texas* (College Station, Texas: Texas A&M Press, 1991). In 1981–1982, he taught documentary photography in the School of Communications at the University of Texas in Austin. From 1982 to 1987, he directed the photojournalism program at the University of Houston Central Campus. In 1964–1966, he was director of the Peace Corps in Borneo. He served as a Marine infantryman in Korea in 1950–1952 and was wounded and decorated numerous times. He is a member of the American Leadership Forum.

WENDY WATRISS
ARTISTIC DIRECTOR AND CO-FOUNDER, FOTOFEST
Wendy Watriss is a co-founder of FotoFest and has served as artistic director since 1991. As project director and curator for FotoFest®, she has developed over 40 international exhibitions since 1990, including path-breaking exhibitions on Latino photographers in the U.S., contemporary Mexican photography, the global environment, photography from Latin America 1865–1994, photography from Central Europe, the visual history of Kurdistan (with Susan Meiselas), contemporary Korean photography, early 20th-century Russian photography, and multimedia/new technology installations. In 1998, she completed the award-winning book *IMAGE AND MEMORY, Photography from Latin America 1866–1994* (Austin, Texas: Univ. of Texas Press, 1998). Since 1992, Wendy Watriss has directed FotoFest art programs and catalogue publications, and she has supervised the Literacy Through Photography program with Frederick Baldwin. In 1992–1997 and 2002–2004, she was responsible for the administration of FotoFest. In 1992–2004, she shared responsibility for FotoFest finances with Frederick Baldwin. She began her professional career in the mid 1960s as a newspaper and television journalist covering local, national, and international political events and stories. From 1963 to 1966, she worked as a writer and newspaper reporter on urban politics for the St. Petersburg Times in Florida. From 1966 to 1970, she was a reporter and producer of political documentaries for public television in New York. In 1970–1991, She worked as an award-winning international photojournalist and creative photographer, publishing work on subjects such as political conflicts in sub-Saharan Africa, civil conflicts in Salvador and Nicaragua, the rebuilding of Skopje in Macedonia, Vietnam veterans and the herbicide Agent Orange, and the Vietnam Veterans Memorial in Washington, D.C. Her photographic work has been exhibited around the world, and she has received international awards from World Press Photo, Interpress Photo, Leica Inc., and Mid America Arts/National Endowment for the Arts. In 1971, she began a photography and oral history project in Texas with Frederick Baldwin. The Texas project received fellowships from the National Endowment for the Humanities, The Rockefeller Foundation, and several Texas foundations. It resulted in numerous exhibitions and the book *Coming To Terms, The German Hill Country of Texas* (College Station, Texas; Texas A&M Press, 1991). She is a member of the American Leadership Forum and a recipient of the Women on the Move award.

VICKI HARRIS
COORDINATOR, *FREE ELEMENT: THE SEASCAPES OF DODO JIN MING*
Vicki Harris, is the Director of Laurence Miller Gallery, New York. She organized *Free Element: The Seascapes of DoDo Jin Ming* .Vicki Harris received bachelor's and master's degrees in art history from Florida State University, Tallahassee, and moved to New York 15 years ago.

ELLEN MANCHESTER
CO-DIRECTOR, WATER IN THE WEST PROJECT
Ellen Manchester is an arts administrator, photography curator, and environmental activist. She was co-founder and project director of the *Rephotographic Survey Project*, published as *Second View* (Albuquerque: Univ. of Mexico Press, 1984). She and her husband, Robert Dawson, were co-directors of the Water in the West Project. She was a founding board member of Earth Island Institute and has served as a guest curator for the Oakland Museum, Oakland, California; de Young Museum, San Francisco; and numerous non-profit galleries and art centers. She is the author of *Arid Waters: Photographs from the Water in the West Project* (Reno: Univ. of Nevada Press, 1991); photographic editor for the book *Colorado: Visions of an American Landscape* (CCASLA, 1991); and co-curator of the University of Colorado, Boulder, exhibition and book *The Great West: Real/Ideal* (1977).

SCOTT MCLEOD
CURATOR, *SHIPBREAKING*, EDWARD BURTYNSKY
Scott McLeod is the director/curator of the Prefix Institute of Contemporary Art (ICA), Toronto, a nonprofit organization dedicated to the appreciation and understanding of photographic, media, and digital art. In this capacity, he edits and publishes the award-winning periodical Prefix Photo, named Best New Magazine by the National Magazine Awards in 2002. An accomplished artist and composer, he has dedicated much of the past 10 years to facilitating the work of other artists. He has curated more than a dozen exhibitions, including the touring exhibitions *Feeding the Fire and Rare (Ad)diction*, and has authored more than 30 catalogue essays and articles for publishers such as YYZ Books, Warwick Art Centre, and Pleasure Dome. Upcoming curatorial projects include Yael Bartana's *Trembling Time* and Stan Douglas's *Every Building on 100 West Hastings* for Prefix ICA. A member of IKT, International Association of Curators of Contemporary Art, Scott McLeod lives and works in Toronto.

TOMÁS RODRÍGUEZ SOTO
CURATOR, *MEMORÍAS DEL AGUA*, EDGAR MORENO
Tomás Rodríguez Soto was born in Ciudad Bolivar, Venezuela, in 1970. He received a degree in literature from the Universidad Central de Venezuela [Central University of Venezuela], Caracas. He has worked in the Museo de Bellas Artes [Museum of Fine Arts] in Caracas since 1991, holding the positions of assistant curator of photography, curator of photography, director of curatorial works, and currently chief curator of photography. He has curated many exhibitions of photography and has coordinated many national and international projects on photography with accompanying catalogues and publications. He has been a juror on many national prizes, including Premio nacional de fotografía [National Prize for Photography], and the Concurso de fotografía latinoamericana Josune Dorronsoro [Josune Dorronsoro Competition of Lain American Photography] in Caracas. Tomás Rodríguez Soto is a member of the editorial board of the Venezuelan photography magazine *Extra-cámara*.

ACKNOWLEDGEMENTS

FOTOFEST 2004 EXHIBITIONS

Joanna Chain, *Trizec Office Properties*

Elsiau Cozens, *The Menil Collection*

Volker Eisele, *ArtScan Gallery, Houston*

Bob Eury, *Houston Downtown Management District*

Eunice Fang, *Erie City Ironworks*

Bill Franks, *Spire Realty*

Kimberly Gauss, *Crescent Real Estate Equities*

Michael Golden, *Art Department, Houston Community College, Central Campus*

Jennifer Greene, *Water Institute of Blue Hill, Maine*

Joyce Harberson, *Reliant Energy Plaza, Houston*

Guy Hagstette, *Houston Downtown Management District*

James and Ann Harithas, *The Station, Houston*

Janet Heitmiller, *University of Houston Downtown*

Tex Kerschen, *The Station*

Jane Kim, *Gallery Xippas, Paris*

Julie Kinzelman, *Kinzelman Art Consulting and McCord Development Inc., Houston*

Institute for Flow Sciences, *Wolfram Schwenk, Andreas Wilkens*

Rick Lowe, *Project Row Houses, Houston*

Scott McCloud, *Editor, Prefix Photo*

Anne Olson, *Buffalo Bayou Partnership, Houston*

Yolanda Londoño, *J.P. Morgan Chase Bank, Houston*

Armando Palacios and Cinda Ward, *New World Museum, Houston*

Winifred Riser, *Buffalo Bayou Partnership, Houston*

Brett Rogers, *British Art Council*

Sally Sprout, *Williams Tower Gallery, Houston*

Frank Staats, *Crescent Real Estate Equities*

Ernest Thompson, *Vine Street Studios, Houston*

Mark L. Tompkins, *McCord Development*

Joel Savary, *Cultural Attache, The French Consulate, Houston*

Denis Simmoneau, *Consul General, The French Consulate, Houston*

Fletcher Thorne-Thomsen, Jr., *Vine Street Studios*

Aaron Tuley, *Buffalo Bayou Partnership, Houston*

Kaveh Kane Coffee, Houston

Rhonda Wilson, *Rhubarb*

Geoff Winningham, *Department of Visual Arts, Rice University*

2004 BIENNIAL SPECIAL EVENTS

Dr. John and Beverly Berry

Julie and Markley Crosswell

Cherry Eno, *Greater Houston Convention and Visitors Bureau*

ArtsHouston, *Chas Haynes, Rosemary Panacanti and Molly McBurney*

Anthony Martinez, *The Menil Collection*

Apama Mackey, *MacKay Gallery*

Bill Thomas, *Photography Department, University of Houston-Central*

Deborah Velders, *The Menil Collection*

Libby Weathers, *D.E.D.A. and The Main Event*

Jill Wood, *Lawndale Art Center, Houston*

Anderson Wrangle, *Artist, Houston*

SPECIAL PROGRAMS

Lucinda Cobley

Keith Hollingsworth, *Hollingsworth Art Services, Houston*

David Lerch, *Axiom Design Group, Houston*

Haesun Kim Lerch, *Mountain Dog Design, Houston*

Lisa Lerch, *Production Artist, Houston*

Jim Walker, *Earth Color, Houston*

David Tarnowski, Sr., *Masterpiece Litho Houston*

David Tarnowski, Jr., *Masterpiece Litho*
Houston

THE GLOBAL FORUM

ORGANIZING COMMITTEE

James Blackburn, *Blackburn &
Carter LLP, Houston*

Dr. Paul Harcombe, *Center for the
Study of Society and the Environment,
Rice University*

Dr. Walter Isle, *Center for the Study
of Society and the Environment, Rice
University*

Dr. Neal Lane, *James A. Baker
Institute, Rice University*

Dr. Mark Wiesner, *Environmental
and Energy Systems Institute, Rice
University*

Christian Holmes, *Shell Center for
Sustainability, Rice University*

Janice Van Dyke Walden, *Van Dyke
Walden Assocs.*

Dale Cordray, *Blackburn & Carter,
Houston*

Clayton Forswall, *Rice University, Houston*

Christine Gardner, *Rice University,
Houston*

Karen and Arnaud Dasprez, *Manzanita
Creative, Houston*

David Gresham, *Citizens Environmental
Coalition*

Terry Hershey

Wendy Kelsey

Mary Stark Love

Ann Olsen, *Buffalo Bayou Partnership,
Houston*

Aaron Tuley, *Buffalo Bayou Partnership,
Houston*

Mary Ellen Whitworth, *Bayou
Preservation Association, Houston*

Megan Wilde, *Rice Univesity, Houston*

AUCTION COMMITTEE

Susie and Sanford Criner, *Chairpersons,
2004 Fine Print Auction*

Denise Bethel, Auctioneer, *Vice President
of, Department of Photography, Sotheby's Inc.*

Garry Bauman, *The Warwick Hotel*

Allison Ayers

Franny Koelsch, *koelsch gallery*

Maria Ines Sicardi, *Sicardi Gallery*

Kimberly Gremillion, *Gremillion & Co.
Fine Art*

W.H. Hunt, *Ricco-Maresca Gallery*

Joseph Bock

Mike Cades

Beth Carls

Rose Cullinan Hock

Susan Davis

Nancy Dukler

Linda Foot

Irene Liberatos

Stephen Longoria

Amy Looper

Sharon Lynn

Melissa Martinez

Ken and Nancy Parker

Leila Perrin

Marilyn Perry

Nancy Rhodes

Arturo Sánchez

Lorna Schnase

María Ines Sicardi

Royce Ann Sline

Vanita Smithey

Mary Stark Love

Heidi Straube

Jennifer Vodvarka

MEETING PLACE VOLUNTEERS

Larry Albert

Cyndy Allard

Tiina Anttila

David Britton

Barbara Busbey

Lucinda Cobley

Susan Davis

Duane Douthit

Nancy Dukler

Travis Errard

Sarah Fenoglio

Linda Foot

Karla Held

Carola Herrin

John Herrin

Rose Cullinan Hock

Sandra Holland

Judy Hungerford

Bert Hungerford

Jill Hunter

Steve Laedtke

Danielle Lemuth

Mary Stark Love

Mickey Marvins

Melissa M. Martinez

Evan Miller

Betty Mooney

Jake Mooney

Nancy Parker

Ken Parker

Paul Perez

Eduoard A. Philippe

Heather Reynolds

Alma Rosas

Ana Carolina Sánchez

J.J. Savarino

Royce Ann Sline

Oluwole Sokoya

Janice Stacy

Heidi Straube

Ellis Vener

Brian Viney

Ann Williams

Dave Wilson

2004 MEETING PLACE REVIEWERS

Darsie Alexander, Baltimore, MD

Kostis Antoniadis, Thessaloniki, Greece

Kathy Aron Dowell, Kansas City, MO

Joe R. Arredondo, Lubbock, TX

Pascal Beausse, Paris, France

Linda Benedict-Jones, Pittsburgh, PA

Lucia Benická, POPRAD, Slovakia

John Bennette, New York, NY

Gay Block, Santa Fe, NM

Sian Bonnell,Weymouth, Dorset, U.K.

Sue Brisk, New York, NY

Stephen Bulger , Toronto, Ontario, Canada

Marilyn Cadenbach, Cambridge, Massachusetts and New York, NY

MaryAnn Camilleri, New York, NY

Xavier Canonne & Marc Vausort, Charleroi, Belgium

Jean Caslin, Houston, TX

Alejandro Castellanos, Mexico City, México

Fernando Castro, Houston, TX

Beate Cegielska, Arhus, Denmark

Gary Miles Chassman, Burlington, VT

Darren Ching, New York, NY

Brian Paul Clamp, New York, NY

John M. Cleary, Houston, TX

David Coleman, Austin, TX

Christopher Coppock, Wales, U. K.

Charlotte Cotton, London, U. K.

Alan Dorow, Silver Spring, MD

Janet Dwoskin, San Francisco, CA

Catherine Evans, Columbus, OH

Burt Finger, Dallas, TX

Missy Finger, Dallas, TX

Blake Fitch, Winchester, MA

Roy Flukinger, Austin, TX

Alasdair Foster, Sydney NSW Australia

Christine Frisinghelli, Graz, Austria

Juan Alberto Gaviria, Medellin, Columbia

Gail G. Gibson, Seattle, WA

Marnie Gillett, San Francisco, CA

William Greiner, New Orleans, LA

Anna Gripp, Hamburg, Germany

Meg Handler, New York, NY

Elda Harrington, Buenos Aires, Argentina

Gary Hesse, Syracuse, NY

Eva Marlene Hodek, Prague, Czech Republic

W.M. Hunt, New York, NY

Karen Irvine, Chicago, IL

Fran Kaufman, New York City, NY

Sarah Kehoe, San Francisco, CA

Kay Kenny, New York City, NY

Julie Kinzelman, Houston, TX

Michael Koetzle, Munich, Germany

Dewi Lewis, Manchester, U.K.

Kevin Longino, Houston, TX

Jan-Erik Lundström, Umeå, Sweden

Celina Lunsford, Frankfurt am Main, Germany

Vaclav Macek, Bratislava, Slovakia

James Maloney, Houston, TX

Lesley A. Martin, New York, NY

Aleksander Matczewski, Kraków, Poland

Tanya Mathis, Boston, MA

Scott McLeod, Toronto, Canada

Anne McNeill, York, U.K.

Kate Menconeri, Woodstock, NY

Michel Métayer, Toulouse, France

Niki Michelin, London, U.K.

Kevin Miller, Daytona Beach, FL

Yossi Milo, New York, NY

Sarah Motherland, New York, NY

Joan Morgenstern, Houston, TX

Andreas Mueller-Pohle, Berlin, Germany

Mathias Niehoff, Berlin, Germany

Ute Noll, Frankfurt, Germany

Alison Devine Nordström, Rochester, NY

Edward J. Osowski, Houston, TX

Deborah Paine, Seattle, WA

Joaquim Paiva, Brazilia, Brazil

Ann Pallesen, Seattle, WA

Lee Ann Peavy, Mason, TX

Stephen Perloff, Langhorne, PA

Gus Powell, New York, NY

Alan E. Rapp, San Francisco, CA

Christopher Rauschenberg, Portland, OR

Rixon Reed, Santa Fe, NM

Miriam Romais, Bronx, NY

Judith Rosenbaum, New York, NY

Francois Saint Pierre, Lectoure, France

Joël Savary, Houston, TX

Rudolf Scheutle, Munich, Germany

Thomas Seelig, Winterthur, Switzerland

Ariel Shanberg, Woodstock, NY

George Slade, Minneapolis, MN

Mark Sloan, Charleston, SC

Mary Virginia Swanson, Tucson, AZ

Barbara Tannenbaum, Akron, OH

Finn Thrane, Odense, Denmark

Jimo Toyin Salako, London, U.K.

Juan Travnik, Buenos Aires, Argentina

Anne Wilkes Tucker, Houston, TX

Ricardo Viera, Bethlehem, PA

Enrica Viganò, Milano, Italy

Lynne Warberg Nations, Sarasota, FL

Katherine Ware, Philadelphia, PA

Clint Willour, Galveston, TX

Rhonda Wilson, Birmingham, U.K.

Tim B. Wride, Los Angeles, CA

Cynthia Young, New York, NY

Marilyn A. Zeitlin, Tempe, AZ

Manfred Zollner, Hamburg, Germany

BIENNIAL VOLUNTEERS

Steven Longoria

Amelia Jayanaty

Danielle Jayanty

Justin Ward

PRESS

Dancie Peruginni Public Relations, Houston

    Marta Fredricks

    Christy Guth

    Jami Mabile

Janice Van Dyke Walden, *Van Dyke Walden Assocs.*

Bill Dawson

Rene Magdaleno

Haesun Kim Lerch

FILM AND VIDEO

Diane Barber, *Visual Arts Director, DiverseWorks Art Space*

Frankie Black, *KUHT-Houston PBS*

Serena Lin Bush

Charles Dove, *Rice Cinema Director, Rice University Media Center*

Sarah Gish, *Gish Creative*

Meg Glew, *Aue Design Studio*

Andrea Grover, *Executive Director, Aurora Picture Show*

Papa Josh, *Promotions Director, Alamo Drafthouse Cinema*

Sara Kellner, *Executive Director, DiverseWorks ArtSpace*

Chelby King, *Executive Director, Lawndale Art Center*

Patrick Kwiatkowski, *Co-Founder, Microcinema International*

Carlos Lama, *Volunteer Coordinator, Aurora Picture Show*

Mary Lampe, *Southwest Alternate Media Project*

Mark Larsen, *Founder, The Artery*

Ken Lawrence, *Director of Programming, KUHT-Houston PBS*

Megan Lembeke, *Promotions & Community Relations Manager, Angelika Film Center*

Toby Lister, *Co-Owner, Dean's Credit Clothing*

Marian Luntz, *Curator of Film and Video, Museum of Fine Arts, Houston*

Nusrat Malik, *Managing Director, Voices Breaking Boundaries*

Mohit Mehta, *Voices Breaking Boundaries*

Sehba Sarwar, *Artistic Director, Voices Breaking Boundaries*

Gina Sonderegger, *Development Assistant, DiverseWorks ArtSpace*

Jennifer Sukis, *Aue Design Studio*

David Wilcox

Jill Wood, *Assistant Director, Exhibitions and Programming, Lawndale Art Center*

LTP 2004 BIENNIAL PROGRAMMING

Kristopher Benson, *NOAA Fisheries Restoration Center*

Buffalo Bayou Partnership

Mark Cervenka, *O'Kane Gallery, UHD*

Fuji Photo Film USA, Inc.

Galveston Bay Estuary Program

Galveston Bay Foundation's Bay Ambassador Program

Galveston Independent School District

Peter Goin, *Photographer*

Wanda Hammerbeck, *Photographer*

Harris County Department of Education, CASE

Sant Khalsa, *Photographer*

Karla Klay, *The Artist Boat*

Ellen Land-Weber, *Photographer*

Lone Star Chapter of the Sierra Club

Mark Nelson, *Photographer*

Tina Proctor, *The Artist Boat*

Dr. Robert Sanborn, *Education Foundation of Harris County*

Linda Shead, *The Trust for Public Land*

Martin Stupich, *Photographer*

University of Houston Downtown

Upper Texas Coast Water-Borne Education Center

UTMB NIEHS Center / Sealy Center for Environmental Health and Medicine

LTP GENERAL PROGRAMMING

Shannon Bishop, *Harris County Department of Education, CASE*

Meredith Bossin, *LTP Intern*

Blair Bouchier, *Manzanita Alliance*

Lisa Caruthers, *Harris County Department of Education, CASE*

Darlene Casas, *HISD–Central District*

Maria DeLeon, *Harris County Department of Education, CASE*

Megan Doherty, *LTP Intern*

Ted Estrada, *Jefferson Davis High School*

Kelly Farmer, *Ketelsen Elementary School*

GoBase2

Marian Harper, *Houston Astros*

Lisa Hooten, *Project GRAD Fine Arts Program*

Catherine Ketelson, *Project GRAD*

David Lerch, *Axiom Design Houston*

Danielle Nygren, *LTP Intern*

Ernest Ortiz, *HISD–North District*

Ann Parker, *Project GRAD Fine Arts Program*

Ping's Design Studio

PARTICIPATING SPACES—FOTOFEST 2004

Since the beginning of FotoFest Biennials in 1986, the participation of Houston's museums, galleries, artist and educational organizations, corporate and retail spaces have been essential to the breadth and diversity of the citywide Biennial. The range of artists and participating spaces is a testament to the vitality of the arts in Houston and the creative energy of the city. It is also a reflection of the growing number of artists who are choosing to study and work in Houston. The active inter-relationship of educational institutions, artist spaces, commercial galleries, and museums is essential to building and maintaining strong art communities in an urban environment. Government and corporations are key to the promotion and visibility of the arts in an urban environment. Art is not a marginal element in urban life, it is essential to a city's ability to creatively confront its own future.

FotoFest 2004

CONTENTS

1

MUSEUMS AND UNIVERSITIES

MUSEUMS AND UNIVERSITIES 1

MANUAL: TWO WORLDS

The Collaboration of Ed Hill and Suzanne Bloom

ARTISTS: MANUAL (ED HILL AND SUZANNE BLOOM)

The phrase "new media" is widely used to designate electronic artworks that depart from conventional media. While the term is relatively recent, in many respects Suzanne Bloom and Ed Hill have been making new media for over a quarter century. *MANUAL: Two Worlds—The Collaboration of Ed Hill and Suzanne Bloom* brings together more than 100 works in a range of media including traditional and digital photography, video, and digital animation.

Lovis Corinth in Vermont is a seminal work from an equally seminal series, *Art in Context: Homage to Walter Benjamin*, a group of images begun at the very beginning of MANUAL career and continued into the early 1980's. The image is unique among the series in its incorporation of an original drawing rather than a reproduction or simulation of a famous artwork. The framed drawing, an actual graphite self-portrait by German pre-Expressionist artist Lovis Corinth, has been removed from the gallery wall, taken outdoors, and tied to a birch tree whose trunk is wrapped in the arms of a teenage boy wearing a new soccer shirt. The effect is a mood of contrasts created by the dim light of the woods, the soft shades of the framed picture, and the bold stripes of the jersey. The drawing—and the art of *drawing* itself—is bound to nature while simultaneously being embraced by the personified "younger" art of *photography*, who wears the expressive portrait as a mask.

This retrospective, the first comprehensive assessment of MANUAL's 30-year collaboration, was curated by Edward W. Earle and organized by the International Center of Photography in New York, where it was presented in 2002. Anne Wilkes Tucker, The Gus and Lyndall Wortham Curator of Photography at the Museum of Fine Arts, Houston, is the coordinating curator in Houston.

Anne Wilkes Tucker
Museum of Fine Arts, Houston

Edward W. Earle
International Center of Photography, New York

MANUAL • *Lovis Corinth in Vermont* from the series *Art in Context*, 1974 •
Toned Silver Gelatin Print

HUNGARIAN AVANT-GARDE PHOTOGRAPHERS
from The Manfred Heiting Collection

ARTISTS: GROUP SHOW

Modern Hungarian photography developed primarily in the 1920s, with photographers such as István Hanga, Imre Kinszki and Kata Kálmán working well into the 1930s. The works on display reveal that Hungarian photographers were connected to the modern artistic and aesthetic dialogues occurring in Europe at the time. While increasingly interested in sharp images that were often in the documentary genre, the photographs often focus on dramatic shadows or feature unusual perspectives to energize an image. At times, the images produced using these techniques moved the images toward abstraction. While capturing casual street scenes and everyday objects, and documenting roaring locomotives as well as modern architectural elements, these photographers favored strong, design-oriented compositions. The 35 photographs on display at the Museum of Fine Arts, Houston, March 1, 2004 - May 23, 2004, represent a generation of Hungarian photographers whose works exhibit, both aesthetically and in their choice of subject matter, a concern with the modern.

Marisa Sanchéz
Museum of Fine Arts, Houston

IMRE KINSZKI, HUNGARIAN, 1901-1945 • *MAN ON A SWINGBOAT*, 1930S • SILVER GELATIN PRINT
GIFT OF MANFRED HEITING, THE MANFRED HEITING COLLECTION

LUISA LAMBRI: LOCATIONS

ARTIST: LUISA LAMBRI

At first glance, Luisa Lambri's photographs of architectural interiors might appear to be yet another example of the austere, depopulated spaces found in much of today's photo-based work. They are, however, eminently different in both conception and execution, at once deeply personal and ethereal, rather than wholly impartial and concrete; they are suffused with a delicacy and intimacy that is diametrically opposed to the stark realism found in the works, for example, of Thomas Ruff or Candida Höfer. Since Luisa Lambri initiated what has become a sustained engagement with modernist architecture and photography in 1997, she has endeavored to strike a subtle balance between objectivity and subjectivity, creating interpretations of spaces rather than documents of them, eliciting something minimal, abstract, and nonspecific that is imprinted by memory and desire.

Born in Como, Italy, in 1969, Luisa Lambri studied languages and literature at universities in Milan and Bologna, Italy, and now resides in Berlin and Milan. Her inventory of projects include Le Corbusier's apartment blocks in Chandigarh, India (1997); Alvar Aalto's Finlandia Hall in Helsinki (1998); Wittgenstein House in Vienna (1999); Mies van der Rohe's Villa Tugendhat in Brno, Czech Republic (1999); and two Richard Neutra houses in Palm Springs, California (2002).

For The Menil Collection, Luisa Lambri has been commissioned to photograph the residence designed by Philip Johnson for John and Dominique de Menil in 1951. This new work will be presented along with a selection of previously unpublished projects, including Richard Neutra's Strathmore Apartments in Los Angeles and Oscar Niemeyer's house in Rio de Janeiro, Brazil. *Luisa Lambri: Locations* is organized by Matthew Drutt and will be accompanied by a fully illustrated catalogue.

Matthew Drutt   **Andriano Pedrosa**
The Menil Collection

LUISA LAMBRI • UNTITLED (*MENIL HOUSE #1*), 2002 • LASERCHROME PRINT

MUSEUMS AND UNIVERSITIES

SHARPENING THE POINT

University of Houston Photography and Digital Media Graduate Thesis Show

ARTISTS: WALT BISTLINE, LAURIE EMERY, JASON NEUMANN, BONNIE NEWMAN, SOODY SHARIFI, CHRISTOPHER TALBOT

This exhibit presents work by six members of the Master of Fine Art program in Photography and Digital Media at the University of Houston, held in conjunction with the University's 2004 MFA Thesis Show.

COASTAL ESSENCE

Exploring the Texas Gulf Coast Photographs by Jim Olive

ARTIST: JIM OLIVE

While giving life and sustenance to plants, animals, and people, the bays and estuaries of Texas have other stories to tell—stories about freshwater inflows, deep port construction, disappearing oyster beds, beach resorts, and pollution control. At a certain point, each story brings opposing forces in play to debate the future of some of our most valuable and irreplaceable resources. The images in this exhibition are a tribute to the Texas coast and to those who work to sensibly use and preserve it.

Jim Olive's stunning photographs present us with a dramatic perspective on our life along the ocean and remind us of both the grandness and the fragility of our coastal treasures. The works in this exhibition were originally created for the Galveston Bay Conservation and Preservation Association and are included in *The Book of Texas Bays* by Jim Blackburn, with photographs by Jim Olive. The book will be published in Fall 2004 by Texas A&M University Press in College Station.

A native Houstonian, Jim Olive has relentlessly examined and photographed the city's development and growth. He is a life member of the Galveston Bay Foundation and actively promotes the preservation and conservation of endangered coastal ecosystems.

Jim Blackburn

The Houston Museum of Natural Science exhibition is underwritten by Houston Endowment Inc.

JIM OLIVE • *COLD PASS*, 2000 • C-PRINT

JOHN HEARTFIELD

Photomontage and the Art of Resistance

ARTIST: JOHN HEARTFIELD

John Heartfield's photomontages provide a clever commentary on his era. During the 1930s, his works challenged Hitler and the Nazi party. This collection of his work, owned by the Museum of Fine Arts, Houston, shows how the main modernist movements of the day, Expressionism, Cubism, and Futurism, influenced John Heartfield and were incorporated into his montages.

Steve Johnson

JOHN HEARTFIELD • *AND AFTER HITLER'S OFFERS OF PEACE, THERE "EVENTUALLY" FOLLOW HIS DOVES OF PEACE*, 1936 • PHOTOMONTAGE MAGAZINE COVER

THERE IS NO WHY HERE

ARTIST: KARL KOENIG

Artist Karl Koenig uses his discerning photographic eye and the remarkable effects of his gumoil printing technique to explore the architectural remains of the Nazi concentration camps. His photographic style and expressive print-making method allow him to offer a unique interpretation of what these buildings may have been like for the condemned, however brief and/or painful their experiences were. Not incidentally, the pictures also suggest what a dehumanizing existence it would have been for many of the imprisoned.

Karl Koenig

KARL KOENIG • *THE SS FIRE BRIGADE'S WATER SUPPLY DISGUISED TO LOOK LIKE A PRISONERS' SWIMMING POOL*, AUSCHWITZ, POLAND, 2000 • GUMOIL PHOTOGRAPHIC PRINT

MUSEUMS AND UNIVERSITIES

DOWN IN HOUSTON

Documenting a Blues Community — James Fraher, Roger Woods

ARTIST: JAMES FRAHER

In the clubs, ballrooms, and barbecue joints of neighborhoods such as Third Ward, Frenchtown, Sunnyside, and Double Bayou, Houston's African-American community gave birth to a vibrant and unique slice of the blues. Ranging from the down-home sounds of Lightnin' Hopkins to the more refined orchestrations of the Duke-Peacock recording empire and beyond, Houston blues was and is the voice of a working class community, an ongoing conversation about good times and hard times, smokin' Saturday nights and Blue Mondays.

Since 1995, Roger Wood and James Fraher have been gathering the story of the blues in Houston. In their book *Down in Houston: Bayou City Blues* (Austin: University of Texas Press, 2003), they draw on dozens of interviews with blues musicians, club owners, audience members, and music producers, as well as dramatic black and white photographs of performers and venues, to present a lovingly detailed portrait of the Houston blues scene, past and present. Text by Roger Wood accompanies the photographs.

Roger Wood

JAMES FRAHER • *HENRY HAYES AT HOME THIRD WARD*, 1997 • SILVER GELATIN PRINT

A FLUID HISTORY

Water Under the Big Sky

ARTIST: MARCY JAMES

Nestled below the crest of the Continental Divide in Montana, the city of Butte once rivaled Chicago as a thriving center of commerce and culture. From the mid 19th century to the 1980s, the extraction of gold, silver, and copper created fortunes for men and women who built imposing mansions, hotels, banks, shops, and civic buildings over and around the mines of the city. Although protected as national landmarks, most of the stately structures have been boarded up. The abandoned mineshafts and the enormous open pit mine, the Berkeley Pit, are so utterly polluted that Butte is now considered one of the largest Superfund sites in the United States

In 1997, photographer Marcy James arrived in Butte to explore the history of "the richest hill on earth." To fix the haunting emptiness of the private, interior spaces of historic Butte, she works alone in darkness. She actively participates in the illumination of the architectural details and human detritus of the past by setting a long exposure on her medium format 2 1/4 Pentacon and walking through the picture with artificial light. For the public facades of these magnificent buildings, Mary James uses her homemade pinhole cameras. Found pieces of transparent material, such as glass, paper, or fabric, become the lens for her exposures of the raw building fronts. Recently, she has turned her attention to the contaminated natural settings for these manmade constructions. The hollowed out passages under Butte are filled with poisonous water, and at the site of Montana's deepest body of water, the Berkeley Pit, toxic water percolates up through the deserted mineshafts. Standing on the arid surface of Butte's city streets, Mary James is photographing through lenses of water to evoke the precarious foundation of Butte's future.

Valerie Hedquist, Ph.D.
University of Montana, Missoula

MARCY JAMES • *CONTINENTAL PIT, VIEW FROM THE LANDSLIDE*, 2003 • PINHOLE CAMERA • CIBACHROME

WALKING IN THE FOOTSTEPS

ARTIST: STEPHEN MARC

Stephen Marc is a photographer/digital montage artist whose work has focused on exploring the African diaspora in a personal search and cultural affirmation of his extended community. His work varies from the traditional black and white documentary photography in the series *The Black Trans-Atlantic Experience*, his investigation of Ghana, Jamaica, England, and the United States, to Soul Searching, a surreal patterned digital weaving of family, found antiques, and self-portraits with scanned objects, drawings, and sections of his documentary photographs.

Since 2000, Stephen Marc has been photographing sites connected to the Underground Railroad, following the routes that fugitive slaves traveled to freedom prior to the Civil War and emancipation. The resulting work is a digital documentary series of composites and montages, describing the Railroad through a strategy that is both factual and metaphorical. The Railroad composites use several angles and views to describe the individual stations that provided shelter. The different images depict hiding places, tunnels, and other significant features in order to provide interpretative overviews of these sites. The montages metaphorically blend together images that address the Railroad and slavery with other references to the African diaspora and contemporary culture. The supplementary role of the montages is to inform the audience regarding the complex nature of the Railroad, which required tactics of concealment, disguise, and evasion (including organized misdirection), as well as the use of secret codes and signals.

Stephen Marc

STEPHEN MARC • UNTITLED, 2002 • DIGITAL MONTAGE, ARCHIVAL PIGMENT

TROY HUECHTKER

ARTIST: TROY HUECHTKER

Troy Huechtker's stunning photographs mesmerize the viewer with their marvelously abstracted images and sensuously rich color. Although visually reminiscent of modernist Color Field paintings, his work is not about the existential transcendence of painterly compositions but is unabashedly a celebration of beauty. However, the creative and cognitive processes that he employs to produce his photographs complicates this sensibility of what some might perceive as mere beauty.

Troy Huechtker's *Untitled Series* consists of images from the 2001 World Series between the New York Yankees and Arizona Diamondbacks. He photographed his television set while the games were being broadcast, yet the final images obscure their origin. The singular moment of capturing a play to broadcast it to televisions across America results from fast-paced production decisions and satellite feeds. While Troy Huechtker's photographs document the live transmission of the baseball game, his use of long exposure times layered the transmitted images, thereby abstracting the composition and obfuscating the concept of time and space. Only the occasional lines of static and reflected images of the artist photographing betray that he shot the images from the television. The final photographs do not document an event or present moment; rather, they convey the dynamism of the game in play, fans cheering, and advertisements flashing. This simulacrum of images invites the viewers to look and then speculate, discovering their own visceral and intellectual reactions to the works.

Equally tantalizing is Troy Huechtker's *Preterition Series:* an exploration of the unseen and overlooked banalities of daily life. In this body of work, he photographed used as well as disregarded domestic items and spaces, including bedsheets, beds, furniture, appliances, and banal household objects. Similar to the previous series, these seductive photographs are abstracted images that cause the viewer to question the referent. The muted light and seemingly silhouetted images provoke the viewer's curiosity and a desire to gaze at the enticing compositions: the images actually appear to be mystical and ethereal landscapes. The enchanting quality of this series makes the photographs less about documenting domestic space and more about the presentation and reception of beauty. Troy Huechtker invites viewers to daydream and create their own narrative.

The captivating quality in Troy Huechtker's oeuvre is that each photograph presents imagery suggesting its own cosmology. This ephemeral imagery invites the viewer to gaze, dream, and contemplate. The viewer is an active participant, not just a voyeur looking through a window. Seeing his work in a gallery, where the viewer is forced to deal with the glare of the walls and the "white cube" environment of the gallery space, while the inaccessible worlds in the photographs are safely ensconced in their frames, makes Troy Huechtker's photographs all the more seductive: the desire of wanting something unobtainable.

Jennifer Vanderpool

TROY HUECHTKER • *UNTITLED SERIES,* 2002 • C-PRINT

NON-PROFIT SPACES

NON-PROFIT SPACES 2

WE ARE THE CAMERA

ARTISTS: F&D CARTIER AND JOY GREGORY

All three artists in this exhibition work without a camera, creating one-of-a-kind photograms by placing objects directly on light sensitive paper and exposing it to natural light.

Symbolizing the "absent body," f&d cartiers' photograms reflect on gender roles and conjure thoughts of femininity. By recording feminine objects, such as handmade Barbie clothes in the series *Someday*, the Cartiers investigate the emphasis placed on exterior beauty, idealization of the female image, and the role of dress as a social indicator. In another series, *Boys Do Not Cry*, images of delicate handkerchiefs bring to mind societal restrictions on gender. Their conscious mishandling of the chemistry while developing the gelatin silver paper results in their signature rose-toned work.

Joy Gregory, a black artist of Jamaican descent, investigates her heritage and the Apartheid by creating images representing the discarded luxury of English colonials in *The Handbag Project*. While on a residency in South Africa, Gregory was able to hear first-hand accounts by local people of life in a colonized society. Armed with this knowledge, she began scouring second-hand stores and came upon accessories once owned by wealthy British women. Gregory began creating photograms that accentuate the aesthetic quality of the handbags and gloves, but

symbolize the wealth and oppression of colonization. Joy Gregory creates one-of-a-kind images by using a unique salt formula she developed that gives her work the abstract effect of translucency.

Houston Center for Photography

F&D CARTIER • *SOPHIA FROM THE SERIES SOMEDAY...,2001* •
PHOTOGRAM

JOY GREGORY • *THE HANDBAG PROJECT SERIES, #1*, 2000 • SALT PRINT PHOTOGRAM

BERTHA ALYCE

A Photographic Biography

ARTIST: GAY BLOCK

Bertha Alyce: A Photographic Biography is a remembrance in words and pictures of the artist's mother. It also serves as an outline of Gay Block's quest to forgive and understand this difficult woman. Confronting her own emotions, Block deconstructs their past relationship, recalling certain events, memories, and conversations. Working on this project for over 30 years, Gay Block has examined human behavior and illustrated her encounter with anger, grief, and forgiveness. This interactive installation features excerpts from Gay Block's award-winning DVD as well as text from the accompanying book, *Bertha Alyce: Mother Exposed* (Albuquerque: University of New Mexico Press, 2003), and includes appropriated images from the family archives. *Bertha Alyce: A Photographic Biography* was curated by Kathleen Howe for the University of New Mexico Art Museum, Albuquerque.

Houston Center for Photography

GAY BLOCK • *MOTHER AT HER 70TH BIRTHDAY PARTY*, 1983-93 • EKTACOLOR PRINT

WOMEN ON THE VERGE OF SOMETHING ELSE

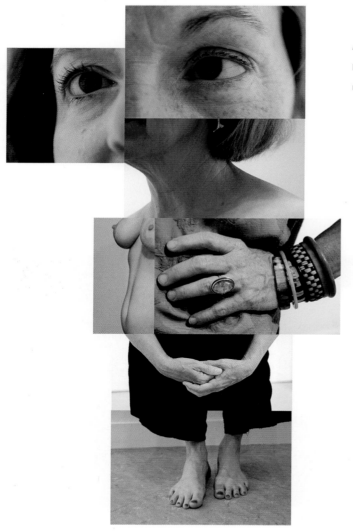

ARTISTS: JEAN CASLIN, MARY MARGARET HANSEN, MAUD LIPSCOMB, BETSY L. SIEGEL, JANICE RUBIN, CAROL VUCHETICH.

JANICE RUBIN • *SIX WOMEN TRANSFORMING,* 2003 • PIGMENTED INK

PG-13

Male Adolescent Identity in the Age of Video Culture

ARTISTS: JANET BIGGS AND BARBARA POLLACK

Power and control, release and chaos—the conflicting impulses fundamental to the male adolescent experience are the primary subjects of this exhibition by video artists Janet Biggs and Barbara Pollack. *PG-13: Male Adolescent Identity in the Age of Video Culture* examines male adolescent experience as represented by, and in contrast to, mainstream popular culture. Using striking juxtapositions of imagery and sound, Pollack and Biggs create a powerful, often unsettling look at how gender is constructed and enacted by preadolescent boys mimicking and embodying expectations of masculinity engendered by sports, video games, and music videos.

Gregory creates one-of-a-kind images by using a unique salt formula she developed that gives her work the abstract effect of translucency.

Diane Barber
DiverseWorks Art Space, Houston

BARBARA POLLACK • *PERFECT DARK*, 2001 • VIDEO STILL

Janet Biggs • *Ritalin*, 2000 • Four-channel video installation • Photo by Owen Slon

NON-PROFIT SPACES

TRANSMIT II

ARTIST: SUSAN DUNKERLEY

Transmit II is an installation of steel-encased, ingotlike slabs of stained glass onto which images have been printed or sandblasted. Each piece is suspended from the ceiling by a stainless steel cable. The collective creates a grove that visitors may freely enter and exit.

Transparency allows for looking within, between, through, and beyond the actual surfaces. Once useful but now forgotten cups, bowls, cutlery, and teapots inhabit the tangled undergrowth of old bottle dumps, crumbling foundations, and abandoned kitchen gardens. Somewhere within this viny and brambled landscape, I am convinced, lie traces of the heart's desires and other such nonsense.

Susan Dunkerley

SUSAN DUNKERLEY • *TWIN BOWLS (VIEW TWO)*, 2003 • SILVER GELATIN EMULSION, ETCHED AND SANDBLASTED STAINED GLASS, GRAPHITE, STAINLESS CABLE, AND STEEL

DEEP EAST TEXAS

ARTIST: MISTY KEASLER

*D**eep East Texas** represents a personal, ongoing document of Misty Keasler's family. It explores familial surroundings in a rural, southern gothic land not too far from the metropolis of Dallas.

Misty Keasler

MISTY KEASLER • *DUCK HUNTING*, 2003 • CHROMOGENIC PHOTOGRAPH
COURTESY OF PHOTOGRAPHS DO NOT BEND GALLERY, DALLAS

CREW

The Men of the U.S.S. Texas

ARTIST: WILL MICHELS

She was a ship — the smartest man o'war afloat, and the best.
A hard, tough, salty, shootin', steamin', fool.
A trophy grabber, a fighter and a he-man battlewagon.

Lieutenant Paul Schubert
U.S.S. Texas Veteran: 1915–1918

I met Bill Reed while working as project architect in charge of the restoration of the battleship Texas. Assigned to Division II during the Second World War, Reed toured me around his former duty stations. He took the time to point out his sleeping quarters. He described the importance of hospital corners at inspection and finished by explaining the trick to climbing onto the second-to-top rack without disturbing his fellow shipmates. Reed was the first crewman I interviewed and the one who taught me that the TEXAS was made of people, not rivets. I feel fortunate to have met and learned from him, although I regret not having the opportunity to take his portrait. Seaman First Class William Reed died three weeks after our meeting.

CREW: The Men of the U.S.S. TEXAS is the culmination of a seven-year photographic and oral history project to document the former crew of the battleship Texas. I started taking these portraits to keep my memory sharp. I wanted to remember this crew, a crew who had shared an experience that I could only imagine. These photographs are my effort to share with others this group of civilians, Marines, and sailors. People who once manned the guns and swabbed the decks of a mighty ship. My hope is that other people will enjoy their faces as much as I enjoyed meeting these men.

Will Michels

WILL MICHELS • *BEURON BOYD – YEOMAN SECOND CLASS, U.S.S. TEXAS VETERAN: 1943-1944*, 1996 • SILVER GELATIN PRINT

GROUP SHOW

ARTISTS: SUZANNE BANNING, CHRISTOPHER OLIVIER, IRENE CLOUTHIER
CARRILLO, DYLAN VITONE

IRENE CLOUTHIER CARRILLO • *BRIDE AND BUTTONS*, 2002 • DIGITAL PRINT/PLEXIGLASS

NON-PROFIT SPACES

DOUBLE LIFE

Gallery: Mezzanine

ARTIST: KELLI CONNELL

In *Double Life*, Denton, Texas-based photographer Kelli Connell exhibits color photographs created by using multiple negatives to construct hypothetical narratives between a model and the model's double. Connell is interested in the dynamics between people as defined by a given situation, particularly roles formed during interpersonal relationships. Whether her model is crying at breakfast with her double, playing strip poker with her quadruples, or seducing herself in a convertible, the artist depicts a wide range of universal occurrences involving intimacy. As her model takes on seemingly infinite familiar roles, the mutability of our own behavior within relationships is hyperbolized.

KELLI CONNELL • *CRYING AT BREAKFAST*, 2002 • CHROMOGENIC PRINTS

ENTRANCE

Gallery: Small

ARTIST: SUSAN SIMMONS

In Lawndale's Small Gallery, Susan Simmons's exhibits *Entrance*, an installation about road travel at dusk that uses video stills, video projection, paintings, and sound. In Simmons's work, journeying by car is a distillation of the experience of time itself, both lightning-paced and halted by the awareness of an image, sound, or event, something that provides a marker. The artist represents this shift in perception by alternating moving images with video stills and paintings on each wall of the gallery.

Jill Wood
Assistant Director, Exhibitions and Programs
Lawndale Art Center, Houston

FOTOFIELD

ARTISTS: OPEN TO ALL INTERESTED ARTISTS

FotoField is a one-day celebration of photography as public art. All interested artists are invited to create a temporary site-specific photographic installation in the Sabine Street ArtPark along Buffalo Bayou, north of downtown between Allen Parkway and Memorial Park. The work can encompass whatever aspects of the photographic arts the artist chooses to incorporate. These can include existing photographs, site-specific work, or performance pieces performed that day and captured on film. The event will begin in the morning and proceed until that evening, when all the work will be taken down and the site will be returned to its normal state. Only the photographic record will survive.

Kevin Jefferies

CHE RICKMAN • UNTITLED, 2002 • PHOTO COLLAGE

DIPTYCH

ARTIST: JOHN BERNHARD

DIPTYCH: A work made up of two matching parts. I utilize the diptych venue as a means of further enhancing a past experience or a "déja vu" perception, making it into a new emotional and enlightening experience.

The correlation of two images brings out a visual duplicity of resembling forms, an intellectual encounter with a reflection on the readability and the meaning of its subjects.

John Bernhard

JOHN BERNHARDT • *WASHINGTON STATE*, 1984 • SILVER GELATIN PRINT

JOHN BERNHARDT • *GULF OF MEXICO*, 1997 • SILVER GELATIN PRINT

NON-PROFIT SPACES

SEEKING REFUGE

ARTIST: RODNEY WATERS

This exhibit of refugee portraits is an extension of a CD project that was created to raise awareness and money for refugees that are resettled in the United States. It is not for or about a particular group of refugees, nor does it attempt to represent all refugee populations. The goal is to use music, poetry, photography, and information to humanize the statistics and to help us realize that our shared bond of humanity is much greater than apparent divisions of culture, nationality, politics, and religion. Helping those less fortunate is only the beginning of what it means to work with refugees. Refugees force us to examine our own lives—our priorities, prejudices, and responsibilities—and to broaden our often too narrow view of what it means to be human and what it means, in any religious context, to be a child of God. More than anything, this is a work about hope. There is so much we can do for refugees in our own communities, not out of a sense of pity, but out of respect and admiration for their remarkable strength and courage. We have all heard the phrase "think globally, act locally". The incredible teamwork that put this project together is proof of what is possible when, faced with the overwhelming situation of refugees worldwide, we look next door and allow a statistic to become a friend. More information about refugees and the CD is available at www.imgh.org and www.rodneywaters.com.

Rodney Waters

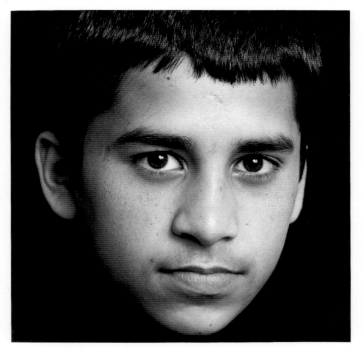

RODNEY WATERS • *JAWAD*, 2003 • MEDIUM TONED SILVER GELATIN PRINT

ONE WORLD, ONE PEOPLE

ARTIST: ARNOLD NEWMAN

One World, One People, an exhibit organized by the Jewish Museum of Florida, features 53 works by world-renowned photographer Arnold Newman. This exhibit is a culmination of the portraits Newman has made of significant individuals over the course of his career. Spanning six decades of work, from the early 1940s to the present, this collection contains portraits of Jewish public figures, from artists to entertainers to philosophers and politicians. All of the portraits, which are of Jews who have made a significant impact in their respective fields, are unique to the personality of the persons they portray.

Arnold Newman is one of the world's best known and most distinguished portrait photographers. He is considered the father of "environment portraiture", a style that places its subjects in a carefully composed setting that captures the essence of their work and personality. There is scarcely a figure of cultural importance who has not sat for Arnold Newman. He has photographed every president since Harry Truman, as well as leaders of countries around the world.

Highlights of the exhibit include photographs of famous personalities such as Yaccov Agam, Woody Allen, Ehud Barak, Saul Bellow, David Ben-Gurion, Leonard Bernstein, Marc Chagall, General Moshe Dayan, Abba Eban, Otto Frank, Chaim Gross, Al Hirschfeld, Danny Kaye, Mayor Teddy Kollek, Jacques Lipchitz, Norman

ARNOLD NEWMAN • *DAVID BEN-GURION*, 1967 • SILVER GELATIN PRINT

Mailer, Golda Meir, Arthur Miller, Zero Mostel, Madame Helena Rubinstein, and Issac Stern.

Each portrait in the exhibit is captioned with personal anecdotes from Arnold Newman on the sitting and its famous subject. Part of his skill resides in his ability to put his subject at ease before shooting.

The exhibit provides visitors with a unique opportunity to view a photographic display of 20th- and early 21st-century Jewish history.

Marcia Zerivitz
Founding Executive Director
Jewish Museum of Florida

JEWISH MOTHERS

Strength, Wisdom, Compassion

ARTIST: LLOYD WOLF

Jewish Mothers: Strength, Wisdom, Compassion honors and examines the lives and experiences of contemporary American Jewish mothers. Photographer Lloyd Wolf and interviewer Paula E. Wolfson have captured the rich diversity of America's Jewish mother in compelling personal stories and poignant black and white photographs. The book is a celebration of Jewish mothers: their accomplishments, their religious and family heritage, their values, their challenges, and their triumphs.

Deutser Gallery

Excerpted from the press release for *Jewish Mothers: Strength, Wisdom, Compassion*, Chronicle Books.

LLOYD WOLF • *PATRICIA LUNIOR*, 1999 • SILVER GELATIN PRINT

WATER BABIES

Avery Danziger

AVERY DANZIGER • *TWINS WITH K9* FROM THE SERIES *WATER BABIES*, 2003 • ULTRACHROME COLOR PRINT

Avery Danziger • *Twins See-Saw* from the series *Water Babies*, 2003 • Ultrachrome Color Print

COMMERCIAL GALLERIES

COMMERCIAL GALLERIES 3

MANUAL

Q & M

Q: the blurry figure in the picture, who is it?

M: not relevant

Q: is it relevant that the figure is male or female?

M: to the extent of being one of two possibilities

Q: what is he/she doing?

M: she's walking into the scene

Q: the scene?

M: a park in Moscow by the river

Q: is that relevant?

M: all specific facts constitute the reality of what we see —
place, time, weather and woman

Q: but the picture is so fuzzy that all the details are unreadable

M: on the contrary, each detail of the event is rendered
perfectly by the camera

Q: but the picture ....

M: it's not a picture, in every sense it's a photograph completely
photographic in identity

Q: a photographic event?

M: a very ordinary event — a woman takes a walk and someone
with a camera follows her, continually photographing as she
moves forward into the landscape

Q: what is that object in the lower part of the photograph?

M: a "blob" — an architectural blob coursing and spinning
through dark space — and it's not a photograph

Q: if not then what?

M: a frame render

Q: which means...?

M: an entirely different kind of event in a very different virtual
world

Q: two worlds in motion

M: a dualistic image

Q: dualism in a pluralistic world

M: a conflicted pluralistic world in which every faction desperately
wants to assert its monistic absolute

Q: and the title of the picture?

M: no title yet — or shall we call it Q&M?

THOMAS JOSHUA COOPER

THOMAS JOSHUA COOPER • *AN INDICATION PIECE – CABOT STRAIT – LOOKING N., N.E. – TOWARDS THE OLD WORLD, CAPE NORTH, CAPE BRETON ISLAND, NOVA SCOTIA, CANADA,* 1999-2001 (ONE OF THE TWO NORTHENMOST POINTS OF NOVA SCOTIA AND ALONG THE SITE OF JOHN CABOT'S CANADIAN DISCOVERIES AND EXPLORATIONS OF THE NEW WORLD FOR THE ENGLISH), 1999-2001 • SELENIUM TONED, SILVER GELATIN PRINT

SUBTERRANEA

Photographs by Sally Gall

ARTIST: SALLY GALL

SALLY GALL • *OASIS*, 1999 • GELATIN SILVER PRINT
COURTESY JULIE SAUL GALLERY, NEW YORK

Sally Gall is a noted photographer who has always sought the inexplicable in nature, finding beauty in things terrestrial, a beauty defined and enhanced by its opposite: the unsettling, the precipitous, the fearful. Here, in a remarkable series of images of the underworld taken over a four-year period in Mexico, Belize, Southeast Asia, the United States, and Europe, she explores a spiritual realm informed by the history of early human passage, myth, and transcendence.

In *Subterranea*, the objective universe is gone, and only the subjective remains. Eternal time is frozen in a fantastic and otherworldly architecture: crumbling walls, stalactites and stalagmites coated with icy limestone, and calcite formations gloaming in the darkness, bleached white as chalk. With each image, Sally Gall draws us deeper into a city forgotten. Somber and mortuary thought seems natural and right in these great spaces— thoughts of Aeneas and Charon, the boatman at the mouth of Hades, and the shades waiting to be rowed across to the eternal beyond, as well as a recognition that we all come at last to darkness and silence.

Umbrage Editions
New York

WEEGEE, THE FAMOUS

ARTIST: WEEGEE

Weegee (born Arthur Fellig), a tough, wisecracking news photographer from New York, received his nickname—an allusion to the Ouija board—because he often arrived early at the scenes of newsworthy crimes or catastrophes. Regardless of whether it was a mystical connection or a radio constantly tuned in to police calls that got him there, this ability, along with his 1945 book *Naked City*, made him a celebrity. His photographs of children playing in the streets, gawking onlookers at crime scenes, firemen with body bags, and other daily events in New York were habitually caught using on-camera flash lighting that isolated his subjects in a blast of light against a dark background, giving his images a stark, punchy quality.

John Cleary Gallery
Houston

WEEGEE • *CHILDREN SLEEPING ON FIRE ESCAPE*, 1941 • GELATIN SILVER PRINT • © PHOTOGRAPHS BY WEEGEE (ARTHUR FELIG), COPYRIGHT 1994, INTERNATIONAL CENTER OF PHOTOGRAPHY, NEW YORK, BEQUEST OF WILMA WILCOX

TOM BARIL • *Solarized Calais Lilies*, 1995 • TONED SILVER GELATIN PRINT
COURTESY OF THE RALLS COLLECTION

TOM BARIL

10 Years: From Pinhole to Wet Plate

ARTIST: TOM BARIL

Tom Baril celebrates the history of the photographic image, paying homage to the past
masters of the medium. The still-lifes of Karl
Blossfeldt and Edward Weston, the modernist urban landscapes of Alfred Stieglitz,
and the early Pictorialists are all present in his work.

Using the best modern papers and unique toning
techniques, Baril strives to achieve the depth and luster
of a fine vintage print. In an age when the medium is
becoming more and more high-tech, he even as he uses
modern materials to achieve a look that is both contemporary and faithful to the past. Tom Baril aspires to create something that is uniquely his.

Marsha Ralls
The Ralls Collection

JAY MAISEL, 50 YEARS

ARTIST: JAY MAISEL

I was born in 1931 in Brooklyn, New York, and moved to Manhattan as quickly as possible. In high school I studied graphic design with Leon Friend. I studied painting with Joseph Hirsch, painting at Cooper Union, and painting at Yale University with Josef Albers. The day I got my degree in painting was the day I decided to be a photographer.

My photographic quest is easily explained. Every once in a while, I'll be walking with someone, and seeing something wonderful, I'll point and say, "Hey, look." I have a desire to share what moves me. Degas wrote, "It is not what we see, but what we make others see."

I am not the least bit interested in showing you how clever I am, or how well I can change, improve, or manipulate the image. I'd rather point out how wonderful this visual feast is that passes before our eyes.

I have no particular aesthetic ax to grind. I have no particular subjects that entrance me to the exclusion of all others. I try to go out as empty as possible, without preconceptions, in order to be open to whatever happens. Therefore, for better or worse, the work is unclassifiable. Subject matter and formal intent run a wild gamut. Labels applied to my work have included "too diverse," "too arty," "too commercial," "too blithely idiosyncratic," and (my favorite) "too rooted in beauty and reality." Great! That's what I'm all about.

I don't have a game plan in terms of subject matter. A museum director once said to me, "I'd like to give you a big show, but I don't know which of you to exhibit." The major motivations for me are visual joy, perception, and investigation. The search is for, and the inspiration comes from, light, gesture, and color. Add to this a preoccupation with negative space, optical illusions, and allusions, and you have it. I have no hidden agendas, no deep psychological implications, and no deeper meanings. What you see is what you see. Enjoy.

Jay Maisel

Jay Maisel • *Blue Wall and Doves*, Early '70's • Epson Digital Pigment Print

STALKS AND WATER

ARTIST: TERRY VINE

In his most recent body of work, Terry Vine engages the floral still-life in a refreshing way. This new series of color work explores the genre with a Queen of Hearts "off with their heads!" approach. All of his subjects have been decapitated, and we are left observing the abstracted lines of the stalks and stems, often with obfuscating condensation on the vase. The viewer is also left to deal with reflections on the surface and information hidden behind the vase. Terry Vine has ventured into the realm of Adolf de Meyer, Josef Sudek, Andre Kertesz, Irving Penn, and Robert Mapplethorpe with a fresh eye and an adventurous spirit.

Clint Willour
Executive Director/Curator
Galveston Arts Center

TERRY VINE • *ROSES, STUDY NO. 1,* 2002 • CHROMOGENIC PRINT

TERRY VINE • *AMARYLLIS STUDY, No. 1,* 2002 • CHROMOGENIC PRINT

INEFFABLE DIALOGUE

ARTIST: CHRISTINE BRUNI FONDREN

The images in Christine Bruni Fondren's series *Ineffable Dialogue* are meditative. Their paradoxical title reveals these images are about inspiration rather than information.

Spirituality is the deep human longing to transport the transcendent into the immanent through experience and reflection. Through images, we attempt to experience the mystery about which we cannot speak. Fondren's abstracted images of water are natural metaphors for the transformation process. They are familiar, yet pull viewers away from their everyday experience. By rotating her images vertically, she draws the viewer in to experience the spiritual, which is symbolically associated with vertical dimension.

Images are innately healing: they carry messages from the vast inner world of the psyche. Nature symbolizes our mother who bequeaths us four elements: earth, water, wind, and fire. Water heals through its oceanic power of inspiration, allowing the mind to give voice to that which is difficult to put in words—the ineffable. The waters of the creation story, the evolutionary water, the amniotic fluid of womb life, all are elements of birth. Just as mar is sea, Mar-y is the archetypal great mother. Depth psychology uses the sea as a symbol of the maternal unconscious out of which consciousness is born. Water cleanses, thus the ritual process of baptism. Water heals through its literal cleansing agency, but more so by its oceanic power of inspiration.

The vertical alignment and abstract form of Fondren's images allow the viewer to find his or her own perspective. C. G. Jung proposed an analytic method called active imagination. This concept requires that one enter a meditative state in which the ego is relaxed and the participant free associates to images. The method is based upon the incumbent healing function of the imagination. Transformations occur to consciousness that might not otherwise. Christine Bruni Fondren's images invite the viewer to begin their own inspired ineffable dialogue.

J. Pittman McGehee
Former Dean of Christ Church Cathedral
Jungian Analyst and Professor, University of Houston

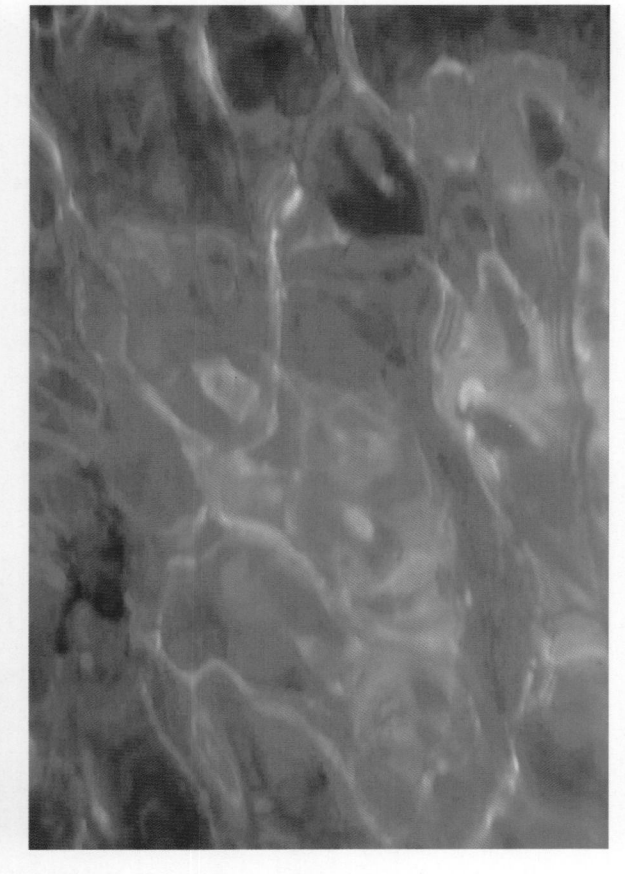

CHRISTINE BRUNI FONDREN • UNTITLED FROM THE SERIES
INEFFABLE DIALOGUE, 2002 • C-TYPE PHOTOGRAPH

CHRISTINE BRUNI FONDREN • UNTITLED FROM THE SERIES
INEFFABLE DIALOGUE, 2002 • C-TYPE PHOTOGRAPH

COMMERCIAL GALLERIES

CROSS CURRENTS

ARTISTS: BRYAN KUNTZ, TOMMY EWASKO, MICHAEL HART, GEORGE HIXSON, JANICE RUBIN, SUZANNE BANNING, PHYLLIS LIEDEKER FINELY, DELILAH MONTOYA, THEO STANLEY, IRMA MARTINEZ SIZER, MIA UNVERZAGT, PAUL ZEIGLER

When asked about his work based on reflections and atmosphere, Andre Kertesz offered a reason why he created art in the way that he did. He stated that he had no explanation other than pure ... instinct. The subject offered itself and he took advantage. The Texas artists in this exhibition arrive from varied backgrounds and implement their craft through various means, whether capturing chance slices of everyday life or manipulating arranged settings. Many of the photographs present the subject of water, as a medium of both transport and distortion, showing figurative images in ritualistic and cleansing baths. Some of the artists arrange and combine a multitude of singular images in order to create new works that represent the movement of time and matter. The creations of these very talented photographers are truly extraordinary.

GUS KOPRIVA
Redbud Gallery, Houston

SUZANNE BANNING • *FEMALE FORMS 01*, 2002 • C-PRINT

STREETS

ARTIST: SUZANNE PAUL

Suzanne Paul began in San Francisco photographing her dogs, which took her to the local parks and beaches. Eventually she summoned the courage to photograph complete strangers around the North Beach, Market Street, Chinatown, and Tenderloin areas. One of the first "assignments" she gave herself was a peace march in the late 1960s, which began in Golden Gate Park and ended at the Civic Center downtown.

She found it very hard at first to aim the camera at strangers, hesitant to invade their privacy and knowing that they would surely find out she was not a "real" photographer. But her love of this genre has deepened over the years, the adventure of stalking the unknown appealing to her sense of risk, which remains the challenging and rewarding, even intoxicating focus of Suzanne Paul's creative expression.

The appeal of being an "observer," having the ability to create order out of chaos, and the pleasure of discovering those exquisite moments of grace and preserving them for all time in photographs that can then be shared with others are both joyous and purposeful. Suzanne treasures those moments that come and go in infinitesimal increments of linear time. This will always be her first love while collecting images.

Street includes current images from 2000–2003—Houston's streets from a Holga point of view—as well as photos from the 1970s, 1980s, and 1990s shot with 35mm film in New York, New Orleans, Mexico, and Houston. It provides a brief overview of Suzanne Paul's work in street photography.

Suzanne Paul

SUZANNE PAUL • *NATE ON SKATEBOARD*, 2002 • SELINIUM FELATIN SILVER PRINT

STORM WASHED TALKING POLES

ARTIST: EGABRAG

Exploring the subtleties that exist between "reality" or "truth" and "illusion," or more specifically what the French deconstructionists refer to as *vrais* and *vraisemblent*, artist George Szepesi creates a representation of what he deems "truth"—what he sees—and then attaches it literally to the "truth" itself. His conceptual public art piece for FotoFest 2004, titled *Storm Washed Talking Poles*, addresses something that is commonplace and familiar, yet rarely revisited. While telephone poles serve as vehicles for electronic communication, they also serve as temporal signposts for communication at street level. The staples that remain in telephone poles after the messages on paper they once held have been removed, function as a remembrance, a path of what was, of what is no more. All that remains is a random pattern of staples—some relatively new and shiny, others rusting and in varying states of decay—that fastened what is now a forgotten message.

Szepesi captures images of these staples, photographed on their communicative poles along Montrose Boulevard in Houston, and then reattaches them by stapling the photographs back onto the staple-covered poles.

Wade Wilson

GEORGE SZEPESI • *STORM WASHED TALKING POLES, SERIES STAPLES, MONTROSE AVE.*, 2004 • CIBACHROME PRINT

NICARAGUA

John Bernhard

JOHN BERNHARD • *#1 FROM THE CHILDREN SERIES*, 1984 • ARCHIVAL INK PRINT

COMMERCIAL GALLERIES

REVERIE

ARTIST: FREDERIC WEBER

Frederic Weber's work seems familiar and mysterious at the same time. The familiarity stems from the influence of figurative work by such photographers as Alfred Stieglitz, Edward Weston, Harry Callahan, and Eadweard Muybridge. The mystery flows from the Pictorialist depiction that is a continuation of Frederic Weber's earlier techniques. The softness of the image places the viewer at a remove from contemporary ways of looking at photographs of the nude, but does so without requiring the artist to resort to antiquated photographic processes. The primary color is blue, but the spectral range (from violet and lavender to indigo and gray) is also a continuation of Frederic Weber's palette from previous work. There is a sensuality in the blue palette that ties it to transitory times of day (before sunrise or dusk), but also conveys the essence of that ephemeral glimpse we intellectually recognize as memory before it fades and disappears.

R. Eric Davis
Hooks-Epstein Galleries, Houston

FREDERIC WEBER • UNTITLED *No. 10* FROM THE SERIES *REVERIE*, 1998-2003 • SILVER DYE BLEACH PHOTOGRAPH
COURTESY OF THE ARTIST AND HOOKS-EPSTEIN GALLERIES

THE EASTER CELEBRATION, GUATEMALA

ARTIST: FERNANDO STEIN, M.D.

Every year during Easter week, the Passion of Christ is commemorated in Guatemala with processions that carry the statues of Christ, the Virgin Mary, and the apostles through the streets on platforms called *andas*. The carefully decorated *andas* are made of wood and carried on the shoulders of hundreds of men and women in a parade that goes around the city for an entire day. Along the parade route, each family is responsible for covering the front of their property with a carpet made of sawdust. The sawdust is collected throughout the year, stained with bright colors, and arranged in beautiful shapes that form these carpets. The carpets are the objects of this exhibit by Fernando Stein

Fernando Stein, MD

FERNANDO STEIN M.D. • *THE PROCESSION*, 1997 • GICLÉE PRINT

PARALLEL ALCHEMY

The H₂O Triple Point & 3 Icons Transformed

ARTIST: JIM WISE

Water's laboratory "triple point" only seems impossible. It is no more unlikely than mixed media art combining painting, digital photography, and inkjet printing. Water freezes; ice melts. Water boils; steam condenses. The appearance of one depends on the transformation of another. But under precisely controlled laboratory conditions, all three states of H₂O coexist in the same chamber.

In these works, a computer disc was produced from a painting. An inkjet print was produced from a disc. And another painting was inspired by the print. The appearance of one depends on the transformation of another, but all may be examined at once. The digital and photographic technologies employed allow the painter and the viewer alike to get a closer look at the art of painting.

Fine, you might say, but why were Albert Einstein, Madonna, and Pablo Picasso chosen as subjects? This unlikely group forms a personal iconography, representing my life of three careers, a life in which the appearance of one career was dependent on the transformation of another. I studied the scientific genius of Einstein in school, experienced backstage pop culture as a lawyer representing Madonna, and later analyzed the artistic innovation of Picasso.

But the true subject of the exhibit is experimentation and discovery. The places in which these works were produced and are now shown are like laboratories, abounding in possibilities, with atmospheres as rich and rare as the chambers of ancient alchemists.

Jim Wise

JIM WISE • *3 ICONS TRANSFORMED*, 2003 • INK JET PRINT

OASIS

ARTISTS: JEAN CASLIN, JEROME CROWDER, JIM DILGER, HERMAN DOBBS, CHARLOTTE RANDOLPH, DAVID VAUGHAN, LINDA WALSH, RODNEY WATERS, DOROTHY WONG

One definition of oasis is something that provides relief from boring or dreary routine. Within this general framework, the photographers in this show developed their ideas of an oasis in very different ways that range from the intimate to the distant, from the everyday to the unusual.

Linda Walsh

HERMAN DOBBS, CHARLOTTE RANDOLPH, DAVID VAUGHAN, LINDA WALSH, DOROTHY WONG • *OASIS*, 2003 • COLLAGE OF GROUP WORK: DOBBS, RANDOLPH, VAUGHAN, WALSH, WONG • DIGITAL PRINT

WATER EX-VOTOS

ARTIST: FRANCISCO LARIOS

The representation of appearances is ceasing to be the incontrovertible basis of evidence or truth about phenomena in the world. We are seeing the rapid devaluation of sight as the fundamental criterion for knowledge and understanding."[1]

This series of ex-votos uses water as a principal theme to sustain a narrative of petitions, desires, miracles, and so on. The petition and the penitent move into a second plane where the virtual image, in an apparent reality, establishes itself so that the object, saint, and miracle may be revealed, making them exist beyond the faith itself.

With an appealing syncretism, Francisco Larios puts forth this series of 24 "digital votive offerings," which at the same time are not intended to achieve the masterful similarity generated by computerized graphics. Why imitate the human body from the realm of virtuality if the practice of cloning is already upon us? Likewise, he does not pretend to structure gratitude from the more orthodox perspective of an ex-voto (if that were even possible); instead he does it by using an ironic tone, an unabashed reflexiveness.

It is complicated, for sure, to perceive the level of veracity that exists in each ex-voto. We know that some at least are closely related to real occurrences, even though the fakeness makes clear the latent and intentionally structured deceit. Another point is to ensure that the arsenal of virgins and saints is not so overwhelming that we find ourselves lost. Larios opts to focus on just a few recurring images, while suggesting that their familiarity is not a simple thing. To the contrary, he uniquely gives them "appropriate authority."[2]

If digitalization of the popular ex-voto reawakens sympathy, even though it may be more through the irony of the radical change of language (without altering the essential properties of the genre) than through the quality of the conceded favors, it is not just because Larios parodies (mechanizes) the primitive pictographic features of the traditional origins, but because he also transposes the simplistic narrative of the primitive popular painter into a sophisticated technological context.   Above all, it is because his work typifies, by the minuteness of its dilemmas, a socioeconomic class that now barely believes in divine intervention. What exists is cybernetic devotion. It implies, for example, that a deprivation of access to the Internet could be as painful or fatal as a life-threatening infirmity or the loss of a limb or a loved one, a few among the infinity of ex-voto motifs. Larios may be expressing the magnitude of his frivolity, but also his profound faith in what it conveys.[3]

Francisco Larios

[1] Kevin Robbins, *Will Image Move Us Still?*, *from The Photographic Image in Digital Culture*, *Routledge*, London, 1995, Martin Lister, editor
[2] Marco Granados, *Post Magazine*, Mexico, 2002
[3] Luis Carlos Emerich, *Cuenca Benl*, Ecador, 2001

Blessed Holy Spirit, I request to present this altarpiece of peace to you in consolation of my anguishes since false testimony has been raised against my freedom where I undergo humiliations, slander, abuse and insults. Since I do not cry out the offenses that have been committed against me, I request mercy to you for my accusers, lawyers, criminals and the police and that the day will come soon when this false slavery is understood. Thank you and Amen. Jacobo Steinberg, Mexico D.F., 2000.

FRANCISCO LARIOS • *EX-VOTO # 21*, 2003 • DIGITAL IMAGE
COURTESY OF MACKEY GALLERY

Dear God, through this image/ex-voto, I ask the Holy Spirit to guide the hands of the plastic surgeon that will fix my face so that I may have a better social acceptance and triumph in the frivolous and empty art world and at least get the status that I have always wished for. I give to you this present as devotion and faith in you. Raymundo Ortigos, Monterrey, Mexico 2001.

FRANCISCO LARIOS • *EX-VOTO # 13*, 2002 • DIGITAL IMAGE
COURTESY OF MACKEY GALLERY

STILL CHAMBERS

ARTIST: LUCIANA ABAIT

Moving under the surface, my work explores themes of presence and absence through architectural landscapes found underwater in swimming pools. Walls, ladders, numbers, and lines lose their sense of usefulness underwater and attain a symbolic quality. Swimmers become anonymous simple beings, insect-like, moving across vast liquid masses. Light is essential, creating surreal and theatrical atmospheres

With the ambiguity that these liquid-filled scenes present, water can be viewed as air, the sky, clouds; a swimming pool itself becomes a room, a box, a theatre stage, a womb. The works aim at eliciting from spectators their most basic emotions, feelings, instincts, and thoughts. It is the viewer, contemplating my paintings, who ultimately determines the message traveling beneath the surface of the water.

Featuring views of swimmers and swimming pools, these pieces capture the isolation and silence of being underwater and use this as a metaphor for a more general sense of aloneness.

Luciana Abait

Luciana Abait • Untitled, *But Number 27*, 2003 • Photograph and Mixed Media on Canvas
Courtesy of Mackey Gallery

COMMERCIAL GALLERIES

FLUID, FLOW, FLUSH

ARTISTS: KELLY GALE AMEN, SCOTT GRIESBACH, BARBARA JONES

Three artists from three disciplines converge at the KGA Compound to create an atmosphere heavy with visuals.

Kelly Gale Amen from Houston is widely recognized for work in the traditional realm of creating fine art objects, for his Art Furniture, and for creating intense living and working spaces. His previous contribution to FotoFest was his tribute to fire in which he set his soft sculpture Art Furniture ablaze to photograph the action and create a tangible body of work relating to the performance. Here he has created a montage of images, drawn from his Art Furniture and displayed in video form within an installation at the KGA Compound.

Scott Griesbach of Santa Monica, California, has contributed new work from his well-respected digital manipulations as well as a video created from, and inspired by, The Orange Show's Art Car Parade, Spring 2003, in Houston. His work is in a variety of collections including the KGA Compound, Pinnacle Financial Strategies, and the Museum of Fine Arts, Houston,

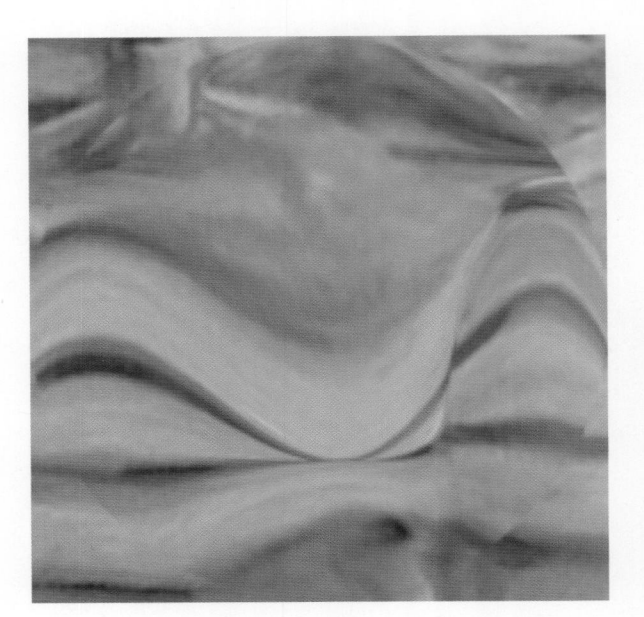

BARBARA JONES • *WATER FOR ALL, DETAIL*, 2003 • MIXED MEDIA
COURTESY OF KGA COMPOUND

KELLY GALE AMEN • *THE FLOW*, 2003 • VIDEO
COURTESY OF KGA COMPOUND

Barbara Jones from Houston, is best known for her paintings. She has created an all-encompassing installation in a single room at the KGA Compound. Using digital photographic imagery she has collected in her work as a painter, she has created a "water world" in which the viewer experiences a virtual drenching.

The convergence of these artists has prodded each to reinvent his or her perception of, and place in, the arena of fine art as it relates to the theme of this exhibition and each other. As they collaborate and separate, mesh and divide, Kelly Gale Amen, Scott Griesbach, and Barbara Jones come together through their respective efforts and solutions to meet the challenges of this exhibition.

While each artist has roots in diverse media, videos and installations bring this small group together under one roof for their contribution to FotoFest 2004.

KGA Compound
Houston

Scott Griesbach • *Omniscient Narrator of Detail*, 2003 • Inkjet Photograph • Courtesy of KGA Compound

COMMERCIAL GALLERIES

SOUTH

ARTIST: STEVE HARRIS

Water in its truest form and place is within the ocean. In its most beautiful and magical state, the raw power of the ocean descends upon coastal formations to create waves that can be ridden. Surfing. The art and sport of surfing as we know it today was a subculture not long ago, an alternative lifestyle reserved for wayward individuals—as most of us are still, in our own way.

Being a surfer for three-quarters of my life and a photographer for almost as long, I decided that the two things for which I have such a passion made a perfect match for a documentary project. My travels have taken me around the globe searching for the elusive perfect wave. What I've put together for this project is a glimpse of the surfing and the traveling life style through Mexico, Costa Rica, Europe, and North Africa. Enjoy the trip.

Steve Harris

STEVE HARRIS • *IF THE CONDITIONS ARE RIGHT, YOU'LL WALK AWAY FROM ANYTHING TO GET THERE – SOUTH,* 1989 • C-TYPE PRINT

ARCTIC LIGHT, ARCTIC TIME

ARTISTS: LINDA WALSH

Linda Walsh has been photographing Alaska for many years. Her most recent travels brought her to Alaska's far northern coasts, from the mining community of Nome on the Bering Sea, to the native villages of Barrow and Kaktovik on the Arctic Ocean, to Icy Reef, a long spit of land between the Beaufort Lagoon and the Arctic Ocean in the Arctic National Wildlife Refuge. Her landscapes explore the dimensions of light and time, whether the soft light of long northern summer days or the deep dusks of its nights.

Walsh's photographs underscore the tensions that exist in the relationship between humans and the land, especially in those places where human influence is less obvious. At times the two interact in ways that enhance the land and the lives lived on it. At other times the interaction may degrade the land. In contested places, such as the Arctic National Wildlife Refuge, the argument is how to preserve the right relationship to the land. She focuses on these complex issues with her photographs of wetlands and industrial debris, the sea and civilization's trash, and the land and our enjoyment of it.

Linda Walsh

LINDA WALSH • *MEMORIAL DAY, NOME, ALASKA 1:30 A.M.*, 2002 • DIGITAL PRINT

COMMERCIAL GALLERIES

FRAGMENTS OF WATER

ARTIST: CLAUDETTE CHAMPBRUN GOUX

How is it possible to capture the vibrations of the air, the constant, subtle changing tones of the light? How can we render the impalpability, which is between our eyes and the object?

As we look closer and closer, the beautiful texture of infinite variations of colors shifting, breaking, and recomposing the water surface can only be unveiled by inquisitive observation and extreme scrutiny.

But our eyes can only glance. It cannot capture the fugitive, ephemeral nuances of the fragmented light. Through the lens of the camera, these minimal textures of Nature appear, and their abstract shapes and intense vibrating colors can be fixed on the print like on canvas.

These photographs are the result of a long meditative observation, as I was looking at the vibrating surface, receptive to its slightest changes, depending on time, the season, the atmosphere, and the wind

Claudette Champbrun Goux

CLAUDETTE CHAMPBRUN GOUX • *BLUE/GREEN FRAGMENT #2*, 1998 • TYPE C-PRINT

MALE NUDES

John Bernhard

JOHN BERNHARD • *#4 FROM MALE NUDE SERIES*, 2002 • ARCHIVAL INK PRINT

COMMERCIAL GALLERIES

WATERWORKS

ARTIST: VINCENTE WOLF

New York City based photographer Vicente Wolf is at the center of one of the most frenetic cities in the world. His images, taken in remote parts of the planet, are a contrast to today's global upheaval because they bring serenity, which is harder and harder to find in our society. He touches the subconscious and evokes a sense of dreams with his water landscapes. These bold images are windows into the wild.

Ikletik Designs

VICENTE WOLF • *SETTINGS 8,* 2002 • COLOR PHOTOGRAPH

REVIVING DOWNTOWN

My Address Book

ARTIST: MARIPOL

For 20 years, I have shot small SX70 color Polaroids of New York's downtown scene. Hearing that Polaroid was going out of business, I decided to experiment with giant Polaroids (20 x 24 inches) in black and white. This new work documents people from all ages and backgrounds within a specific, tightly controlled format. The subjects came from my address book: artists, family, friends, and acquaintances. During the shoot, I asked everyone, "Where are you at this moment?" and they gave me a quote. The resulting black and white images became my photo journal. The work is my response to living in downtown New York after September 11. It celebrates our community, its courage, and the importance of going on with everyday life. I've entitled this project *Reviving Downtown.*

Maripol
New York City

In June 2001, I attended the grand opening of the film *Downtown 81*, which Maripol co-produced, at the Screening Room in New York. In conjunction with the release of the film, Deitch Projects mounted an exhibition of still photography from the film, highlighting Maripol's outstanding Polaroid collection. For FotoFest 2002, we brought this show to Houston, curated by Maripol, in conjunction with the film, which screened at the Angelika Film Center. Both the film and the Polaroid series explore the extraordinary, real-life, hip, arty Manhattan club scene in the post-punk decade. Maripol was at the center of the creativity, excess, and edgy glamour that defined the era. She was friends and collaborators with Andy Warhol, Jean-Michel Basquiat, Keith Haring, Debbie Harry, and Madonna (who styled herself then as the ultimate Material Girl).

I am proud and privileged to introduce of her latest works at FotoFest 2004, a document of the brave new world that is 21st-century Manhattan.

Deborah Colton
Iklektik Designs
Houston

AQUA REVELATIONS

ARTIST: VAN VU

Born in Vietnam in 1932, Van Vu started his photographic career in 1955, and his foremost photographs, *Dreaming in motherly love and Lonely*, were exhibited at the International Photographic Salon of Saigon. *Lonely*, in particular, the photo of a torn-jacketed child selling bread and walking under a heavy night rain in a small flooded street, received special acclaim. Van Vu won gold and sliver medals simultaneously.

Motivated by this success, Van Vu dedicated himself to further study and to a deeper exploration of the field of fine art photography. In April 1975, Van Vu came to the United States as a refugee and worked first at the school Pictures Inc. and Money Lab as a supervisor, then at Darkroom, Inc. in Jackson, Mississippi. In 1981, he moved to Houston and worked at The Color Place.

Van Vu graduated with a degree in professional photography from the New Jersey School of Modern Photography in 1978 and from the Advanced Color Lab at Rochester Institute of Technology, New York, in 1980. Thirty-six years of hard work, relentless study, and extensive experience led Van Vu in 1982 to open Southwest Photo Lab in Houston.

He researched and developed darkroom techniques, creating contemporary colors through new technical lines. As a professional photographer, as well as an experienced lab technician, Van Vu combined both advanced techniques of picture taking and darkroom processing to achieve the desired results.

Van Vu

Van Vu • *Autumn Pond*, 2001 • C-Print

AQUA REVELATIONS

ARTIST: ZENA STETKA HOWE

Delving beneath the surface of the expected, Zena Stetka Howe uses her camera as a paintbrush to gently excavate the details of the ordinary. She composes paintings that jolts us into the exquisiteness of the mundane, as the most sententious objects become photogenic phenomena through her lens. Her detached acumen comes full circle when the observer is transformed into an accomplice in a new reality on her photographic canvas.

Zena Stetka Howe

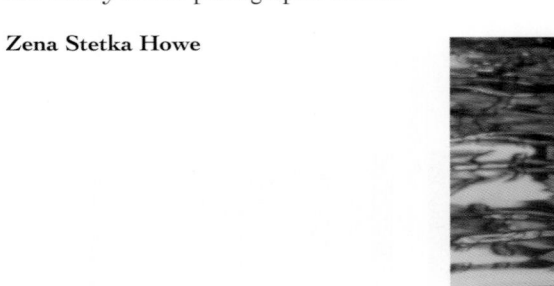

ZENA STETKA HOWE • *SAN ANTONIO*, 2003 • C-PRINT

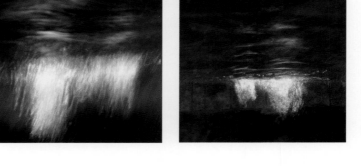

SUSANNE YORK • *SPLASH TRIPTYCH*, 2003 • PIEZO PRINT

RAPTURE OF THE DEEP

ARTIST: SUSANNE YORK

Water as calligraphy, as form frozen in stop-time motion; water as memory and as exclamation. The infinite shapes that water can take or create is the essence of what Susanne York seeks in these photographic creations. Meticulously technical in execution, yet painterly in appearance, these images inhabit the space between figuration and abstraction, reality and fantasy.

Deep within, we all have memories of passing moments or feelings that are somewhat connected to water: in swimming pools, at the beach, in a lake, or on a river. It could be nothing specific; it could be a childhood experience; or it could be just an idea of a feeling. In these photographs, Susanne York simply asks us to experience, recall, and give in to the mystery and beauty that is to be found within this watery world.

Thom Andriola
New Gallery, Houston

SUSANNE YORK • *APPARITION, 2003* • PIEZO PRINT

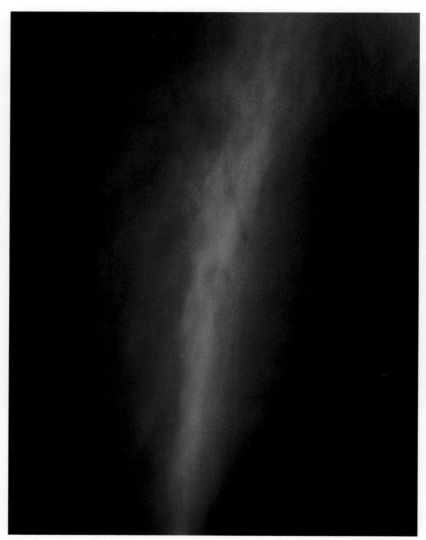

Elinor Carucci • *Swimming Pool*, 1999 • Cibachrome Print • Courtesy of Ricco-Maresca Gallery, New York

Elinor Carucci

OTHER RAPTURES

NEW GALLERY

≈ WATER

COMMERCIAL GALLERIES

PATRICK MEAGHER • *BASEL NO. 10, 2001, 2003* • C-PRINT

WATER WALL

Patrick Meagher

GALLERY SONJA ROESCH

CONTEMPORARY RUSSIAN PHOTOGRAPHY

Vintage Photographs and Photocollages — Zofia Rydet

ZOFIA RYDET • *ANNIHILATION I* FROM *THE WORLD OF FEELINGS AND IMAGINATION*, CA 1970 • VINTAGE SILVER
GELATIN PHOTO COLLAGE

CONTEMPORARY RUSSIAN PHOTOGRAPHY

Thumbtacks and Modernism—Andrey Chezhin

ANDREY CHEZHIN • *HOMAGE TO ROBERT MAPPLETHORPE,* 1999 • HAND TONED SILVER GELATIN PRINT

SOVIET PHOTOJOURNALISM

Samariy Gurariy

SAMARIY GURARIY • *KHRUSHCHEV AT TASHKENT AGRICULTURAL CONFERENCE*,
CA 1960 • SILVER GELATIN PRINT

CORPORATE
SPACES

CORPORATE SPACES

DIVING DREAMS, STEAMS AND OTHER WATER THINGS

ARTIST: OLIVER

Oliver has his own vision and tweaks the image until he feels he has reached a satisfactory solution. He challenges the edges, making us think as we keep an eye on his sensual, colorful images. While initially resistant to digital imagery in any form, I am becoming more accepting of it. Indeed, one of my favorite pieces in my personal collection is a work by oliver.

Jacqueline Hamilton, 2003
Art Consultant

oliver is a very dynamic and gifted artist. We are pleased to add his creative imagery to our gallery here in Cayman.

Marianne Hill Kennedy, 2003
Gallery Grand Cayman, BWI

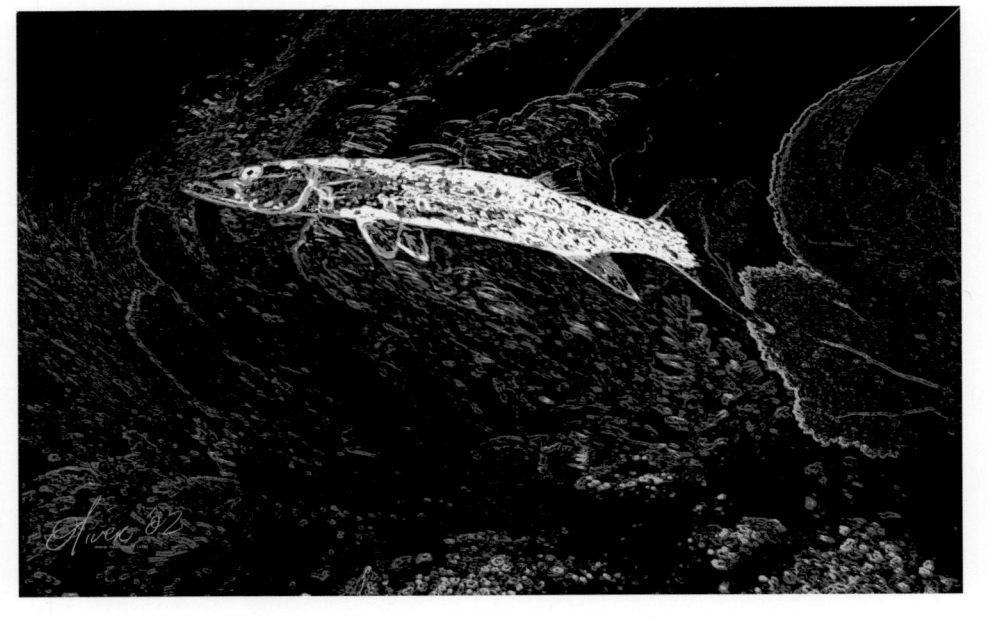

OLIVER • *DWM23*, 2002 • DIGITALLY MANIPULATED SLIDE PRINTED ON CANVAS

13 CURRENTS

ARTIST: MARK L. TOMPKINS

Water, a few gallons
(More or less),
Dust, a handful,
Recipe my soul's choice
For a body.

Is the force of this pull
Water calling to itself,
So tightly bonded
I often confuse it for me,
Or calling to the truth of me?

The pull to water,
When I answer,
I come to wash,
Wash myself in peace

MARK L. TOMPKINS • *PULL*, 2003 • LIGHT JET PRINT

On behalf of McCord Development, Inc., this exhibition has been organized by Kinzelman Art Consulting.

SURFACE

ARTISTS: HARRY KALISH, ALAN LEMIRE, ERNESTINE RUBEN, PAUL SMEAD, FANNIE TAPPER, SARAH VAN KEUREN, WILLIAM WYLIE

Surface is a group exhibition referencing the simple beauty of water in its fluid, ever-changing forms, rendered through traditional, pinhole, non-silver, and digital photographic methods. *Surface* goes beyond the textural studies of water to include photographs whose process literally depends upon the surface of the paper. This blend of photographers' works, each exploring unique methods of image making, successfully invokes the meditative qualities of water. Among these artists is a divergence in both the technical process and the aesthetic effects used to inquisitively observe the infinite variations of color, texture, and light found on and beyond the surface of water.

Julie Kinzelman
Kinzelman Art Consulting, Houston

On behalf of McCord Development, Inc., this exhibition has been organized by Kinzelman Art Consulting.

WILLIAM WYLIE • UNTITLED *223*, 2000 • SILVER GELATIN PRINT

PAUL SMEAD • UNTITLED, 2003 • SILVER GELATIN PRINT

SARAH VAN KEUREN • *RISING VAPORS #4*, 2001 • CYANOTYPE AND GUM BICHROMATE PRINT

CORPORATE SPACES

MYSTICAL DREAMSCAPES

ARTISTS: ELLIOTT MCDOWELL

I improvise. It's my greatest talent. I prefer situations to plans, you see. . . Really, I've had to deal with givens. I can sort a great deal of information . . . very quickly.

William Gibson, *Neuromancer* (Ace Books, New York, 1995)

 No scene that Elliott McDowell depicts ever existed. His images emerge from inside his head. An only child and inveterate fantasist, he's most at home in the spirit world. At age six, looking into a Brownie camera, he marveled to discover "a real safe place."

He tried becoming a classic American photographer, lens-faithful, devoted to black and white. The straight, "f-64" style was good training in technical perfection, but conventional photographic realism didn't interest him for long. He was drawn to Jerry Uelsmann's revolutionary combination printing. The seamless joining of figures, landscapes, and interiors conjured worlds beyond normal perceptive consciousness, beyond "the thing itself" or the banalities of decisive moments.

Surrealism was marginal in the American photographic credo. A visionary and an addict of the superreal, Elliott McDowell prefers the margin. His sources are art history, spiritual literature, the silence of redwood forests, and Robert Monroe's workshops that directed him in out-of-body experiences.

Elliott McDowell is a digital painter, a surgical splicer of non sequiturs. He collects these informational bits in slide transparencies by the thousands and, like a painter, he chooses and arranges them as if they were colors from a palette. Whether the photographic bits originate in Missouri, Ireland, Italy, Jackson Hole in Wyoming, the French catacombs, or a Paris hotel is unimportant. His "trees" may have been painted on an old vase. His "suns" may belong to some bibelot from his vast collection of ornamental objects. Combined, they become virtual geographies, virtual light and weather, cooked-up mosaics resembling tarot cards or mandalas. Extremely plastic, like out-of-body experiences, his "places" are off the edge of the known map. As mystical dreamscapes, they evoke fairy tale settings where it's eerily damp and wizards speak in rhyme.

Comfortable with these energy systems, he chooses colors from television—kaleidoscopic, flashy, decadent. Lurid electric blues and greens, tropical pinks, and Arizona reds collide in magnetic force fields. He invents a new kind of hot-core romance of layers, motion blur, radial blur, and lowered opacity. Nothing is inviolate. His consuming question: How subtle a form can these manipulations take? "Christ, you think that looks real?" cries Case in *Neuromancer*, to which his girlfriend replies, "Naw, but it looks like you care enough to fake it."

Elliott McDowell cares enough to amuse and confuse with visual contradictions. Bringing nonphysical energies to photography, silver paths of the nerves, he toys with the fact that we and the world are more than mere bodies. "We stopped what you call 'dying' a long time ago," the elementals in his acid-green woods might say. "Eat? Sleep? I gave those up years back." He works best in winter. When the weather is nasty, cold, and dark, he shuts himself away, plying his enchantments like an alchemist.

Eugenia Parry

ELLIOTT McDOWELL • *The Prophetic Pine, 2002* • DIGITAL PHOTO COMPOSITE

RESTAURANTS AND COMMERCIAL SPACES

5 RESTAURANTS AND COMMERCIAL SPACES

FLUIDITY

ARTISTS: AMERICAN SOCIETY OF MEDIA PHOTOGRAPHERS, GROUP SHOW

The American Society of Media Photographers (ASMP) proudly presents *Fluidity*. This juried exhibition of images includes works on the FotoFest theme of water as interpreted by Houston-based commercial photographers.

Members of ASMP are among the world's most accomplished photographers. They work in the many facets of publication photography, a field that includes photojournalism, advertising, studio photography, product photography, and corporate communications. For its 5,000 members nationally, ASMP fosters creative excellence and an environment in which commercial photography can thrive.

Rocky Kneten
President, ASMP/Houston

CLOCKWISE FROM TOP LEFT: MIKE DUHON, ROCKY KNETEN, DAVID NANCE, JIM CALDWELL, JANICE RUBIN, NASH BAKER, RODOLFO HERNÁNDEZ, THAINE MANSKE, SCOTT KOHN, BERYL STRIEWSKI, JOHN SMALLWOOD, BOB GOMEL, MICHAEL HART

PHOTOGRAPHS BY WALT BISTLINE

ARTIST: WALT BISTLINE

I first visited South Padre Island along the Texas Gulf Coast near Mexico in 1979. For the past decade, I've gone there four or five times a year. While the beachfront has become congested with high-rise condos, the island's bayside, which faces the mainland across the Laguna Madre, remains quieter. A nature preserve offers long boardwalks through a saltwater marsh to the edge of the Laguna, with tattered bird blinds for watching the herons, egrets, gulls, and various migratory birds that make the Rio Grande Valley their winter home.

Three interests of mine led to this series. First, I am primarily a landscape photographer and I have photographed in and around the South Padre nature preserve for years. Second, as an artist I am intrigued by modernism's fascination with the grid, from Piet Mondrian's De Stijl paintings to the Minimalist sculptures of Donald Judd and Carl Andre to Agnes Martin's quest for the "abstract sublime". Third, I seek ways to layer my works (without digital manipulation), so that they engage the viewer's eye for a bit longer than the brief time otherwise needed to simply recognize a landscape. In these photographs, the landscape is always present, but it is seen through the filter of the gridlike structures of the blinds, which fragment the world outside. Some pieces of the landscape appear clearly through rectangular, man-made openings, others are seen through the random openings that nature has created over the years, and some are only seen faintly through the veil of the netting.

Walt Bistline

WALT BISTLINE • *SOUTH PADRE ISLAND (03-3A-6)*, 2003 • INK JET PRINT

VISIONS OF SPIRIT

ARTIST: KAREN SACHAR

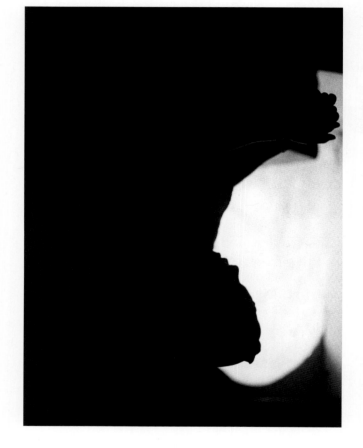

KAREN SACHAR • *MAMA, THE ZULU HEALER*, 1997 • SILVER GELATIN PRINT

F rom the monks of Ethiopia to children dancing on the beach in Galveston, Texas, may you happen upon a glimpse of the soul reflected in the images before you and be reminded of how generously the spirit lives in our lives.

It is through tiny footsteps and giant leaps that we become who we are. The greatest gift we are given is the opportunity to discover. We are presented with a path that guides us, and as we go along, step by step, we encounter moments that help us define who we are, what we believe, and where it is we want to go next. They are moments that lead us to truths.

As elders and as children, we are the bridge between yesterday, today, and tomorrow. With the opening of our hearts, the spirit of the heavens dances through our soul, rekindling parts of ourselves, asking us to remember, to seek and to reconnect with the source of our knowingness. It is my hope that as you venture through the places and faces of the moments that have crossed my path, something may spark within you and take you toward a new horizon on your journey.

This work is inspired by the spirit of humankind. While on this journey, Karen Sacher's hope is to embrace the soul and discover the heart of spirit that dances with one and all.

Karen Sachar

NATURAL DICHOTOMIES

ARTIST: COLIN BLAKELY

This series deals with cultural and political perceptions of nature. It involves photographing undeveloped areas near my home. With the help of photographic strobes, I use composition and lighting to manipulate the scene. The resulting tension between the natural and artificial in the images reflects the duality inherent in all landscapes. Even the most remote reaches of the globe are affected by the hand of mankind. The artificial is part of all that we have come to think of as nature.

Colin Blakely

COLIN BLAKELY • *42° 16' 21" N, 85° 46' 01" W*, 2003 • PIGMENT INK JET PRINT

FROM THE CENTER

ARTIST: LESLIE FIELD

This series suggests the sensory delight that comes with contemplating an object of beauty. The poppy's grace, elegance, and implied movement show flirtatiousness and sensuality. It is a reminder of the ephemeral and a stimulus for joy. A poppy's opiate quality also implies a heady, dreamlike state in which memory and forgetfulness interplay. Perhaps this is the same place of creativity and transcendence that the experience of art provides.

Leslie Field

LESLIE FIELD • *POSTURING*, 2003 • PIGMENT INK JET PRINT

RESTAURANTS AND COMMERCIAL SPACES

WATER WITCHERY

ARTIST: FANNIE TAPPER

Water as a metaphor brings to life the flow of human emotions: the sense of the pull of the unknown; the exhilaration of domination felt by a sailor; the flow of time felt by the disheartened. The rhythmic rippling across still waters satisfies the urge to flee the routine to reflect, to feel the upsurge of joy at the contemplation of beauty, to sense the eternal.

The images presented here are of bodies of water—large and small, imposing or insignificant. They are a subset of my ongoing efforts to capture the magic, and the witchery of water, creating ever new shapes that are ephemeral, seen and forgotten in seconds as new shapes form unless they are rescued by the eye and hand of the artist.

Fannie Tapper

FANNIE TAPPER • *WATER WITCHERY*, 2003 • COLOR GICLÉE ON SILK

DOMESTIC ISOLATION

ARTIST: WENDY LEVINE AND LAURA BURLTON

Wendy Levine's witty still lifes of domesticity are filled with details of a life with children. She is a great narrative photographer who can spin a tale without ever showing a person. The photographs are distinguished pictorially by her keen appreciation for the interplay of primary colors. They first appeal to the viewer on a purely primitive sensual level—the way a bright red apple does. But upon closer reading, each image delivers a humorous reflection upon parenthood.

Laura Burlton's gelatin silver prints are sometimes haunting in their diminutive scale, deriving an ethereal quality from the Holga's haphazard vignetting. She achieves effective juxtapositions through sharp angles and broad tonal ranges in work that says, unapologetically, "This is my life".

Both women's photographs record medium-format scenes of the domestic. Laura Burlton's images are small-scale black and white images of children, while Wendy Levine's large C-Prints offer evidence of children only through their absence from the frames, documenting instead quirky still lives of familial detritus.

The exhibit clearly illustrates how a domestic existence has altered and enhanced the visual palettes of two female artists.

Wendy Levine
Essay based on reviews by Kathy Ryan, Photo Editor, New York Times Magazine, and Beverly Conley, BC Photo

WENDY LEVINE • *DOLLY BATH*, 2002 • C-PRINT

LAURA BURLTON • *ANGLES*, 2002 • SILVER GELATIN PRINT

THE ART OF MUSIC

ARTIST: GERRY GRAPHIA

GERRY GRAPHIA • *EDDIE VAN HALEN*, 1998 • C-PRINT

Being a musician all of my life, I naturally have a passion for music and the musicians that influenced me during my career. After the heyday of my rock band 2-4-1 in the mid 1990s, I took a more serious approach to my photography and pursued any magazine that would let me cover the major venue music scene, both photographically and editorially.

I feel it is much easier to photograph musicians when you are one with them because you understand how music is structured and can anticipate the artists' movements. The results are the images on display in this exhibit of music icons of all genres who have influenced generations of musicians and have brought much joy and happiness to fans.

Because I am a purist at heart, the photographs contained in this exhibit were taken with high-speed film and available light, depicting the emotion and intensity of each artist at a critical moment in the performance. Each photograph is accompanied by a description of what was going on at the time of exposure.

One of the greatest compliments that I have ever received was from someone viewing my photographs of artists in performance who said they made viewers feel as if they were at the concert themselves. The artists in this exhibit give everything they've got to the audience, night after night. The purpose of my photography is to convey the excitement, joy, emotion, and intensity offered to the masses by these music icons.

Gerry Graphia

RESTAURANTS AND COMMERCIAL SPACES

PARTICIPATING SPACES NOT IN CATALOGUE

UNIVERSITIES, NON-PROFIT ART SPACES

125 Gallery at the Cultural Arts Council of
Houston/Harris County
5004 Feagan
Estrada-Solis Studios
Kingwood College, Fine Art Gallery
MBS Studios
Mother Dog Studios
Negative Space
Raw Space
Rice University Art Gallery
Stages Repertory Theatre
Southmore House Gallery
The Arts Alliance Center at Clear Lake
The Cloister Gallery at Christ Church Cathedral
The Jung Center
UT Health Science Center at Houston
University of St. Thomas, Jones Gallery

COMMERCIAL GALLERIES

Barbara Davis Gallery
Blossom Street Gallery
Booker-Lowe Gallery
Dean Day Gallery
DNM Art Group
Gibson-Riley Gallery

Goldesberry Gallery
Houston Studio Glass
Joan Wich & Co. Gallery
Lowell Collins Gallery
McClain Gallery
Mixture Contemporary Art
Poissant O'Neal Gallery
The Tirr Gallery
Watermark, Fine Art Photographs and Books

CORPORATE AND RETAIL SPACES

Capella's Salon
City Gallery at Wells Fargo Plaza
Cosmos
Croissant Brioche
Daily Review Café
Dean's Credit Clothing
Dramos Studios
Hollywood Frame
Hungry's Café and Bistro
Mo Mong
Post Office Street Cafe
The Raven Grill
SOK, the Salon On Kirby
Xnihilo
Zana

ARTIST BIOGRAPHIES

Museums and Universities

WALT BISTLINE (ALSO AT MICHAELINE'S RESTUARANT)

Born in 1950, Walt Bistline has been photographing seriously since 1994. His show at FotoFest 2004 in the participating space Michaeline's Restaurant will be his eighth solo exhibition. His work has also been included in numerous group exhibitions, including recent shows in France, Florida, Oregon, and various cities in Texas. He received his undergraduate degree in English literature from Emory University, Atlanta, and holds a law degree from Boston University, Boston. He is currently in the third year of the M.F.A. program in photography at the University of Houston, where he is a teaching fellow.

JAMES FRAHER

Born in 1949 in Chicago, James Fraher resides in Grayslake, Illinois. He is the author of *The Blues is a Feeling: Voices and Visions of African-American Blues Musicians*. Fraher's photographs have appeared on the covers of *Living Blues* magazine and on over 150 music recordings. In 1996, he received a Keeping the Blues Alive Award from the Blues Foundation in Memphis. Photographs by Fraher have been exhibited in museums and galleries in the United States, Ireland, France, Italy, and Scotland.

JOHN HEARTFIELD

John Heartfield was born Helmut Herzefelde on June 19, 1891 in Berlin, Germany. Like so many of his generation, World War I had a profound effect on both is political beliefs and artistic endeavors. He became close friends with George Grosz and was inspired by Dadaism, Futurism and Cubism. He was among artists who simultaneously developed photomontage, and created pointed commentaries against the rise of Hitler and Fascism in Europe appearing on the cover of *Der Arbeiter-Illustrierte-Zeitung* (Workers Illustrated Newspaper) among other publications. He returned to Germany in 1950 and taught at Humboldt University of Leipzig. He continued to participate in art exhibits throughout Europe until his death in 1968.

TROY HUECHTKER

Troy Huechtker is an artist living and working in Houston. Although he is a native Texan, he has only recently returned to Texas after completing an MFA at the University of California, Santa Barbara, and a BFA at the School of Visual Arts in New York. His work contemplates issues of space, intimacy, media, nature, perception, and reception. Troy Huechtker's work has been exhibited in New York and Los Angeles.

MARCY JAMES

Marcy James is currently living in Montana and pursuing an M.F.A. at the University of Montana, Missoula. Her path to fine art photography follows professional work that includes commercial and journalistic photography, including photography from the 1990 Gulf War. Her background in these other fields of photography continues to influence the anthropological tendencies in her work and allows her to pursue a more expressive and personal style in her "societal landscapes."

KARL P. KOENIG

Karl P. Koenig holds a Ph.D. in clinical psychology from the University of Washington, and he taught at Stanford University and the University of New Mexico in the psychology and psychiatry departments. In 1981, he left teaching and research to enter private practice in Albuquerque. Photography, painting, and drawing are among his lifelong interests. He learned about alternative photographic printing methods in 1989 and 1990, which led him to the discovery of gumoil. As an artist he continues to write and teach, produce new works and exhibit while continuing to experiment with gumoil and other methods outside of mainstream photography.

LUISA LAMBRI

Born in Como, Italy, in 1969, Lambri studied languages and literature at universities Milan and Bologna. She a resides in Berlin and Milan. Her inventory of projects includes Le Corbusier's apartment blocks in Chandigarh, India (1997); Alvar Aalto's Finlandia Hall in Helsinki (1998); Wittgenstein House in Vienna (1999); Mies van der Rohe's Villa Tugendhat in Brno, Czech Republic (1999); and two Richard Neutra houses in Palm Springs, California.

MANUAL (SUZANNE BLOOM AND ED HILL)
(ALSO AT MOODY GALLERY)

Suzanne Bloom and Ed Hill began their artistic collaboration in 1974 and chose MANUAL as their collective name. MANUAL has worked with various imaging systems, first among these systems are photography and video. In 1985, they began to utilize computers. Along with a handful of other artists, they are considered pioneers of digital photography. Through the years they have continued to expand their use of digital media to include interactive multimedia and, recently, programmed digital still-frame animation. The content of their work has consistently revolved around the complex relation between Nature, Culture, and Technology. Their mixed and multimedia installations, photography works, videotapes, interactive computer programs, and programmed digital animations have been seen in 39 solo and over 200 group shows. Their retrospective exhibition, *MANUAL: Two Worlds - the Collaboration of Ed Hill and Suzanne Bloom*, organized by the International

Center of Photography (ICP) in New York City, was shown in 2003 at ICP. In addition to the catalogue accompanying the retrospective, *MANUAL errant arcadia*, their on-line catalogue raisonné may be seen at www.manualart.net. MANUAL is represented by the Moody Gallery in Houston, Texas.

STEPHEN MARC

Stephen Marc is a professor in the School of Art at Arizona State University, Tempe, where he joined the faculty in 1998. For 20 years (1978–1998), he taught at Columbia College in Chicago. He received his M.F.A. from Tyler School of Art, Temple University, Philadelphia, and his B.A. from Pomona College, Claremont, California. Marc's work bridges documentary photography and digital imaging, with recurring emphasis on visual explorations of the African diaspora. Marc has published two photographic books: *Urban Notions* (Champaign: University of Illinois, 1983) and *The Black Trans-Atlantic Experience* (Champaign: University of Illinois, 1992). Recently Marc has been actively involved in community-based projects, often related to his current investigation of the Underground Railroad. Since 2000, he has created residency/commission works for Mississippi State University, CEPA Gallery, The Center for Photography at Woodstock, Lycoming College, Jamestown Community College, and the "America 24/7" documentary project. He has had numerous exhibitions of his work, including *Committed to the Image* at the Brooklyn Museum of Art, Brooklyn, New York; the Smithsonian's traveling show *Reflections in Black, Color, Culture, and Complexity* at the Museum of Contemporary Art, Atlanta, Georgia, 2003; and FotoFest 1998 at the Community Artists Collective, Houston.

JASON NEUMANN

Jason Neumann has an undergraduate degree in photography from Sam Houston State University, Huntsville, Texas, and is currently a third-year graduate student at the University of Houston. Neumann teaches photography full time at Jersey Village High School and has been in numerous group shows at Harris Gallery, Houston, where he is represented. Neumann's photographs have been acquired by the Museum of Fine Arts, Houston, and by various private collectors.

BONNIE NEWMAN

Born in Houston in 1944, Bonnie Newman was a recipient of an Individual Artist Grant from the Cultural Arts Council of Houston/Harris County in 1993. She was a MacDowell Colony Fellow in 1987. She attended the Skowhegan School of Painting and Sculpture, Skowhegan, Maine, in 1982. She earned her B.A. in painting and drawing from the University of California at Berkeley and holds an M.F.A. in painting from the University of Houston, 1994. Currently she is an M.F.A. candidate in photography at the University of Houston.

JIM OLIVE

For photographer Jim Olive, a life spent in the outdoors experiencing nature in all it's grandeur and beauty coupled with the need to share and inspire others became a commitment to do his best technically and aesthetically in his profession. He has used his talent and experiences to present a dramatic perspective of life on the Texas gulf coast, reflexing the grandness and fragility of coastal resources. A native Houstonian, Jim has relentlessly photographed our city's growth and development while concurrently documenting the coastal environment. He was chosen by the EPA to document the environment for Project Documerica where his images were displayed at the Corocoran Gallery in Washington D.C. and are cataloged in the Library of Congress. His work has appeared in numerous publications including *Time-Life, Paris Match, Field and Stream, Texas Parks and Wildlife, Sierra Club, Tide* and others. His photographs are included in the collections of many of Houston's leading corporations including energy companies, hospitals, law firms and others.

SOODY SHARIFI

Soody Sharifi was born in Iran. She moved to Houston in 1974. She is presently a teaching fellow at the University of Houston. She was a recipient of a 2002 fellowship from the Houston Center of Photography. Her work has been published nationally and internationally.

CHRISTOPHER TALBOT

Born in Portland, Oregon, in 1971, Christopher Talbot has always worked in photography and education. He earned his B.F.A. in photography in 1995 from Brigham Young University, Provo, Utah. After continuing his photographic work and teaching in Central America for four years, he returned to the United States and is currently completing work on his M.F.A. in photography and digital media at the University of Houston. Talbot is a teaching fellow at the University of Houston and a digital imaging consultant at Que Imaging of Houston.

ROGER WOOD

Roger Wood's articles on Houston's blues, zydeco, and jazz history have appeared in numerous books, periodicals, and CD liner notes. A Houston resident, he has taught literature and writing at Houston Community College, Central College in Third Ward, since 1981.

Non-Profit Spaces

SUZANNE BANNING (ALSO AT GALLERY 101)

Born in 1973 in Hengelo, The Netherlands, Suzanne Banning received her B.F.A. in 1998 from the Art Academy in Arnhem, The Netherlands. Since July 2000, she has lived and worked in Houston. For a long time, Banning has been intrigued by the visual effect of movement in photography; by experimenting, she uses it to capture reality in a new way. Soon after her first show, she was awarded first

prize in an exhibition juried by Marysol Nieves (Senior Curator, Bronx Museum of the Arts, Bronx, New York). Since settling in Houston, Banning has been part of over 20 group shows, including several Visual Arts Alliance shows in Houston, 2001-2003 (juried by Sharon Kopriva, Marysol Nieves, Clint Willour, and Polly Hammett) and two *Assistance League Celebrates Texas Art* exhibitions (Williams Tower Gallery, Houston, 2002 and 2003). In addition, her work has been featured at Wheeler Bro's Studios, Lubbock, Texas; Dishman Art Gallery, Beaumont, Texas; Lowell Collins Gallery, Houston; Redbud Gallery, Houston; and the Art League, Houston.

JOHN BERNHARD (ALSO AT BERNAHE SOMOZA AND DEFROG GALLERIES)

John Bernhard has been pursuing the art of photography for over 20 years. His work has won numerous awards and has been exhibited and published throughout the United States and Europe. In addition, his photographs are included in museums and private collections. His work was part of *Body Work*, curated by Christian Peterson, a 120-year survey of photographs of the nude using the work of 12 photographers selected from the permanent collection of the Minneapolis Institute of Arts, Minneapolis. Bernhard has had three books published: *Nudes Metamorphs* (EMCO Press, Houston, TX, 2002), a compilation of seven years' work on nude bodies and transformations using elements of the earth; *Polo Watercolor Series* (DeFrog Gallery, Houston, TX, 2002), a compilation of 13 years' work when he was the official photographer of the sport of polo in Houston; and *Nicaragua — A Journey to Remember* (funded by The Nicaragua Children Texas Benfit Fund, Houston, TX, Drake Printing, Pasadena, TX, 2002) a reflection of his travels to Nicaragua depicting his strong social concerns. He is at present working on a new book, *Diptych* (Elite Edition, Houston, TX, 2004), which emphasizes the correlation of two images with the visual duplicity of resembling forms. He is represented by J.J. Brookings Gallery in San Francisco. Bernhard resides in Houston, where he has designed and built his studio and art gallery.

JANET BIGGS

Janet Biggs has been exhibiting her work since 1987. Recent solo exhibitions include *Respiridone* at Cornell University's Herbert F. Johnson Museum of Art, Ithaca, New York (2002), a three-channel video installation at Team Gallery, New York (2001), and shows at Plains Art Museum, Fargo, North Dakota (2001) and Western Gallery, Bellingham, Washington (2001). Her work has also been featured in numerous group exhibitions throughout the United States and Europe, including *Romper Room*, a 1997 exhibition at DiverseWorks, Houston. Biggs recently served as an artist-in-residence with the Wexner Center Media Arts Program, Ohio State University, Columbus, Ohio.

GAY BLOCK

Gay Block began her career in 1973, photographing her own affluent Jewish community in Houston. During the years 1973–1976, she studied photography with Geoff Winningham, Garry Winogrand, and Anne Tucker. Block has been the recipient of two National Endowment for the Arts grants and has published two books in col-laboration with writer Malka Drucker: *Rescuers: Portraits of Moral Courage in the Holocaust* and *White Fire: A Portrait of Women Spiritual Leaders in America*. A touring exhibition of *Rescuers* appeared at over 50 venues, including the Museum of Modern Art, New York; Corcoran Gallery, Washington, D.C.; and Museum of Fine Arts, Houston. Block presented a slide lecture on *Bertha Alyce* as a work-in-progress at the national Women in Photography Conference, organized by Houston Center for Photography in 1994. In 2003, the University of New Mexico Press in Albuquerque published her book *Bertha Alyce: Mother exPosed*, which includes the award-winning DVD *Bertha Alyce*. Block's work is in numerous collections, including the Museum of Modern Art, New York; Museum of Fine Arts, Houston; and San Francisco Museum of Modern Art, San Francisco.

FRANÇOISE AND DANIEL CARTIER

Collaborating since 1995, Swiss artists Françoise and Daniel Cartier fused their separate mediums—sculpture and photography—to become one creative entity: f&d cartier. Their collaborative method of creating photograms with natural light is similar to Henry Fox Talbot's early "photogenic drawings." The artists deal with contemporary themes of identity and gender that are invoked through their pink-toned photograms. Daniel was awarded the Swiss Federal Grant of Applied Arts in 1977 and 1980. Collaboratively they have received the "The Selection vfg. 2001" Swiss Foundation of Photography/Zurich Prize as well as Geneva's Michel Jordi Photographic Award in 1998. Through the Landis & Gyr Foundation, they spent six months in 1999 as artists-in-residence in London. Featured in numerous public and private collections, their work has been exhibited throughout North America and Europe. Yossi Milo Gallery, New York, represents them in the United States.

JEAN CASLIN (ALSO AT GALLERY 3)

Jean Caslin received a B.A. in English literature and fine arts from Boston University, Boston, and then studied photography and photographic history while pursuing an M.A. in art history at Stanford University, Stanford, California. Caslin began her arts administration career as Assistant Director of the Photographic Resource Center at Boston University in 1979 and became Executive Director/Curator of the Houston Center for Photography in 1988. Her photographic work has been featured in group exhibitions in participating spaces at FotoFest 2000 and 2002, and in group shows in Houston for the Texas Photographic Society, Rice University, Glassell School of Art, koelsch Gallery, and Studio E.

IRENE CLOUTHIER CARRILLO

Irene Clouthier was born in Culiacan, Sinaloa, Mexico, in 1974. She is currently living and working in Virginia. Her work has recently been shown at the *V International Digital Art Exhibit* and *Colloquium* in Havana, Cuba, and the Anchorage Museum, Anchorage, Alaska. Irene's exhibition *Our Voices, Our Image* showed at the Inter American Development Bank Cultural Center Art Gallery through the Washington, D.C., Commission for the Arts and Humanities with the collaboration of the Virginia Commission for the Arts. Clouthier

received her B.F.A. in 1997 from the University of Monterrey, Mexico, during which time she was awarded the Academic Excellence Award in 1998. She is at present working on her M.F.A. in visual information technologies at George Mason University in Fairfax, Virginia.

KELLI A. CONNELL

Kelli A. Connell received a B.F.A. in photography and visual art studies from North Texas State University, Denton (1997), and an M.F.A. in photography from Texas Woman's University, Denton (2003). Connell was recently featured in a solo exhibition at Barry Whistler Gallery, Dallas (2003) and McKinney Avenue Contemporary, Dallas (2003). She has been included in group shows at McNeese State University, Lake Charles, Louisiana (2003); Creative Artists' Network, Philadelphia (2003); Dallas Center for Contemporary Art, Dallas (2003 and 2002); and Arlington Museum of Art, Arlington, Texas (2002). She has curated exhibitions at the University of Texas at Dallas Art Gallery, Dallas (2001); the Haggerty Gallery at the University of Dallas, Irving, Texas (2001); and the Arlington Museum of Art, Arlington, Texas (2000). Connell currently resides in Youngstown, Ohio, where she is an assistant professor of art at Youngstown State University.

AVERY DANZIGER

Avery Danziger was born in Chapel Hill, NC in 1953 and now lives in Columbia, Missouri. He has been a photographer and photographic instructor for over 30 years and a documentary filmmaker for the last 15 years. His photographs are in many international collections and museums, including: Museum of Modern Art, NYC; Corcoran Gallery, Washington, DC; National Museum of American Art, Washington, DC; Bibliotheque Nationale, Paris; Stedelijk Museum of Modern Art, Amsterdam.

ERINA DUGANNE

Erina Duganne is a doctoral candidate in the Department of Art and Art History at The University of Texas at Austin. She received her B.A. from Reed College, Portland, Oregon, and M.A. from The University of Texas at Austin. She is currently working on her doctoral dissertation entitled *Looking In/Looking Out: The Representation of Race in 1950s and 1960s U.S. Photography*. In addition to teaching at The University of Texas at Austin, Duganne has served as a curatorial intern in the Department of American and Contemporary Art at the Jack S. Blanton Museum of Art, Austin, Texas, and recently curated *Beyond the Academy: Encouraging New Talent From Texas at Arthouse*, Jones Center, Austin, Texas.

SUSAN DUNKERLEY

Susan Dunkerley was born in Galveston, Texas, in 1964. She has had solo exhibitions in numerous venues including Silver Eye Center for Photography, Pittsburgh, and the Houston Center for Photography, Houston. In 2000, Dunkerley was a FofoFest- sponsored artist. Her photographs have been included in group exhibitions in the United States and Europe. Her work is in the collections of the Brooklyn Museum of Art, Brooklyn, New York; Philadelphia Museum of Art, Philadelphia; and Museum of Fine Arts, Houston. Since 1997, Dunkerley has lived in Waco, Texas, where she is currently an associate professor of art at Baylor University.

JOY GREGORY

Born in England to parents of South African origin, Joy Gregory sees her work has being influenced by a combination of race, gender, and aesthetics. She attended the Royal College of Art, London, where she was awarded a master's in photography in 1986. Gregory has exhibited internationally, including in Cape Town, South Africa, where she completed her series *Lost Histories*, reflecting on colonization and its effects on culture and self-image. In 2002, Gregory received the NESTA (the National Endowment for Science, Technology and the Arts) Fellowship that enabled her to combine her unique 19th-century printing process with digital media. Her monograph, *Objects of Beauty*, is scheduled to be published in Spring 2004 by Autograph/Chris Boot. Gregory's work is featured in the collections of the Victoria and Albert Museum, London; Institute of Modern Art, Brisbane, Australia; and Yale University, New Haven, Connecticut. She lives and works in London.

MARY MARGARET HANSEN

A Houston photographer and visual artist, Mary Margaret Hansen recently created www.pursestories.com, an interactive Web site that explores the handbag—that private space we sling over our shoulder or hang from our wrist. The Web site grew from *Purse Stories*, an installation exhibited in *Mama Said…Nine Interpretations* during FotoFest 2000, and from an earlier collaboration with Weave Dance Company, Houston. Hansen has exhibited in participating spaces at FotoFest 1986 and 1988 and at the Houston Center for Photography.

MISTY KEASLER

Misty Keasler received her B.A. from Columbia College in Chicago. She has achieved a great deal at the age of 25, including the prestigious Lange-Taylor Prize, an annual award given to a photojournalist and writer who collaborate on a photographic project. *Photo District News* included her in its selection of "25 Up-and-Coming American Photographers" in 2003. Her Dallas Museum of Art DeGolyer Grant and inclusion in the *New American Talent* exhibition at the Austin Museum of Art, Austin, Texas, have all been achieved within the past two years. Her photographs are included in the collections of the Museum of Fine Arts, Houston, and the Kiyosato Museum of Photographic Arts, Kiyosato, Japan. She is represented by Photographs Do Not Bend Gallery, Dallas.

ORLANDO LARA

Hecho en Mexico and reared in Houston, Texas, Orlando Lara is an artist, scholar and writer. He earned a B.A. in Chicana/o studies from Stanford University in 2003 where he focused on border and migration studies. At Stanford University, he has exhibited prints and photography such as *La Lucha Continua* in commemoration of Cesar Chavez and *Floricanto* where he displayed himself as a *mojado*

museum specimen. As an artist/scholar in residence with the Border Arts Workshop/Taller Artístico Fronterizo he lived in El Poblado Maclovio Rojas, a "squatter" community in Mexico. From this experience, he created a video installation for the "Art Defends" exhibit at Southwestern College in San Diego. *The Trail of Thirst* installation represents four years of undergraduate study and a lifetime of growing up among an extended family of Mexican immigrants.

MAUD LIPSCOMB

Maud Lipscomb is a Houston visual artist who studied photography in the Continuing Studies program at Rice University, Houston, as well as photography and art at the Glassell School of Art, Museum of Fine Arts, Houston. Her collages employ both original and found images utilizing the transfer process. Lipscomb has exhibited her work in numerous photography and mixed-media exhibitions including *Mama Said* in a participating space at FotoFest 2000 and at the Houston Center for Photography.

WILL MICHELS

Will Michels, a native Houstonian, received a bachelor's of architecture degree with honors from Pratt Institute, Brooklyn, New York. In 2000 Michels was awarded two separate grants from the Summerlee Foundation and Houston Endowment Inc. to photograph the veterans of the battleship *Texas*. He enjoys taking portraits most of all, and he teaches photography at the Glassell School of Art, Museum of Fine Arts, Houston. Michels's work is represented in numerous collections including the Museum of Fine Arts, Houston.

DELILAH MONTOYA (ALSO AT GALLERY 101)

For artist Delilah Montoya, transforming the past is a communal act in which revered symbols and their mystical and spiritual qualities are reborn in photographic representation. Montoya was born in Fort Worth in 1955. Her work makes use of alternative approaches that incorporate mark-making and printmaking skills with photographic processes such as the collotype. This process is the 19th-century printmaking technique developed in France to produce a stable/archival continuous tone graphic print. By using this vintage technology, she has produced an intimate portrait series of two girls caught in motionless stares, trapped perpetually in their youth. Currently Montoya's work is in the Los Angeles County Museum of Art, Los Angeles; Museum of Fine Art, Houston; Mexican Museum, San Francisco; Bronx Museum, Bronx, New York; Smithsonian Institute; Washington, D.C.; UCLA Wight Gallery, Los Angeles; Stanford University Libraries, Stanford, California; Armand Hammer Museum of Art and Cultural Center, Los Angeles; National Hispanic Center of New Mexico, Albuquerque; and Museum of Fine Arts, Santa Fe. Her work has been exhibited throughout New Mexico, Texas, New York, California, France, and Mexico.

ARNOLD NEWMAN

Arnold Newman was born in New York in 1931. The family settled in Miami Beach in 1936. Newman studied art at the University of Miami. Forced to leave school for economic reasons, he became an apprentice in a photo studio, where his love for photography began. Newman went to New York in 1941, and his talent was discovered by Alfred Stieglitz and Beaumont Hall who gave him his own show. He developed the technique of "environmental photography," in which portraits of people are made in their own surroundings. This work has won many international awards. His work has appeared in publications such as *LIFE, Look, and Harper's Bazaar,* and is included in the collections of museums and private collectors worldwide. Newman and wife, Augusta, have two sons and four grandchildren. He continues to work as vigorously as ever.

CHRISTOPHER OLIVIER

Native Houstonian Christopher Olivier uses two monikers for his work: Bexar and Olivier. The Bexar work is manufactured from discarded electronic devices such as faxes, copiers, and computers. The pieces take on a new life as sculpture. The Olivier work is in paint and abstract digital photography. He began his dual art career in the *Fourth Annual Open Show* in 1997 at Art League Houston. Olivier and Bexar were chosen as two of the 20 artists selected. Since then he has displayed his work in juried competitions and other venues. In June 2003, he was selected for DiverseWorks' Creative Capitol Workshop, Houston. He was awarded second prize in the Visual Arts Alliance exhibition juried by Lynn Herbert from the Contemporary Arts Museum, Houston. His paintings, sculpture, and photography are in private collections in Colorado, Texas, California, New York, Holland, and France.

BARBARA POLLACK

Barbara Pollack's work has been the subject of solo exhibitions at Esso Gallery, New York (2001); Thread Waxing Space, New York (2000); Meyerson Gallery at the University of Pennsylvania, Philadelphia (2000); and Wesleyan University's Zilkha Gallery, Middletown, Connecticut (1999). A recipient of fellowships from the Ragdale Foundation (2001) and MacDowell Colony (1994, 1996, 1997), she has work in the collections of the Solomon R. Guggenheim Museum, New York; Brooklyn Museum of Art, Brooklyn, New York; and Museum of Fine Arts, Houston, among others. She recently served as artist-in-residence at The Kitchen, New York. Pollack teaches at the School of Visual Arts, New York, and writes extensively on photography and contemporary art.

JANICE RUBIN (ALSO AT GALLERY 101)

Janice Rubin is a Houston-based photographer. Her work has been exhibited internationally, and her photographs are included in the permanent collection of the Museum of Fine Arts, Houston, as well as many private collections. She is the recipient of a National Endowment for the Arts Fellowship. Her work has appeared in publications in the United States and Europe including *Smithsonian, Newsweek, Town and Country, Fortune, Rolling Stone,* and *The New York Times.* Her 1987 exhibition, *Survival of the Spirit: Jewish Lives in the Soviet Union,* toured 17 cities in North America.

BETSY L. SIEGEL

Betsy Siegel earned an M.F.A degree in film at Brandeis University, Waltham, Massachusetts. A working photographer, she is known for her documentary work. Siegel has exhibited in numerous group shows including independent exhibits at FotoFest in Houston and art spaces in New Mexico. Her work has been published regionally and nationally.

SUSAN SIMMONS

Houston-based artist Susan Simmons received a B.A. in philosophy from Agnes Scott College, Decatur, Georgia (1990), and worked as a graphic designer from 1991 to 1999. She was featured in a solo exhibition at Terlingua House Projects Gallery, Alpine, Texas (2001) and group shows at Commerce Street Artist Warehouse, Houston (2002), and Studio 424, Galveston, Texas (2001).She currently resides in Douala, Cameroon.

DYLAN VITONE

Documentary photographer Dylan Vitone presents traditional subjects in a nontraditional way. His work features a full 360-degree view of his subjects, as can be seen in his project *Photographs from South Boston*, an exploration of life and its idiosyncrasies in an impoverished, insular community. Dylan Vitone holds an M.F.A. in photography from Massachusetts College of Art in Boston, and a B.A. in photo-communications from St. Edward's University in Austin, Texas. He has shown nationally at places that include the Photographic Resource Center at Boston University, Boston, and RISD (Rhode Island School of Design, Providence). He is scheduled for upcoming shows at Blue Sky Gallery, Portland, Oregon, and Notre Dame University, Notre Dame, Indiana.

CAROL VUCHETICH

Carol Vuchetich received an M.F.A. from the University of Houston and has exhibited her work in the United States and abroad. For her work documenting life in the inner city, she received grants from the Texas Council on the Humanities, the National Endowment for the Arts through the Cultural Arts Council of Houston/Harris County, and the Houston Center for Photography. She currently teaches at Galveston College, Galveston, Texas; the Glassell Junior School of Art, Museum of Fine Arts, Houston; and the Continuing Studies program at Rice University, Houston.

RODNEY WATERS (ALSO AT GALLERY 3)

Photographer and pianist Rodney Waters is a native of Lubbock, Texas, and he earned his bachelor's and master's of music from the Mannes College of Music in New York. A self-taught photographer, Waters has exhibited work in several galleries in the Houston area as well as at the Buddy Holly Center in Lubbock, Texas. His volunteer work with refugees resettled by Interfaith Ministries for Greater Houston has resulted in the creation of several large-scale projects designed to use the arts for humanitarian and interfaith goals. He performs regularly with Context and the Houston Symphony, and his

recording with Curt Thompson of the complete Sonatas for Violin and Piano by American composer Charles Ives was recently reviewed by Naxos. The CD *Seeking Refuge* is available from Interfaith Ministries for Greater Houston.

LLOYD WOLF

Lloyd Wolf is an award-winning photographer whose work is in major public and private collections. His work has appeared in *The Washington Post Magazine, Jewish Monthly, The Forward, People, Vogue,* and many other publications. He received a National Endowment for the Arts grant in 1980. His documentary projects include a prison drug-rehab clinic, the Moroccan Jewish community, the March of the Living, Operation Understanding (on Black-Jewish relations), and "Grandma's House" about a program that cares for HIV-positive babies. He collaborated with Paula Wolfson on the book *Jewish Mothers: Strength Wisdom Compassion* (San Francisco, Chronicle Books, 2000). His first book, *Facing the Wall: Americans at the Vietnam Memorial* (in collaboration with Duncan Spenser), was published by Macmillan in New York in 1986.

Commercial Galleries

LUCIANA ABAIT

Luciana Abait, born in 1971, is an Argentine artist who has resided in Miami since 1997. She earned her master's degree in Painting at the National School of Fine Arts Prilidiano Pueyrredon, Buenos Aires Argentina in 1996. Among her solo exhibitions are *Liquid* at Mackey Gallery, Houston; *New Works*, Jean Albano Gallery, Chicago; *Swimming Rooms*, Miami-Dade Department of Cultural Affairs, Miami; and *Visual Fields*, TaiKoo Place, Hong Kong. She has recently participated in group shows at Rice/ Polak Gallery, Provincetown; Fredric Snitzer Gallery, Miami, and the National Gallery of the Cayman Islands. Her work has been reviewed by publications such as *Art Nexus, Ming Pao Hong Kong, Miami Herald, Chicago Reade,* and *Art in America.* Abait's works are held by private, public and corporate collectors from the United States, Europe, Latin America and East Asia.

KELLY GALE AMEN

Kelly Gale Amen, a native of Weatherford, Oklahoma, has been an influential participant in the Houston arts community for decades, noted for his strong support of the arts and his active participation as an artist and a creator of Art Furniture and sculpture. Amen enjoys a reputation for cutting-edge concept and design.

SUZANNE BANNING (SEE NON-PROFIT SPACES)

TOM BARIL

For the last 10 years, Tom Baril has used pinhole cameras, solarized Polaroid negatives, and the wet plate collodion process. Always working in large formats, he uses his work to confront head-on the history of the medium. The ghosts of Alfred Stieglitz, Edward Weston, and Karl Blossfeldt can be felt in his images of New York and

in his still-lifes. Though there is a distinct respect for the past, if not a direct reference to it, evident in Baril's work, his pictures are always his own. Baril was born in Connecticut in 1952. In 1980 he received a B.F.A. in photography from the School of Visual Arts in New York. While still a student at Visual Arts, he began working as Robert Mapplethorpe's printer. Baril has since been credited with developing the lush quality of the late photographer's black and white prints. He was soon recognized as a master printer, and other artists and galleries sought his printmaking skills. Although known primarily as a master printmaker, taking pictures has always been Baril's true passion. Initially he avoided the studio to distance himself from Mapplethorpe's work; he focused instead on landscapes and urban architecture. His photograph of the Chrysler building became one of the best-known images of that frequently photographed building. In 2000 and 2001, he was commissioned to photograph San Francisco and Boston. Baril eventually shifted his focus to the studio where he began photographing still-lifes, nudes, and curious objects with a pin-hole camera. In 1994, he began to photograph flowers. A monograph, now sold out, was published in 1997 by 4AD. A second book, *Botanica*, was published by Arena Editions, New York, 2001 in May 2000. Baril's work is featured in many prestigious private and public collections worldwide, including the Los Angeles County Museum, Los Angeles; Museum of Fine Arts, Houston; Stedelijk Museum, Amsterdam; Philadelphia Museum of Art, Philadelphia; Fogg Museum at Harvard University, Cambridge, Massachusetts; Elton John Collection; Polaroid Collection; and Center for Creative Photography, Tucson. He has had solo exhibitions in major cities throughout the United States and select cities in Europe. His work has been featured in numerous publications.

JOHN BERNHARD (SEE NON-PROFIT SPACES)

CLYDE BUTCHER

Born in Missouri in 1942, Clyde Butcher graduated from the California Polytechnic University, San Luis Obispo, in 1964 with a degree in architecture. After multiple ventures in architecture and commercial photography in California, he moved to Florida in 1980. In Florida, he switched to black and white photography exclusively and devoted most of his time to documenting the Florida wilderness. Butcher has published several books, including *Clyde Butcher Portfolio I* (Shadetree Press, Fort Myers, FL, 1994), *Nature's Places of Spiritual Sanctuary* (University Press of Florida, Gainesville, FL, 2003), and *Clyde Butcher: Florida Landscapes* (Cypress Gallery, Ochopee, FL, 2001). He is the recipient of many awards, including the Sierra Club's prestigious Ansel Adams Award for Conservation Photography in 2000. Butcher lives and works in southern Florida where he keeps his studio and gallery at the Big Cypress Gallery and Venice Gallery and Studio.

KEITH CARTER

Born in Madison, Wisconsin, in 1948, Keith Carter moved to Beaumont, Texas, at the age of five and has lived there since. He developed his talents as a photographer essentially in isolation, with advice from David Cargill, an artist and teacher at Lamar University in Beaumont. Today, Carter is an internationally recognized photographer and educator. He holds the endowed Walles Chair of Art at Lamar University, and eight books on his work have been published. His photographs are included in numerous permanent collections and have appeared in a multitude of solo and group exhibitions in the United States and abroad. The Wittliff Gallery of Southwestern and Mexican Photography at Southwest Texas State University, San Marcos, houses his major collection.

ELINOR CARUCCI

Born in 1971 in Israel, Carucci lives and works in New York. she earned her B.F.A. degree at Bezalet Academy of Art in Jerusalem. Carucci has participated in several solo shows, including exhibitions at the Photographers' Gallery, London; Fotografie Forum, Frankfurt; Prague House of Photography, Prague; Ricco/Maresca Gallery, New York; and National Arts Club, New York. She has exhibited her work in group shows at the Brooklyn Museum of Art, Wookstock Center for Photography, New York; The Museum of Israeli Art, and The Israel Museum. Carucci has published work in several books and other publications and is represented in collections in the United States, Europe, and Israel. She won the Guggenheim Fellowship in 2002, the Friends of Photography (SF) Special Honorable Mention–Ruttenberg Award in 1999, and won the Memorial Foundation for Jewish Culture project grant in 1998.

JEAN CASLIN (SEE NON-PROFIT SPACES)

ANDREY CHEZHIN (ALSO IN FOTOFEST-SPONSORED EXHIBIT)

Internationally renowned conceptual photographer, Andrey Chezhin was born in St Petersburg, Russia, in 1960. He created his beloved character, Thumbtack in the 1990s to symbolize a nameless, faceless individual in a big state machine. The 50-image series *Thumbtacks and Modernism* is the most recent part of the *Thumbtack* trilogy. Here, Chezhin pays homage to the outstanding masters of 20th century art by creating portraits of the *Thumbtack* in the style characteristic of each artist. All images are executed by purely photographic means— multiple exposures, collages, hand toning. Chezhin's work has been widely exhibited and collected internationally, including Museum of Fine Arts, Houston; Brooklyn Museum of Art, Brooklyn, NY; Columbus Museum of Art, Columbus, OH; Muzeo Ken Damy, Brescia, Italy;The Navigator Foundation, Boston, MA; The Norton and Nancy Dodge Collection, The Jane Voorhees Zimmerli Art Museum at Rutgers, New Brunswick, NJ; Southeast Museum of Photography, Daytona Beach, Daytona, FL;The State Russian Museum, St. Petersburg.

THOMAS JOSHUA COOPER

Thomas Joshua Cooper was born in San Francisco in 1946. As a member of the Cherokee Nation and son of a U.S. naval officer, Cooper spent his childhood living on Indian reservations throughout

the western United States. He studied at Humboldt State University and the University of New Mexico, graduating in 1972 with distinction in photography. In 1982, he founded the department of photography at the Glasgow School of Art in Glasgow, Scotland. As current director of the department, Cooper resides in Glasgow while traveling throughout Europe and North America working on photographic projects, some of which are many years in the making. Cooper uses a field camera from the 1890s and makes glass negatives, often making a single long exposure. His work has been exhibited widely in museum and galleries around the world, most recently at the College of Santa Fe, New Mexico, and the Sean Kelly Gallery, New York. The artist has an upcoming show at the Dia Center for the Arts, New York. The work is included in museum, public and private collections worldwide.

JEROME CROWDER

Jerome Crowder was born and raised in Houston, and has been taking photographs since he was 11 years old. He has taught anthropology in the Semester at Sea program sponsored by the Institute for Shipboard Education and at the University of Houston. Crowder's photographic work explores migration and urbanization in La Paz, Bolivia, where he has been working since 1989, and in Peru. He is currently a lecturer in the Department of Anthropology at the University of Houston.

JIM DILGER

Jim Dilger is a native Houstonian. He started photographing in 1998 and began attending Continuing Education photography classes at Rice University, Houston, in 2001. Along with pursuing an interest in travel photography, Dilger has completed a photographic series *Houston at Night*.

HERMAN DOBBS

Herman Dobbs began working in photography three years ago after retiring from a career as a surgeon. He is particularly interested in images pertaining to human manipulations of the natural world. He works with black and white film and traditional printing methods.

TOMMY EWASKO

Tommy Ewasko was born in Scranton, Pennsylvania, in 1958 and currently resides in Houston. He received a B.S. from Rochester Institute of Technology, School of Photographic Arts and Sciences, Rochester, New York. Ewasko has received numerous grants, including the Kodak Award of Excellence and the Xerox Achievement Award, as well as awards from the Art Directors Clubs of Houston, New York, and Louisiana, and the International Association of Business Communicators (IABC) Award of Excellence. The integration of style and substance in his work is a reflection of his continuing growth as a photographic artist. His clients include Hyatt Regency Hotels, Motorola, Sysco, Coca-Cola, and Getty Images. His work is part of the permanent collection at The George Eastman House International Museum of Photography and Film, Rochester, New York.

PHYLLIS LIEDEKER FINLEY

Born in Marshall, Texas, in 1945, Phyllis Finley grew up in Corpus Christi, Texas. She earned a B.A. with honors from Sophie Newcomb College, New Orleans, in 1967. Following a career in motherhood, from 1982 to 1984 she did postgraduate work in photography in the Art Department at the University of Texas at Austin. While pursuing her art, Finley also ran a commercial photography business for 10 years in Austin. For 20 years Finley has been photographing in neighborhoods, exploring the meanings of "home" and "heaven." In photographing the commonplace, she finds beauty in ordinary, often overlooked places. She currently resides in Corpus Christi. Her work has been published and exhibited throughout the United States.

CHRISTINE BRUNI FONDREN

Christine Bruni Fondren was born in Houston in 1967. After studying at the Parsons School of Design, New York, she received her degree from the University of Texas at Austin. Fondren has developed a body of work that draws upon her experience and study of fashion, psychology, and spirituality. Although she has participated in group shows and smaller exhibitions, FotoFest 2004 marks her premier solo exhibition. She currently lives and works in Houston as a painter and photographer.

SALLY GALL

Sally Gall has worked as a photographer for over 25 years. In addition to focusing on her own work, she teaches and makes commissioned pieces. Gall grew up in Houston and currently lives and works in New York. Her work is widely exhibited around the country and is in the collections of various museums, among them the Simon R. Guggenheim Museum, New York; Cleveland Museum of Art, Cleveland; New Orleans Museum of Art, New Orleans; Museum of Fine Arts, Houston; and San Francisco Museum of Art, San Francisco. She is the recipient of several awards and fellowships, including a National Endowment for the Arts Visual Artist Fellowship, two MacDowell Colony Fellowships, and a Rockefeller Foundation Residency in Bellagio, Italy. Her most recent book, *The Water's Edge* (Chronicle Books, San Francisco) with an essay by James Salter, was published in 1995.

CLAUDETTE CHAMPRUN GOUX

Born in 1951, Claudette Goux lived in Houston, Texas and now lives in the Los Angeles area. She received, in 2003, a master's degree in art history from the University of California, Riverside. She completed her bachelor's degree in Photography, in 1998, from Rice University, Houston, TX. following study at the New York Institute of Photography, New York City. Prior degrees include a bachelor's degree in philosophy and a bachelor's degree in sociology from the University of Nancy, Nancy, France. Her work has been exhibited in several group and solo shows. Her bibliography includes the *1996 Houston Area Exhibition Catalogue*, the spring 1997 issue of *Heritage Magazine*, and exhibition reviews in *Public News*, *The Press Enterprise* and *The Highlander*. She has been awarded the California Museum of Photography fellowship, the Christine Croneis Sayres Memorial

Award in Studio Art and a prize from the Texas Historical Foundation for a photograph from her series *Places of Worship*. Her work is represented in numerous collections in America and Europe and at The Blaffer Museum of University of Houston, Houston, Texas.

SCOTT GRIESBACH

Scott Griesbach was born in 1967 in Milwaukee. He has pursued an interest in the political as well as the technical aspects of art throughout his career as an artist. Educated at the University of Wisconsin, the University of California, Los Angeles, and the Philosophical Institute. Griesbach is currently a resident of Santa Monica, California. He continues his interest in all things visual with his work in the realm of digital imagery. His digital work was featured in FotoFest 2002, *The Classical Eye and Beyond*.

SAMARIY GURARIY

Samariy Mikhailovitch Gurariy was born in 1916 in the Ukraine. He died in 1998 in New York. Gurariy belongs to the top rank of Soviet photojournalists. Starting in 1934, he worked almost exclusively for *Izvestia* and *Trud*. During World War II, he was dispatched as photo reporter to different fronts. One of the very few artists to enjoy Stalin's confidence, he was appointed special correspondent at the Yalta and Potsdam conferences. In world-renowned photographs, he recorded the official meetings of Stalin, Roosevelt and Churchill, Stalin and Truman, Molotov at the United Nations, Khrushchev hugging Fidel Castro in Moscow, first cosmonauts and their popularity. As Soviet society and political culture evolved following Stalin's death in 1953, Gurariy was on hand to record the changes at every level, including the hidden top strata behind the walls of the Kremlin. Gurariy's own style of work changed during the 50 years of his career and reveals a lively intelligence that was never content to merely repeat successful formulae. After the collapse of Communism, Gurariy left Russia for the United States, smuggling a great number of prints and negatives. In 1995, a book titled *This is History…*, based on his famed political images, was published in Moscow by V.A. Bryntsalov. In 2002, a large collection of his work was exhibited by the Grace Museum in Abilene, Texas, as part of a major exhibition *Soviet Art of the Cold War*.

STEVE HARRIS

Armed with creativity and a passionate vision, Steve Harris set out to make his mark on the world of photography in 1988 after earning a B.F.A. from Parsons School of Design in Paris. His private collection documents his travels throughout Europe, North Africa, the United States, Mexico, and more recently, two mountaineering expeditions he led in Boliva and Peru. His professional background ranges from New York's fashion industry to commercial and advertising work in Houston.

MICHAEL HART

A native of Indiana who had his first paying job in photography at the age of 15, Michael Hart has been a Texan for 35 years. During the past 26 years, he has worked as a professional photographer in Houston, where he specializes in creating images primarily "on location" for design firms, corporations, and advertising agencies. His work has taken him to every state in the union and 30 foreign countries. His photographs have appeared in *Communication Arts Photography Annual, Graphex, PRINT Magazine's Regional Design Annual*, The Dallas Society of Visual Communications show, The Art Director's Club of Houston show, and The Houston Advertising Federation's Addy Awards.

GEORGE HIXSON

George Hixson lives and works making photographs in Houston. Personal projects include essays on the urban landscapes of Houston; the relationships between freeways, architecture, and the primordial bayous and green spaces that surround and run through the city; his travels across America with various performance artists and musicians; and his continuing documentation of the alternative visual and performance arts scene in Houston.

ZENA STETKA HOWE

Zena Stetka Howe was born in Pilzen, Czechoslovakia, and grew up under the artistic influence of her uncle, an accomplished painter and sculptor. She is faithful to his philosophy of expressing one's feelings under any circumstances and through any art form. Fluent in English, Russian, French, and Czech, Zena Howe received her early education in Litomerice, Czechoslovakia, taking advanced studies in Latin and foreign languages. Before coming to the United States in 1975, she worked as a film editor for Czechoslovak TV in Prague. She attended the Fashion Institute of Technology in New York, working part-time as a model. Family and financial difficulties caused her to put her dream of becoming a fashion designer on hold, and she worked as a flight attendant for the next 14 years. With the strength gained from her life experiences and with the support of her family, Zena Howe recently returned to her dream of creative expression.

BARBARA JONES

Barbara Jones, originally a native of New York, has been a resident Houstonian since 1970. A graduate of the University of Houston, she is best recognized as a painter. Jones has always used photographs as source material. Her work consists of the images created in her studio as well as a variety of murals throughout the city.

BRYAN KUNTZ

Bryan Kuntz was born in San Antonio in 1955. He now resides in Richmond, Texas. Kuntz graduated from Texas A&M University, Commerce, in 1979 with a B.A. in photography. He worked with photographers in Dallas and New York before moving to Houston in

...1982 to open his own photography studio. His photography has been published in *Communication Arts Photography Annual*, the *Print Magazine Regional Design Annual*, *Photo Design Magazine*, *Annual Reports 100*, and *Creativity Annual*, and has received awards from the Houston Addy Awards, Dallas Society of Visual Communications, and The Art Directors Club of Houston. His subject matter and style has varied widely over the years. He is currently working on a series of black and white tree photographs as well as a series of Polaroid emulsion transfers on plexiglass.

FRANCISCO LARIOS

Born in Mexico in 1960, Francisco Larios left his native Sonora to complete his studies and finally settled in the city of Monterrey in the industrial north of Mexico, where he became a painter. In 1997, he won first prize at the *Bienal del Museo de Monterrey, Mexico*, and in 1999 an international jury awarded him the *Premio Omnilife* in Guadalajara, Mexico. In 2001, Larios began to work with "new photography" in 3D modeling. His first photographic digital-drawing series, entitled *El ABC de la Evolución [The ABC's of Evolution]*, won first prize at the *Photographic Monterrey Salon*, Mexico, in 2001. With the next series, *Ex-votos*, he won first prize in the *Bienal de Cuenca*, Ecuador. The Cuenca prize proved valuable to his career, as he captured the attention of curators in Mexico and collectors all over the world. In the second *Ex-votos* series, Larios created photographic stories within the context of water. This project was also selected for the *Festival de Artes Electronicas en São Paulo, Brazil*, in 2002. These computer drawings (or new photographs with 3D modeling) consist of game software that has taken Larios six years to perfect. He models virtual objects in scenes: he chooses the type of camera he wants to use and starts working figures from geometrical forms. Larios works in Monterrey and has most recently been honored at the Museo the Arte Contemporaneo (MARCO), Monterrey, Mexico, in their final and fourth installment exhibition *The 20th Century Masters of Mexico*.

JAY MAISEL

Photographer Jay Maisel's name has become synonymous with light, gesture, and color. His images have been used for advertising, editorial, and corporate communications. He has exhibited widely; his prints are in private, corporate, and museum collections. Among his awards are the American Society of Media Photographers (ASMP) and Professional Photographers of America (PPA) Lifetime Achievement awards, ASMP Photographer of the Year, and the International Center of Photography's Infinity Award. He is also in the Art Directors Club Hall of Fame. A graduate of Cooper Union, New York, and Yale University, New Haven, Connecticut, Jay conducts workshops, seminars, and lectures around the world. His most recent books are *Jay Maisel's New York and A Tribute*, about the World Trade Center (New York, Firefly Books, 2000).

MANUAL (SEE MUSEUMS AND UNIVERSITIES)

MARIPOL

New York artist and image-maker Maripol has secured a place in photographic history with her SX70 Polaroids shot during the 1980s. This pivotal series, considered by some as one of the most revealing portraits of New York in the post-punk era, presents known and unknown subjects from the period, straddling the worlds of art, music, fashion, and film. These groundbreaking images have subsequently been shown around the world in leading museums, nonprofits, and galleries, including FotoFest 2002, Houston; Deitch Projects, New York (2001); Frédéric Sanchez Gallery, Paris (2001); Robert Miller Gallery, New York (1997); and P.S.1 Contemporary Art Center, Long Island City, New York (1984). She has an upcoming exhibit scheduled for 2004 in Tokyo. Her most recent work, introducing large-format black and white Polaroids and entitled *Reviving Downtown*, is premiering at Deborah Colton Gallery, Houston, during FotoFest 2004.

PATRICK MEAGHER

Patrick Meagher (pronounced: Mäh'r) was born in 1973 in Manhattan, NY. Meagher studied conceptual art, sculpture, and site work at Carnegie Mellon University; photography and painting at Kunstakademie Düsseldorf, Germany; and Landscape Architecture at Harvard Graduate School of Design. His broader body of work currently consists of digital photo-based art, machine-cut sculpture in EPS Styrofoam, and freehand drawings on paper. Meagher exhibits internationally and has work in the collections of Museo Castello di Rivoli, TATE Modern, Mannesmann Steel GMBH, the U.S. Government, and the National Endowment for the Arts.

DELILAH MONTOYA (SEE NON-PROFIT SPACES)

OSCAR MUÑOZ

Born in Popayán, Colombia, in 1951, Oscar Muñoz had exhibited his work at the Bronx Museum of Art, Bronx, New York; Museo de Arte Moderno, Bogotá; Museo de Bellas Artes, Caracas; Museo de Arte Moderno de Buenos Aires, Buenos Aires; Center for Photography at Woodstock, New York; and the Museum of the Americas, Washington, D.C. A book was recently published about the work of Oscar Muñoz entitled *Volverte Aire* (Ediciones Eco, Bogota, Colombia 2003). His work is included in many important collections around the world. Exhibitions of his work were held during FotoFest 1996 and 2002.

OSAMU JAMES NAKAGAWA

Osamu James Nakagawa is an American-born Japanese photographer. His family moved back to Tokyo soon after his birth in New York in 1962 and returned when Nakagawa was 15. He received his M.F.A. at the University of Houston and is now an assistant professor of photography at Indiana University in Bloomington. Nakagawa's photographs can be found in a number of public collections including

SUZANNE PAUL

Suzanne Paul got her B.F.A. in 1968 at the University of Houston. Primarily showing in noncommercial spaces, she has had several one-person shows at venues that include the Contemporary Arts Museum, Houston, 1976; Fort Worth Museum of Modern Art, Fort Worth, 1985; and FotoFest, Houston, 2001. Art critics have written about Paul's work since 1976. She was the recipient of a National Endowment for the Arts photo survey grant in 1980. She began her "serious," albeit "fun," work on the streets of San Francisco. She has moved from small black and white photographs, showing rarified moments of grace and humorous subtleties of the human experience, to large color photos.

CHARLOTTE RANDOLPH

Since 1993, Charlotte Randolph has enhanced a lifelong interest in the visual arts and her degree in art history by taking numerous photography workshops and classes at Rice University, Houston, and the Glassell School of Art, Museum of Fine Arts, Houston. Her photographs have won awards and been exhibited in several Texas cities. They also have appeared in a number of publications of the American Orchid Society. Currently she is using a vintage 4 x 5 view camera to photograph landscapes; the camera's slow, deliberate function brings her rewarding insights.

JANICE RUBIN (SEE NON-PROFIT SPACES)

ZOFIA RYDET

During her lifetime, the Polish photographer Zofia Rydet (1911-1997) exhibited extensively internationally. From Argentina to Australia. She achieved a degree of fame, with three books and a documentary film. She is represented in museum collections from the Museum of Modern Art, New York to the Centre Georges Pompidou, Paris. Since her photographs have rarely been seen in the U.S., her work has remained largely unknown in the U.S. The last showing of her work was in 1979 at the International Center of Photography, New York, and 2002 at Anya Tish Gallery, Houston. This collection, spanning three decades, features vintage silver gelatin prints ranging from documentary photography to extravagant forays into surrealism, using photo collage. Included are images from some of her most notable photo cycles. They provide a succinct overview of the artist's important and prolific career: *Little Man* (1950s), *The Time of Passing* (1960s), and *The World of Feelings and Imagination* (1970s).

IRMA MARTINEZ SIZER

Irma Martinez Sizer was born in Mexico City and moved to West Texas when she was in her twenties. She attended the University of the Americas–Puebla in Puebla, Mexico, and majored in graphic design. Her work has been exhibited at galleries and museums in Texas and Mexico. Martinez Sizer is currently working on her M.F.A. in photography and printmaking at Texas Tech University, Lubbock, where she is an instructor as well. Martinez Sizer finds herself continuing to learn about American culture even though she has lived in the United States for several years. The differences in the two cultures that influence her are often evident in the everyday things of life.

THEO STANLEY

Theo R. Stanley was born in Colorado Springs, Colorado, in 1976. In the spring of 1994, he graduated from Park High School of Livingston, Montana, with honors and received a national scholarship to attend an Oxford University summer program. He attended the Meadows School of the Arts, Southern Methodist University, Dallas. Stanley graduated magna cum laude in 1998 and received his B.F.A. degree with departmental distinction and a travel award. He moved to New York in 1998, where he worked for, and collaborated with, photographer and filmmaker Bruce Weber. He studied with Weber for four years, leading his team and assuming the responsibility of first assistant for the final two years. Currently he is working on his master's degree. His work addresses the daily situations and gravity of the human predicament. The images are often figurative, but also involve environments and architectures that embody an interior view. Stanley utilizes a diverse range of traditional and alternative photographic techniques along with drawing and painting.

FERNANDO STEIN

Fernando Stein, M.D., a native of Guatemala, paid his way through medical school taking pictures professionally. Today he is Chief of the Critical Care Clinic, among other titles, at Texas Children's Hospital in Houston. He is the author of the recent book *The Art of Texas Children's Hospital* (Herring Press, Houston, TX, 2000).

GEORGE SZEPESI

George Szepesi was born in Caracas. In 1974, he graduated from the University of Houston, cum laude, in architecture. He went on to study at the Center for Advanced Visual Studies at M.I.T., Cambridge, Massachusetts, and received a master's degree in 1978. He founded EGBRAG and A.A.A. (Anonymous Artists Association), creating numerous graphic editions, ephemeral art presentations, outdoor installations, indoor performances, and large-scale works.

MIA UNVERZAGT

Mia Unverzagt graduated from HBK-Saar (University of Fine Arts, Saarbrücken, Germany) in 2002 with a diploma and title as Master Student. In 1998 she was awarded the Fine Arts Award of the Greater District of Saarbrücken, and she received a scholarship from the Rosa Luxemburg Foundation, Berlin, for studies from 1999 to 2004. In 2000 she worked in Havana, Cuba, with a grant from the Ludwig Foundation of Cuba. During this time she organized an exchange of seven Cuban and seven German artists with the purpose of finding

out whether or not artists can communicate through their work only. In 2003 she worked together with eight graphic designers on a project called *Book of Episodes* in which each designer created a little catalogue about a different part of the artist's work. Unverzagt will be in Havana until September 2004 on a one-year scholarship from the Ludwig Foundation of Cuba.

DAVID VAUGHAN

David Vaughan is a photographer with more than 30 years of experience, specializing in portraiture and studio photography. His photographs have been exhibited at the Houston Center for Photography and koelsch Gallery, as well as at other Houston venues. He holds a B.S. from Abilene Christian University, Abilene, Texas, and studied photography at the master's level at the University of Houston.

TERRY VINE

Born and raised in a small town in northeastern Ohio, Terry Vine currently lives and works in Houston, where he has been photographing commercially for nearly 20 years. While his corporate work has taken him around the world and won many prestigious industry awards, his personal work centers on black and white studies of the cities and rural areas of Mexico and Europe. His recent body of work *Stalks and Water* is an exploration of color, structure, and light. In addition to many solo and group exhibitions in the United States and abroad, Vine's work is in the collections of the Museum of Fine Arts, Houston; Denver Art Museum, Denver; Santa Barbara Museum of Art, Santa Barbara, California; and Wittliff Gallery of Southwest and Mexican Photography, Southwest Texas State University, San Marcos, as well as numerous private collections.

VAN VU

Born in Vietnam in 1932, Van Vu began his photographic career in 1955. He came to the United States in 1975 and initially settled with his family in Jackson, Mississippi, before moving in 1981 to Houston. In Houston, he worked for a while at The Color Place before founding his own lab, Southwest Photo, in 1982. Vu's professional photographic experience was enhanced with professional studies at the New Jersey School of Modern Photography in 1978 and Rochester Institute of Technology, Rochester, New York, in 1980. Vu has researched and developed darkroom techniques, creating new technical lines for contemporary colors. He combines these laboratory techniques with his professional photography. He has exhibited at Canon House Gallery, San Francisco; Municipal Art Gallery, Jackson, Mississippi; and Sugar Creek Country Club, Ensearch Tower, Doubletree Hotel, and New Territory Community Center in Houston.

LINDA WALSH

Linda Walsh was born and grew up in Summit, New Jersey. Her passion for photography began while living in New York shortly after graduating from college. Walsh moved to Houston in 1974, where she began photographing western landscapes. Her landscapes include areas of the American West from the Arctic Ocean to the Texas Gulf.

RODNEY WATERS (SEE NON-PROFIT SPACES)

FREDERIC WEBER

Born in 1955, Frederic Weber has been extensively exhibiting his work since 1991. His acclaimed *Reverie* series furthers his investigation of the human form. His work is featured on the cover and interior of the recently released *Curve: The Female Nude Now* (New York: Universe Books, 2003). In addition to appearing in numerous private collections, Frederic Weber's photographs are in such important collections as those of the Museum of Fine Arts, Houston; Manfred Heiting Collection, Amsterdam and Los Angeles; Los Angeles County Museum of Art, Los Angeles; Chrysler Museum of Art, Norfolk, Virginia; Denver Art Museum, Denver; George Eastman House, Rochester, New York; Forbes Collection, New York; Dow Jones Collection, New York; Whitney Museum of American Art, New York; and the Gernsheim Collection at the University of Texas in Austin.

WEEGEE

Weegee Born 1899, Died 1968 Photographer American As legend tells it, Arthur Fellig earned the nickname Weegee during his early career as a freelance press photographer in New York City. His apparent sixth sense for crime often led him to a scene well ahead of the police. Observers likened this sense, actually derived from tuning his radio to the police frequency, to the Ouija board, the popular fortune-telling game. Spelling it phonetically, Fellig took Weegee as his professional name. With his subjects ranging from wild-eyed adolescent onlookers at a late night gangland slaying to glassy-eyed starlets at Hollywood movie premieres, Weegee could be considered one of the first ambulance chasers. He was as flamboyant as some of his subjects, creating his own mythology, reveling in his own notoriety as well as that of his subjects, and even stamping the backs of his pictures with "Credit Photo by Weegee the Famous." Weegee also worked in Hollywood as a filmmaker, performer, and technical consultant. His 1945 book Naked City was the inspiration for the 1947 film The Naked City. The Public Eye (1992), starring Joe Pesci, was based on the man himself.

JIM WISE

Jim Wise is a Houston-based mixed-media artist. Born in 1946, he is a lifelong image-maker who comes to exhibiting his work in a roundabout way. With parallel careers in engineering and law, he studied drawing, painting, and printmaking at the Glassell School of Art, Museum of Fine Arts, Houston, and at the Art League of Houston. "A multicareer life endows any artist with priceless perspective, which I enjoy sharing," he says. He has exhibited works locally in various juried competitions and in alternative spaces. In recent work, he combines his primary interest in painting with digital photography and inkjet printing.

VICENTE WOLF

Vicente Wolf has been photographing for over a decade, creating luminous color imagery inspired by his travels to exotic places such as India, Thailand, Namibia, and Sri Lanka. His past exhibitions include *Bambo*, Pucci Gallery, New York (1999); *Tree Forms and Compositions*,

Homer Gallery, New York (2000); and *Visions*, Pucci Gallery, New York (2002). His newest series, entitled *Waterworks*, features medium-format color prints, which evoke a sense of serenity and stand as bold windows to an inner feeling of peace, harmony, and balance, in contrast to our technological 21st-century world. This series was exhibited concurrently at Naomi Silva Gallery, Atlanta, and Georgia Museum of Art, Athens, in October 2003. Born in Havana, Cuba, Wolf is based in New York, where he directs a thriving and influential international interior design practice. As a designer, he has received many prestigious national awards, including being inducted into the *Interior Design Magazine* "Designer Hall of Fame" in 1998. His recent book, *Learning to See: Bringing the World Around You Into Your Home* (City: Artisan, 2002), features many of his artistic images as well as detailed photos of his interiors.

DOROTHY WONG

Dorothy Wong is a psychologist and an avid photographer. She has said that she will "shoot" anything that does not move faster than the revolution of the earth. Her current favorite subjects are close-ups of flowers, fruits, and vegetables. Wong's work has been featured in group exhibitions organized by the Houston Chinese Photographic Society, Houston Center for Photography, Fourth Wednesday Photo Club, and Beaumont Art League. Her photographs have been published in the *Houston Press* and in the 10th anniversary publication of the Houston Chinese Photographic Society. In August 2003 she had her first solo show, *Mostly Flowers*, at Michaeline's Restaurant, Houston. She also exhibited at the 2003 annual meeting of the Photographic Society of America held in Houston.

SUSANNE YORK

A native Texan, artist Susanne York has been producing photographs for almost three decades. Although formally trained in photojournalism, her experience and talent span many genres including photojournalism, commercial photography, documentary film making, and fine art photography. Her award-winning work has been showcased in several solo and group exhibitions and has been showcased in several solo and group exhibitions and has been featured in newspapers, books and magazines.

PAUL ZEIGLER

Paul Zeigler was born and raised in Butte, Montana, and educated at local parochial schools. Zeigler received a B.A. in history and political science and an M.F.A. in Creative Writing/Poetry from the University of Montana, Missoula, and has published poetry in various small press magazines. He is a self-taught photographer with over 30 years behind the camera. His photographic studies center around abandoned treasures from dried-out flowers to steam trains, to rapidly emptying towns beside the interstate. Zeigler explores the beauty that remains in subjects no longer considered beautiful or useful.

Corporate Spaces

HARRY KALISH

Searching out scenes in nature that indicate the activity of outside forces, Harry Kalish often produces work instilled with a sense of time passing. His work has been seen at venues including the Perkins Center for the Arts, Moorestown, New Jersey, and in Philadelphia at Creative Artists Network, The Philadelphia Art Alliance, and Philadelphia Museum of Art. Kalish's work is included in the permanent collections of the National Museum of American Art, Smithsonian Institution, Washington, D.C.; Philadelphia Museum of Art, Philadelphia; and The Pew Charitable Trust, Philadelphia. The artist currently maintains a studio in Lansdowne, Pennsylvania.

SARAH VAN KEUREN

Sarah Van Keuren completed an M.F.A. in photography at the University of Delaware, Newark, in 1998 and now lives and works in Philadelphia, where she is an adjunct professor of non-silver processes at the University of the Arts. Her pinhole photographs employ a cyanotype and gum bichromate printing process to render subjects in a painterly haze. Van Keuren's photographs have been exhibited extensively at several venues including the Art Institute of Boston; Rantagalleria, Oulu, Finland; The Philadelphia Art Alliance, Philadelphia; Locks Gallery, Philadelphia; and the Contemporary Arts Museum, Houston. Her work is included in collections at the Philadelphia Museum of Art, Philadelphia; National Museum of American Art, Smithsonian Institution, Washington, D.C.; and State Museum of Pennsylvania, Harrisburg.

ALAN LEMIRE

Alan Lemire is a commercial and fine art photographer who lives in Marin County, California. Most of his personal work revolves around southeastern Utah and the Pacific coastline where he explores the landscape through the large-format black and white tradition. He is currently a senior photographer at the digital studio for Gap Inc. Direct. This has allowed him opportunities to photograph in Africa and Central America. In addition, he is also an educator who has taught at the Art Center College of Design in Pasadena, California, and currently teaches at the Academy of Art College in San Francisco.

ELLIOTT MCDOWELL

Born in Evansville, Indiana, in 1948, Elliott McDowell received a B.B.A. degree in 1970 from Southern Methodist University, Dallas. A creative businessman, he was an avid photographer from childhood. After 1970, he studied with Ansel Adams and in Santa Fe with William Clift and Laura Gilpin. His black and white photographs were published in the book *Photographs: Elliott McDowell* (Boston: David R. Godine, 1980). Aberbach Fine Art, New York, subsequently published some of these images in large editions as posters. Distributed throughout the world, they still turn up in unexpected places. McDowell turned to color in the early 1990s, and, by 1995 he

was exploring the digital imaging and photo composites that are his chief interest today. A regular contributor to *Popular Photography and Imaging*, he offers readers digital imagery and composite printing with mysterious, technical artistry. Appearing in many solo and group exhibitions, his work belongs to both public and private American collections. McDowell lives in Santa Fe.

OLIVER

oliver is an artist who uses the tools and techniques of modern photography as his primary mode of expression. oliver returned to professional photography and art in 1997 after a hiatus starting in the late 1970s. oliver's return to photography was induced by the onset of a very painful condition that prevented him from working as an attorney. The digital darkroom seemed a natural place for him, given his background in computers, and it allowed him to focus on images instead of the pain. oliver is influenced by photography, his first love, as well by as painting, sculpture, movies, theater, and other art forms. Fortunate to be able to go back to art full time at mid life, oliver is making progress in the return to his first choice of career. When restarting photography in 1997, oliver abandoned the dark, highly intellectualized images of his earlier period to focus on lighter, more livable sensual art while still retaining intellectual influences.

ERNESTINE RUBEN

Ernestine Ruben's newest imagery combines a 19th-century, historic sensibility with the serene romance of the landscape rendered in washes of gum bichromate, a non-silver printing process. Ruben lives and works in Princeton, New Jersey, and has had recent solo exhibitions at John Stevenson Gallery, New York; Montgomery Museum of Fine Arts, Montgomery, Alabama; Maison Europeène de la Photographie, Paris; and Rodin Museum, Philadelphia. Her work is in collections worldwide including the Philadelphia Museum of Art, Philadelphia; Rodin Museum, Paris; Museum of Fine Arts, Houston; Stedlijk Museum, Amsterdam; and Museum of Modern Art, Paris.

PAUL SMEAD

Paul Smead's photographs impart a sense of contemplation found in the residue of a human presence. Born in 1956 in California, Smead has lived and worked as a designer in Houston since 1998. He earned a B.S. in interior architecture at Arizona State University, College of Architecture, Tempe, in 1979, further studied at the Harvard Graduate School of Design, Cambridge, Massachusetts, in 1986, and presently attends the Glassell School of Art, Museum of Fine Arts, Houston. Smead's work is represented in corporate and private collections, and he continues to exhibit throughout Houston.

FANNIE TAPPER

Born in Temple, Texas, and currently residing in Houston, Fannie Tapper is a native who often escapes the vast spaces of Texas to capture the exotic locales of Haiti and France on film. Tapper uses digital media to alter her photographs and create compositions that explore texture and color to produce feelings of awe and joy. She has exhibited extensively throughout Texas and nationally. Her work can be found in the collections of the Museum of Fine Arts, Houston; Birmingham Museum of Art, Birmingham, Alabama; and South Texas Art Museum, Corpus Christi.

MARK L. TOMPKINS

Mark L. Tompkins is an author and award-winning photographer whose work has been exhibited internationally. Tompkins has pursued his passion for photography and writing since 1975. In his early career, he focused on underwater photography. His more recent work merges black and white photographs with text, resulting in the creation of expressive, multidimensional visual poems. Tompkins's latest work, *Remembering to Live: Visual Poems for the Journey*, has been published as a book. It is a tour of emotional, professional, and spiritual growth experiences that provides lasting solace and insight. The book has been called *The Visual Chicken Soup for the Soul* and received endorsements from Deepak Chopra and Dr. Wayne Dyer. Tompkins was born in Brownsville, Texas, in 1960. Spending most of his life outside the United States until 1979, he attended Tawa Collage in New Zealand and the University of Texas at Austin where he earned a B.S. in chemical engineering. Currently he is a partner in a commercial real estate development firm and resides in Houston.

WILLIAM WYLIE

William Wylie examines the landscape with a sensitivity that captures the sensual qualities of water. His first book, *Riverwalk* (2000), was published by the University Press of Colorado, Boulder, and his second book, *Stillwater* (2002), was published by Nazraeli Press, City. In the past 10 years, he has been the focus of two Public Television documentaries and a Colorado Public Radio feature story on the Poudre River project. His work has been exhibited at various venues including the Amon Carter Museum of Art, Fort Worth; Museum of Contemporary Art, Fort Collins, Colorado; and Print Center, Philadelphia. His work can be found in numerous collections including the Amon Carter Museum of Art, Fort Worth; Saint Louis Museum of Art, St. Louis; and Art Museum at Princeton University, Princeton, New Jersey. Wylie completed his B.F.A. at Colorado State University, Colorado Springs, and his M.F.A. at the University of Michigan, Ann Arbor. He currently teaches at the University of Virginia, Charlottesville.

Restaurants and Commerical Spaces

WALT BISTLINE (SEE MUSEUMS AND UNIVERSITIES)

COLIN BLAKELY

Born in New York, Colin Blakely moved to Houston as a young child and lived there through high school. He received a B.A. from Williams College, Williamstown, Massachusetts, with a double major in studio arts and abstract math. In 2001, he earned an M.F.A. from the University of New Mexico, Albuquerque. He currently teaches photography and digital imaging at Eastern Michigan University in

Ypsilanti, Michigan. His work was shown at FotoFest 2002, Houston; the Society for Contemporary Photography, Kansas City; Albuquerque Museum; and Colorado Photographic Arts Center, Denver. Blakely's photographs have been featured in *Photo District News*

LAURA BURLTON

Beginning with pop magazines and an MTV feature in high school, Laura Burlton veered towards photography early on. A native of Texas, she met and married her British husband after a stint in the United Kingdom. Now a young mother, Laura actively maintains her role in photography. The Glassell School of Art, Museum of Fine Arts, Houston, awarded her Frank Freed Memorial Scholarships in both 2002 and 2003. Burlton's current focus has shifted from scen-esters to domestic scenes, to which she brings a wry perspective.

LESLIE FIELD

A photographer and mixed-media artist, Leslie Field has been working since 1990. Experimental by nature, she works in alternative process-es, photosculpture, and installation. Her work has been exhibited throughout Texas, Vermont, and New York, and has been acquired by numerous private collections. Field's work is also in the permanent col-lections of Congregation Emanu-El, Congregation Beth Israel, and the Museum of Fine Arts, Houston. In addition to being a visual artist, Field is an art consultant and independent curator who works with corporate clients, nonprofit organizations, and private collections.

GERALD (GERRY) GRAPHIA

Born in New Orleans in 1956, Gerry Graphia has been involved in the entertainment industry since he began playing drums at six years old. An aspiring rock musician and Harley-Davidson enthusiast, he says his self-taught photographic skills are rooted in his passion for music, motorcycles, sports, and beautiful women. After his unsigned rock band 2-4-1 achieved notable success by being consistently featured on prime time FM radio, he turned his energy to photographing music and sports superstars and celebrities, as well as editorial endeavors. His photography has been internationally published in several maga-zines and is exhibited in the Hard Rock Café and the offices of major concert promoters. Currently he is the music editor/photographer and sports editor/photographer for *Full Throttle Magazine*, where he covers major music and the NFL's Houston Texans. His photography captures the emotion and intensity of the moment and he is known for being in the "right place at the right time."

WENDY LEVINE

After living much of her life abroad, Wendy Levine was repatriated to Houston with two young children. A documentary photographer in the Middle East and London, she now turned her photography toward her immediate surroundings and began capturing more *nature* themes found in the home. *Photography Quarterly* chose Levine in 2002 as one of five photographers "for images placing unexpect-ed and savvy attention on the ordinary in life." In 2003, she received an Individual Artist Grant from the Cultural Arts Council of Houston/Harris County (CACHH) to continue this theme with a multicultural twist. The latest images show childhood commonalities that resonate worldwide and are on view at CACHH Headquarters in Houston, February–April 16, 2004.

KAREN SACHER

As an artist, Karen Sacher hopes to reflect the essence of the human spirit through photography. Whether she is photographing families at the beach or children from the Dominican Republic, she intends her work to reflect the emotion of her subjects and their experiences. Both her artistic endeavors and her spiritual quests have enabled her to travel the world and enjoy an adventurous life. From the villages of Ethiopia to the mountains of Machu Picchu to a third-grade class-room down the street, Sacher enjoys photographing a diversity of people and places. She has been published in numerous magazines and books, and she works with Hallmark. She enjoys shooting com-mercially as well documenting unique weddings around the world. She has exhibited in Houston and Washington, D.C., and is part of many private and corporate art collections. Sacher has recently founded a nonprofit organization, Heart of Humanity. The purpose of Heart of Humanity is to educate and inspire through photography and creative writing. Photography exhibits, classroom teaching, and collaboration with other nonprofits to creatively tell their stories form the outreach of this program. As a photographer with a background in marketing, graphic design, and creative writing, Sacher sees her goal as to develop national and international projects that will creatively educate. Sacher currently lives in Houston. She was born in St. Louis and received her B.S. in advertising from the University of Texas at Austin. She founded her business in 1995.

FANNIE TRAPPER

Fannie Trapper, a lifelong Texan, was educated at Baylor University, Waco, Texas, earning a B.A. in English literature, and at Rice University, where she received a Ph.D. in French literature. She was a professor of French at the University of Houston from 1969 to 1992 and debuted as a photographer in 1991 as second place winner in the Lawndale Big Show at the Glassell School of Art, Museum of Fine Arts, Houston. Since then she has been represented by galleries and art consultants in Houston, Dallas, and Kansas City. Featured in 19 solo exhibitions, she has also exhibited in numerous national and international group shows. Four previous FotoFest exhibitions (1994, 1996, 1998, and 2000) have included her photography at independent spaces. Her work is represented in four museums (including the Museum of Fine Arts Houston), a dozen other public collections, and private collections in the United States and Europe.

Curators

COLIN KEEL

Colin Keel was born in Amarillo, Texas and graduated from Texas Tech University. As director of changing exhibits at Holocaust Museum, he has worked with a variety of artists in photography, film, painting and collage. 2004 is his second time to participate in Foto Fest as a curator.

ANNE WILKES TUCKER
MUSEUM OF FINE ARTS HOUSTON

Anne Wilkes Tucker was born in Baton Rouge, Louisiana, where she attended public schools. She received undergraduate degrees from Randolph Macon Woman's College and Rochester Institute of Technology. She received a graduate degree from the Visual Studies Workshop, a division of the State University of New York, in Rochester, New York. While in graduate school, she worked at the George Eastman House in Rochester and at the Gernsheim Collection at the University of Texas, Austin. In 1970-71, she was a curatorial intern in the photography department of Museum of Modern Art, New York City. She is currently the Gus and Lyndall Wortham Curator of Photography at The Museum of Fine Arts, Houston where she has worked since 1976. She founded the Photography Department at the museum that now has a collection of over 20,000 photographs. She has curated over forty exhibitions including retrospectives for Robert Frank, Ray K. Metzker, Brassaï, George Krause, Louis Faurer and Richard Misrach, as well as surveys on the Czech Avant-garde, Allan Chasanoff collection, and the History of Japanese Photography. Most recently, she co-curated with D.J. Stout the exhibition *First Down Houston: The Birth of an NFL Franchise* with photographs by Robert Clark. Most of these exhibitions were accompanied by a publication; she has published many articles and lectured throughout the U.S., Europe, Asia and Latin America. She has been awarded fellowships by the National Endowment for the Arts and the John Simon Guggenheim Memorial Foundation and The Getty Center, and received an Alumnae Achievement award from Randolph Macon Woman's College. In 2001, in an issue devoted to "America's Best," TIME magazine honored her as "America's Best Curator".

CLINT WILLOUR
GALVESTON ARTS CENTER

Mr. Willour has been an art professional for the past 30 years, serving in both the profit and non-profit areas. He is the executive director and curator of the Galveston Arts Center, serves on the art board of Houston FotoFest, the program committee of the Houston Center for Photography as well as the photography accessions subcommittee of the Museum of Fine Arts, Houston. He is also an independent curator creating exhibitions for a number of non-profit institutions in the region in a variety of media. He is interested in viewing non-commercial, fine art photography.